The

UNITAR
HIROSHIMA
FELLOWSHIP
for
AFGHANISTAN
(2003~2018)

AN ANTHOLOGY

The Editors wish to thank the United Nations Institute for Training and Research (UNITAR) whose support made the publication of this book possible.

United Nations Institute for Training and Research

Library of Congress Control Number: 2023903243

Azimi, Nassrine and Khan-Kamal, Humaira
The UNITAR Hiroshima Fellowship for Afghanistan, An Anthology
2023

ISBN: 979-8-9878079-0-3 (paper back)
ISBN: 979-8-9878079-1-0 (Ebook)

Cover: theBookdesigners.com
Book layout: theBookdesigners.com

AF🜲P AFGHAN FELLOWSHIP LEGACY PROJECTS

The

UNITAR HIROSHIMA FELLOWSHIP

for

AFGHANISTAN (2003~2018)

AN ANTHOLOGY

NASSRINE AZIMI and HUMAIRA KHAN-KAMAL

EDITORS

SPECIAL THANKS TO
**JENNY XIN LUAN & TAIGA NISHIMURA,
RESEARCH ASSISTANTS**

سوله

انی

صلح

مانی

صلح 平和

TABLE OF CONTENTS

III.

III A.

III B.

IV.

V.

VI.

سوله
مانی
صلح
平和

ACKNOWLEDGEMENTS

It took us many years to rally our Afghan Fellowship community, and indeed ourselves, to carve the time, energy and space to produce this book, the idea of which had been on our minds for long. Then, just as momentum was at its peak, and papers and contributions were pouring in, in August of 2021 the Taliban returned to power in Afghanistan and seemingly undid, in a mere few weeks, what the Fellowship had strived to achieve over close to two decades.

At that point we almost gave up on the book, but for a persistent question that kept haunting us: 'Had it all been a waste then?'

The completion of this manuscript is our response to that question.

A collection of writings by multiple members of the UNITAR Hiroshima Fellowship for Afghanistan (AF), this book covers the period from the inception of the program in early 2002, until the present day. Ironically, over this past year we have found that the need to share its lessons has become ever more critical, precisely because the events of August 2021 in Afghanistan loom so large over everything else. It seemed essential to us to try not just to document but also share widely the Fellowship story, so that future generations may learn from the challenges and accomplishments of an international development effort that, even though small, was path-breaking, long-term, dynamic and most importantly, Afghan-driven.

But the book also tells a compelling human story, a story of different people coming together from around the world, to solve problems and initiate solutions — regardless of language, cultural barriers, age, race or technological challenges.

We both have personal memories and reminiscences of each of the authors in these pages, and in fact of the Afghan Fellowship's more than 500 alumni, mentors, faculty members, partners, and UNITAR staff. It will be difficult to thank every one of them here, but may they know how much they have each influenced us, teaching us to think afresh about international cooperation, human resource development, Afghanistan, Japan and, indeed, life. Two people — Michael Fors and Sabahuddin Sokout — need a special mention, for they were not just pillars of the Fellowship and our advisors throughout, but over time have become like brothers to us.

We are grateful to authorities in Hiroshima and across Japan, Afghanistan and other countries, who unstintingly sustained the Fellowship over the years. Our gratitude to UNITAR, which has been our professional and intellectual home, and to the many colleagues there who supported the Fellowship, and now the Afghan Fellowship Legacy Projects (AFLP), with ardor and intelligence. A special thanks to our young researchers Yuko Baba, Jenny Xin Luan and Taiga Nishimura for their able assistance to this publication, to Mihoko Kumamoto, Sharapiya Kakimova, Lorne Jaques and David Eaton for unstinting moral and material support, to Barbara and Isshu Fujiwara for generously giving of their time and talents, and to Chang Li Lin, for her solidarity and wise counsel over the years.

Finally we are grateful for the chance to work together again, something that over more than 25 years has never failed to bring us personal joy, intellectual camaraderie and professional complementarity. We hope that this book, a labor of love by all who have contributed, builds a realistic narrative of the struggles and successes of a unique community. Its members may now be scattered around the world but they carry within them, and will hopefully bring to fruition one day, the many seeds planted during the exceptional years of the UNITAR Hiroshima Fellowship for Afghanistan.

Nassrine Azimi & Humaira Khan-Kamal
Co-Editors, Hiroshima and Phoenix, October 2022

FOREWORD

FROM HIROSHIMA

On the publication of this book I would like to express my deepest respect to all parties involved in the UNITAR Hiroshima Fellowship for Afghanistan, which for more than a decade and a half was dedicated to developing human resources in Afghanistan.

Since the establishment of the UNITAR Hiroshima Office in July 2003, Hiroshima Prefecture has consistently supported its activities. Among these, the Fellowship for Afghanistan was one of the most important programs that started concurrently with the opening of the office.

Dr. Nassrine Azimi, the co-editor of this publication, served as the first director of the UNITAR Hiroshima Office for six years from its opening in 2003 till 2009. She and her colleagues have contributed greatly to the revitalization of Afghanistan by launching and operating the program.

In this Fellowship, participants from Afghanistan also learned firsthand the hardships that people in Hiroshima experienced, the impacts of the atomic bombing and the process of post-war reconstruction, by holding discussions with hibakusha (A-bomb survivors), visiting bombed sites, and viewing the present state of Hiroshima, which has revived into a beautiful city. I believe that these invaluable experiences encouraged the participants, inspiring them to work for the restoration of their own country.

It is regrettable that since the collapse of the former Afghan government in August 2021, the Taliban authorities have yet to allow much needed human resource development programs, like the Hiroshima Fellowship, to be held for the country's professionals. Despite these challenges however, I believe it is extremely meaningful to publicize the outcomes of the Fellowship, and share globally the unique lessons we have learned through it.

As is evidenced in this book, people in Afghanistan and Hiroshima Prefecture have fostered eternal friendships. I truly look forward to seeing again our friends in Afghanistan here in Hiroshima.

Hidehiko Yuzaki
Governor of Hiroshima Prefecture, March 2022

AFGHANISTAN:
Whither in the Future?

When I was a boy, many decades ago, during the 1960s, my parents took me to live in Iran, a country then experimenting with Western conceptions of modernity, and experiencing both promising and at times distressing results. To its east lay its no less beautiful and engaging neighbor, Afghanistan, a country still, in many ways, resembling its 19th century self, but also, tentatively, seeking to experiment with what economic and social progress could offer it.

Alas, in both countries, political upheavals and deep-rooted resistance interrupted these tentative efforts to compromise between strong and proud traditions on the one hand and the economic and social changes occurring in much of the rest of the world on the other. Self-isolation and rejection of many aspects of the outside world overtook each of these countries, as did, at times, foreign designs alien to the preferences of their peoples.

During my teens and twenties, I returned to both countries, finding them enthralling all over again but each betraying profound under-lying tension that would erupt only a few years later. The fear and reality of outside intervention, political, economic, and occasion-ally military, contributed to a growing sense of instability and siege instigated by the world beyond.

Many decades later, I came to live in Japan, and was delighted to discover its role as host to the UNITAR Hiroshima Fellowship for

Afghanistan, supported by the UN, the role of which was to empower young and accomplished Afghans to imagine the future of their country and to develop strategies for its economic and social progress. Not surprisingly, its participants included a significant number of talented women bursting with ideas, ambition for their country and optimism that its potential could be achieved.

Given the distressing backdrop of the most recent forty years of Afghanistan's history, initiated by political strains within the country that led to a Soviet military intervention as of the late 1970s, their ideas and commitment might have seemed admirable in the abstract but unlikely to bear fruit. Further, recent events might seem to confirm such pessimism.

And yet, with the economic, social and cultural wealth of any nation embodied not just in its human achievements but also in its potential, to which the UNITAR Hiroshima Fellowship for Afghanistan offered so much in encouraging exploration of the options and expanding the potential of the country. This potential, now dormant, will revive in the future, of this we can be sure. Human aspiration can falter, be temporarily frustrated and hope can be lost. But ultimately the human spirit is indomitable and for this reason the Hiroshima Fellowship for Afghanistan can and will influence the future of the country, just as it has contributed excitingly to its recent past.

Several years ago, in Tokyo, I met with a number of Afghan women brought together by the Fellowship to benefit from each other's experience and to compare notes and formulate ideas and projects for the future. The evening proved both inspiring and, I believed (and still believe), promising. It allowed me to learn a lot, a privilege and pleasure for any of us.

My heart and warm thanks go out to its past participants, the follow-up team currently in place, and those who initiated and supported the Fellowship, notably the United Nations Institute for Training and Research, which was founded in the Hiroshima Prefecture and with so many of its hospitable, generous and engaged inhabitants the perfect partners. May their vision for the historic and enthralling country of Afghanistan yet be achieved, and may they all contribute to its progress.

David M. Malone

Rector, United Nations University & Under-Secretary-General, United Nations

Human Resources Development
is the Cornerstone of
Nation Building

The Afghan Fellowship Legacy Projects (AFLP) was launched with a view to capacity building of Afghan professionals and was implemented in Hiroshima, city of the tragedy of atomic bomb atrocity and the symbolic city of revival and world peace. The project was initiated and conducted by Dr. Nassrine Azimi and Ms. Humaira Khan-Kamal, with colleagues at the UNITAR Hiroshima Office.

I had the pleasure and privilege to get acquainted with Dr. Azimi through the National Federation of UNESCO Associations in Japan (NFUAJ) "Mirai – Isan" (Future Legacy) Project. Together with Ms. Tomoko Watanabe, she had initiated and implemented an extremely significant "Green Legacy Hiroshima Initiative," which was selected and awarded as a "Mirai – Isan" prize winner. Highlighting miracle trees surviving the atomic bomb destruction, this project collects seeds from atomic bomb burned trees, sending them, as symbols and hope for world peace, to various places worldwide. The Initiative truly embodies the noble ideals and the spirit of UNESCO.

I am now once again deeply impressed by yet another praise-worthy effort, the "Afghan Fellowship Legacy Projects."

Afghanistan is a country of unique charm, often referred to as the "crossroads of civilizations" and it has enchanted many Japanese scholars over time — scholars like Prof. Takayasu Higuchi, Prof. Kosaku Maeda, Prof. Ikuo Hirayama, to name a few.

The Silk Roads passed through Afghanistan, an important relay point of Western and Oriental civilizations to travel and reach Japan. This is particularly manifested in the introduction of Buddhism — it is said that it took about 1,000 years for Buddhism to reach Japan. The first Buddha statues were created in ancient Gandhara, areas now covering west Afghanistan and Pakistan. The Gandhara buddha statues reflect strong Greco-Roman influence. In the book Beauty of Afghanistan written by Mr. Kiyoshi Tanioka, we see an interesting and symbolic photo of a statue found in Afghanistan: which shows the Buddha guarded by Heracles (hero of the Greek mythology), an eloquent symbol of the fusion of the civilizations of the East and West.

Afghanistan is also a special country for me. My first contact with Afghanistan occurred while I was working at UNESCO Headquarters in Paris as a program specialist in the Education Sector in the 1970s, responsible for a very large UNESCO-UNDP project of teacher training in Afghanistan. Some 20 UNESCO experts were sent to teacher training colleges located in all provincial capital cities there, and I undertook official missions to Afghanistan to monitor the project and meet with the Afghan authorities. Though poor, Afghanistan was a peaceful country at that time and its people were kind and friendly, in those times before the 1979 Soviet invasion. I was enchanted by the beauty of the Afghan traditional art and crafts.

My second intervention with Afghanistan took place after my return to Japan in 2001, having reached the UN retirement age and completed my assignment as Director of the UNESCO Beijing Office. Immediately after my return home, I was appointed professor at Bunkyo Gakuin University in April 2001 and also as Director-General of the National Federation of UNESCO Associations in

Japan (NFUAJ). Earlier the Taliban had seized power in Afghanistan and conducted very severe measures throughout their reign. Awful things happened throughout 2001: destruction of two huge buddha statues in Bamiyan in March by the Taliban regime, and high-jacked airplanes that attacked and destroyed skyscrapers in New York in September shocked the whole world. Around that time, assistance for Afghan refugees was a keen concern of the international community. The NFUAJ also launched a campaign to safeguard the cultural heritage in Afghanistan together with Prof. Ikuo Hirayama, UNESCO Goodwill Ambassador. An exhibition of the Afghan cultural heritage was organized at the UNESCO Headquarters in Paris.

The NFUAJ also launched a nation-wide fund-raising campaign to implement education support projects for Afghan people. On 31 December 2001, together with my colleague, I undertook a mission to Pakistan with a view to starting educational support for Afghan refugees living in extremely severe situations in the suburbs of Islamabad. This was the first NFUAJ educational support for Afghan refugees and in 2002 NFUAJ started "Terakoya Projects" (community learning centers) near Kabul. The Terakoya Projects continued in Kabul and nearby villages for the last 20 years, until the Taliban takeover of government in August 2021. Many Afghans, men and women, boys and girls, have attended classes of the Terakoya Project, and obtained basic literary and useful skills conducive to income generation. This is a truly cooperative project, led by both Afghans and Japanese. Afghan authorities and people involved in the project truly appreciated its values and positive impacts, particularly the grass-roots people-to-people support. Totally non-political and genuine support extended by the Japanese citizens was recognized as manifestation of an honest and true friendship. We Japanese also learned many things through the implementation process.

In 2004, the NFUAJ launched a cultural heritage preservation project in Bamiyan. Thanks to considerable amounts of donations given by the UNESCO association members and the general public in Japan, we established a multipurpose center for the preservation of cultural heritage and educational support for the villagers. I undertook several missions to Bamiyan together with the then Afghan Minister of Culture. This facility was handed over to the Afghan authorities.

The Kabul Museum has a banner, attached at the entrance. It carries an impressive slogan which reads, "A Nation can stay alive when its culture stays alive."

At present, the UFUAJ educational support project in Afghanistan is obliged to stay inactive. This is an awfully sad situation. However I do not think that our efforts have been in vain, same as the laudable Afghan Fellowship Legacy Projects (AFLP). I am confident that the spirit of our projects remains in the heart and soul of our Afghan friends, and I share the same values and convictions with Dr. Azimi and the UNITAR Hiroshima team. I sincerely hope that we can resume our Terakoya Projects as soon as the situation permits.

We, homo sapiens, are the same humankind, one species and belonging to only one remote ancestor. We can understand each other, despite differences of race, sex, color, language, or religion. And, we have to respect and preserve the cultural diversity. UNESCO adopted in 2001 the Universal Declaration on Cultural Diversity.

Let us pray together for the peace and happiness of our Afghan friends.

I close by quoting an enlightening message by the late US Senator Mr. J. W. Fulbright, who established the famous Fulbright Fellowship and Scholarship Program. It is said that Mr. Fulbright believed that if we could just get to know each other better, through educational and cultural exchanges, we could hope to have a world without wars.

> "International educational exchange is the most signifi-
> cant current project designed to continue the process of
> humanizing mankind to the point, we would hope, that
> men can learn to live in peace – eventually even to coop-
> erate in constructive activities rather than compete in a
> mindless contest of mutual destruction..."[1]

Noboru Noguchi
Former Director-General and current Advisor,
National Federation of UNESCO Associations in Japan (NFUAJ)

---

[1] https://eca.state.gov/fulbright/about-fulbright/history/j-william-fulbright/j-william-fulbright-quotes

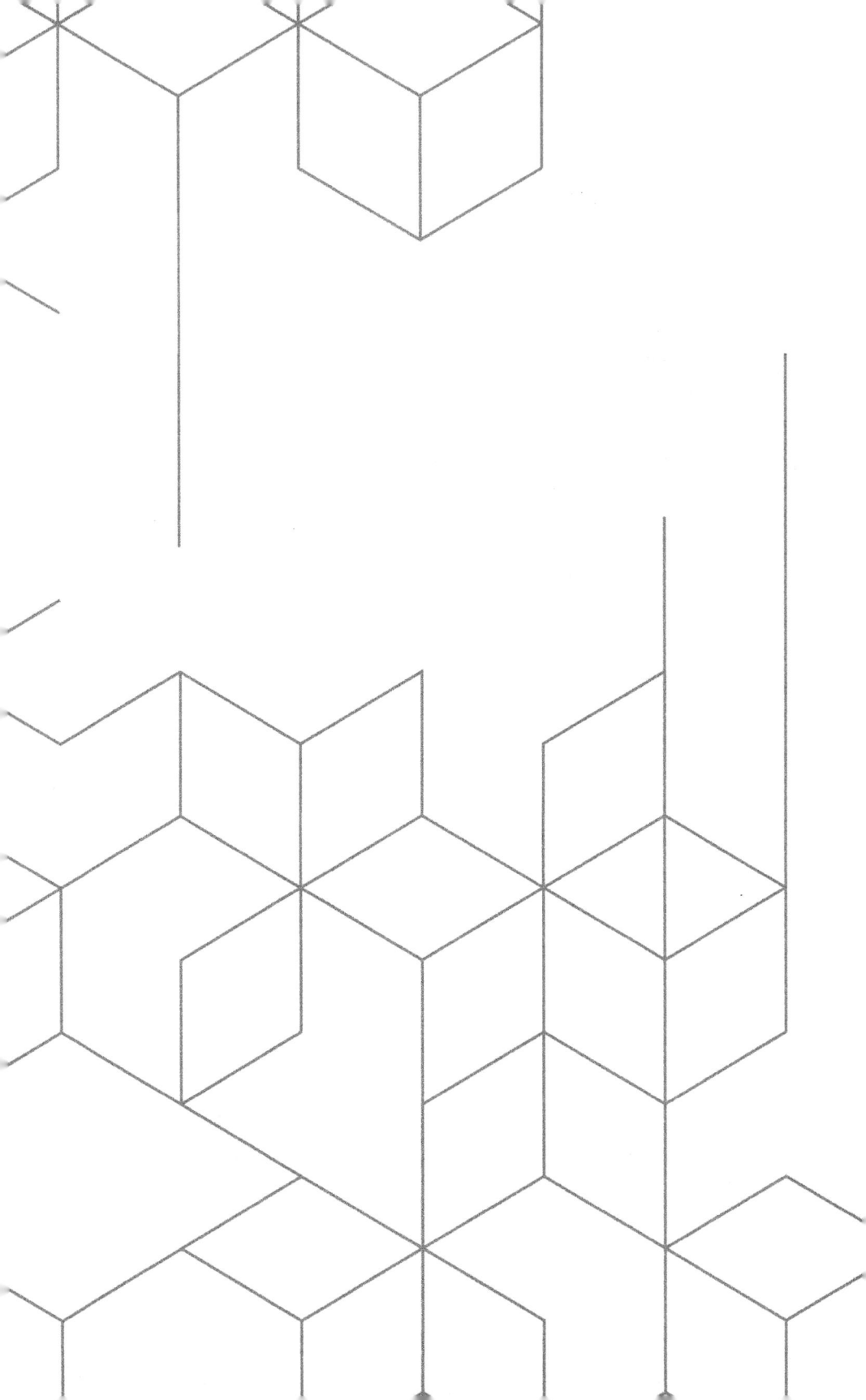

PROLOGUE

PROLOGUE

Nassrine Azimi[2]

Ignorance — God's prison
Knowing — God's palace

Rumi, born 1207 in Balkh (present day Afghanistan)

Over his lifetime the Hiroshima-born painter and narrator of the Silk Road, Ikuo Hirayama, visited Afghanistan numerous times – in 1968 painting the Great Stone Buddha, a majestic statute nestled since the 6th century in a cave overlooking the Bamiyan Valley. The Great Buddha of Bamiyan was mindlessly destroyed by the Taliban regime in 2001, yet another shot in the foot to deprive Afghanistan of its rich heritage, unique source of pride, and revenue, for generations to come.

Hirayama, however, did not abandon the land he so loved. After the fall of the Taliban, he was to return to Afghanistan in 2002, already old and frail, to paint the empty cave left after the destruction of the standing Buddha.

Japan has been for long a trusted friend of Afghanistan. Over the past two decades it has also been one of its most important donors. Part of the reason is practical: twice the size of Japan and with one fourth of the population — 65% of which are under the age of 25 — the country offers a great partner and potential market to aging Japan, with possibilities for investments and sharing expertise in almost every sector imaginable: infrastructure, agriculture,

[2] Senior Advisor, United Nations Institute for Training and Research (UNITAR), Co-founder & Coordinator, Green Legacy Hiroshima Initiative, and Co-founder Afghan Fellowship Legacy Projects (AFLP)

mining, health, services, or education. But the bonds between the two countries are even deeper than these real and expedient considerations. The Japanese have long been intrigued by the cultures of Afghanistan, while the Afghans have great admiration for Japan, which they view — politically and culturally — far more favorably than almost any other economically advanced country.

It was in Japan, and more critically in Hiroshima — alongside Nagasaki one of the only two cities in the world to be destroyed by atomic bombing in August 1945 — that the UNITAR Hiroshima Fellowship for Afghanistan was born. So much meaning, memories, and resonance evoked for me by these few words.

The Fellowship's roots go back to 2002, when UNITAR was preparing to open an office for the Asia-Pacific region in Hiroshima, the first and only UN presence there. Our team was tasked with designing a training program to distill some of Hiroshima's post-war experiences.

We went to Afghanistan and interviewed many, to see how we could best help in rebuilding its broken civil service, despite the catastrophic conditions of the country after 30 years of war. All members of the mission were familiar with the country — in my own case from childhood memories of a visit in the 1960s. The wreckage we saw, despite prior preparations and news coverage, came as a shock. Instead of the tree-lined streets and the crisp, blue skies of the Kabul I remembered, there was the depressing detritus, of decades of war and neglect, bullet-riddled walls across a dusty city bereft of greenery, everywhere the lingering smell of fear and repression.

We interviewed ministers and clerks, academics and businessmen, UN staff, NGO field officers, curators, and ambassadors. It soon became clear that our initial optimistic plans, drawn in the safety of offices back home, were irrelevant. A more flexible strategy, better attuned to Afghan realities, was urgently needed.

The result was an original concept, the UNITAR Hiroshima Fellowship for Afghanistan — year-long cycles of executive training for the country's cadre. It provided core training — from project design, management, report-writing and fund-raising, to accounting and budgeting, team building, and networking. Each cycle included on-site and distance-learning components, and every team was assigned a dedicated group of volunteer mentors, in and outside Afghanistan. Inclusiveness was mandatory — men and women, young and old, Hazara, Pashtun, Tajik, Uzbek, and others, were required to (and did) work together. Each cycle concluded with a final workshop and conference in Hiroshima.

Hiroshima's story of postwar revival greatly affected these trainees, and many would tell us, after visiting the city's Peace Memorial Museum, or listening to the testimony of A-Bomb survivors, "If Hiroshima could revive, then maybe so can we." Hiroshima's efforts to forgo hatred in favor of activism — to forgive but not to forget — echoed strongly with them coming from a country still mired in long-past enmities.

The Hiroshima Fellowship also changed how we came to see international development assistance. It changed us.

What were some of its guiding principles?

First, the Fellowship's core team at UNITAR was enormously diverse and deeply committed: two impressive women, from Pakistan and Kazakhstan, were its early coordinators. Over the years Russian and Ukrainian colleagues, Japanese and Afghans, one Argentinian, one Filipina, a New Zealander and an Australian have worked on it. There were Muslims, Christians and Buddhists, Dari, and Pashto-speakers. An impressive network of instructors —Americans and Canadians, Singaporeans, Japanese, Iranian, Pakistani, and Indians — from top universities, national and international organizations, and even companies like Microsoft — rallied, bringing desperately needed skills *pro-bono* and for the long haul. One may well ask why did they do so? I believe in the beginning because these experts found the narratives of Hiroshima and Afghanistan compelling; later because they too came to feel energized by the Afghans' tremendous desire for learning and for change.

Second, by necessity the Fellowship was frugal, which made it sustainable. Its modest, paced approach proved essential for working in a country that had lost almost everything. We watched over the years as multi-million-dollar, top-down, donor-driven projects were launched with great fanfare, then fizzled out one after the other. Meanwhile the Fellowship just kept building foundations. Though financial resources were limited, thanks to the vision and wisdom of the main donor, the Hiroshima Prefecture, they were long-term. This, alongside significant in-kind support and both the personal and institutional commitment of many partners, meant we could plan ahead, and especially plan for the longer term.

Third, early on the Afghans themselves became an indispensable part of the design and implementation teams. This was not easy at first, but proved crucial, and uniquely successful. The Afghans' intellectual engagement and personal responsibility for the Fellowship transformed its dynamics — we were no longer donor and donee, but part of a single learning community. The Fellowship was first and foremost learner-driven, showcasing time and again the Afghan self-awareness of their own needs and optimal solutions. Our fellows were not passive recipients of top-down assistance. Many in fact risked their lives to assist program events. The Fellowship achieved, in a modest way, what international assistance is notoriously poor at creating — a sense of national ownership. It also validated our UNITAR community's belief, that given equal opportunity everyone aspires to excellence.

Fourth, we constantly strived not to forget Afghan realities, visiting whenever possible. From peaceful Hiroshima it was difficult to imagine the daunting conditions under which Fellows worked: rebuilding institutions in the midst of political turmoil, bomb threats, assassinations, scarce resources and collapsing infrastructure. Their resilience was impressive, but the conditions were indeed drastic. We made sure not to forget this.

Finally, the deep and symbolic significance of Hiroshima provided a larger-than-life context for the Fellowship. I never met a group as visibly affected by Hiroshima's moral stance — or by its revival — as the Afghans.

The Hiroshima Fellowship continued and thrived under my successors at the helm of the UNITAR Hiroshima Office, over its life span providing training for around 500 professionals from government, academia, and the non-governmental sector. We never claimed that Afghanistan's problems were solved, simply because a few hundred professionals across a dozen ministries and institutions completed the Fellowship. But we could say with confidence that there was never a lack of talented professionals in Afghanistan. With a modicum of political stability, they could change their country.

It also helped that the work started by the Fellowship could be transformed and built-upon. A case in point was the Afghan Botanical Garden Network Project (AFLP BG-Net). Since early 2020 and with the help of our alumni and a wide international network of pro-bono botanical garden experts we launched a campaign for Afghan universities, to develop botanical gardens (none exist to-date in Afghanistan), as an extension of their research and conservation efforts.

There are many who have pointed to a lack of progress in Afghanistan after the past two decades. We understand their frustrations, but to forget where Afghanistan was in 2001, and to undermine what has been achieved thus far — it is not just self-defeating, it is also inaccurate. Twenty years ago, only some 900,000 boys attended school. As of August 2021 there were more than nine million schoolchildren

— 39 per cent of whom were girls. These children are neither government nor Taliban, they are all just Afghan children. With peace, education, and opportunity they could turn their country around. Some 42 per cent of the Afghans are under the age of 14, making it one of the youngest nations in the world. One more generation, and progress could take root. It may still not become Sweden, but it could become Vietnam.

My friend the late Sergio Vieira de Melo used to say of the United Nations' work that pragmatism was essential, but that it could not come at the expense of idealism. The Afghans helped us remember our idealism. They also touched our lives in practical ways — with their intelligence, their humor, their hospitality, the way they could sing or recite poetry at every opportunity. They inspired their mentors and Hiroshima hosts with their dignity, their resilience and warmth, their love of learning and wide-eyed admiration for the discipline and technological prowess of Japan. Our bonds with them were sustained over the years not by pity or mere sympathy, but by empathy — their destiny could easily have been ours.

We glimpsed, over the lifespan of the Fellowship, the possibility of a different Afghanistan — a land of peace and prosperity, commensurate with its rich cultural heritage. We will continue to believe in, and root for, that vision of Afghanistan.

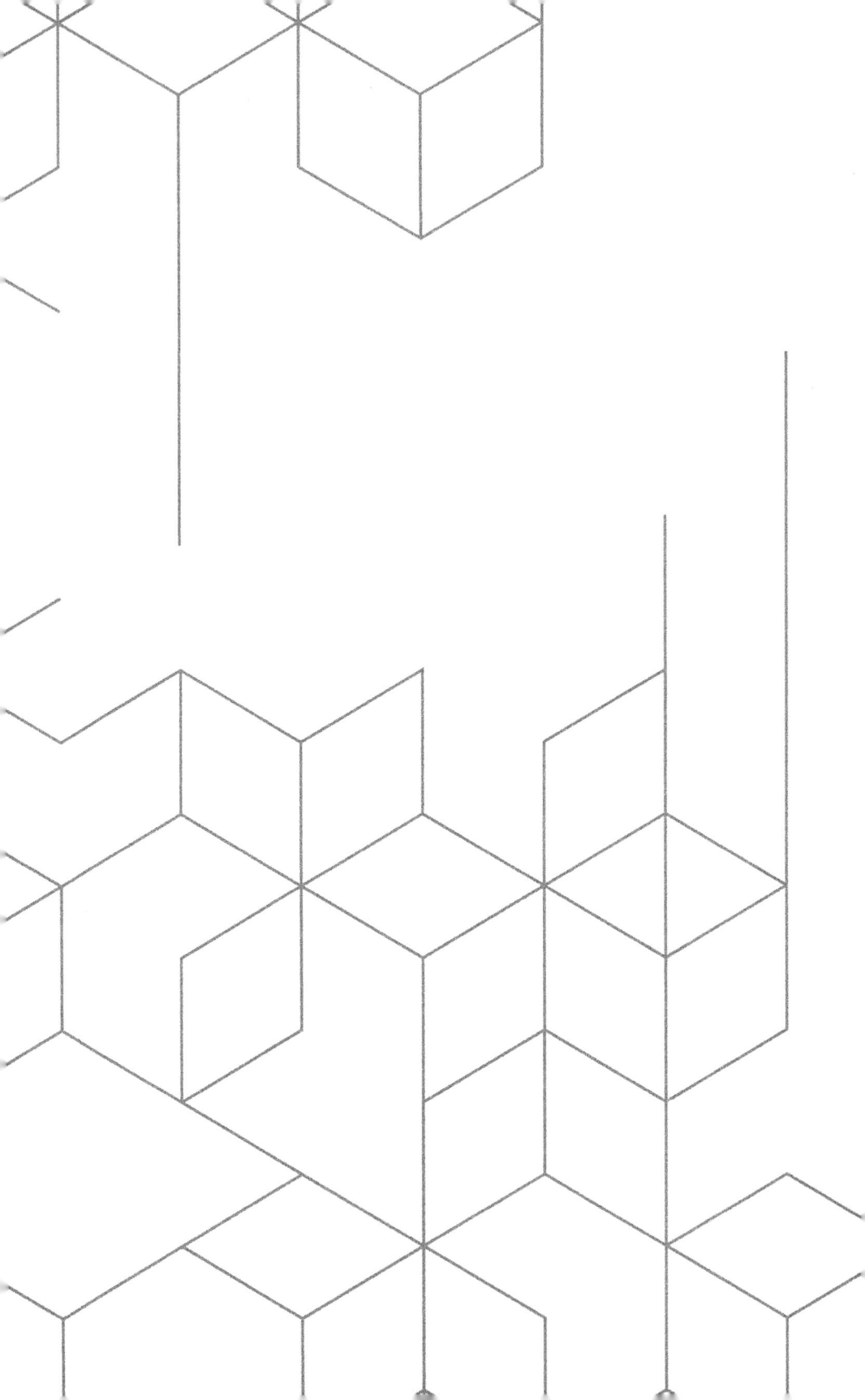

PART I
INTRODUCTION

THE PURSUIT OF MEANING:

The UNITAR-Hiroshima Fellowship for Afghanistan
Humaira Khan-Kamal[3]

This is not a paper on methodology, it is the story of a perfect storm when the best of the human spirit came together from Afghanistan and around the world, bound together in the Pursuit of Meaning[4] that the Fellowship gave to all our lives.

The events of September 2011 in the United States seemed to change everything, spreading ripples around the world. For Afghanistan however it was centuries of the same, the tragic destiny of a country caught in the great global game, not of its making or choice....

But for all those who wanted to help Afghanistan inside and outside the country, suddenly there was also a window of opportunity.

The Afghan Fellowship (AF) community over its fifteen-year duration expanded to around 500 members including 80 or so international Mentors and Faculty members who stayed involved and committed throughout. The leitmotiv through its uniquely long run, that kept the community together, was the unifying belief in the future of Afghanistan. Without ever being explicitly declared, this became the motivation for every contribution and effort, as much by the Afghan

---

[3] Humaira Khan-Kamal, AF Program Leader from inception to 2011; AF Senior Advisor 2012-2016; Co-founder AFLP.

[4] *The Power of Meaning*, Emily Esfahani Smith, Crown Publishers, NY, 2017

Fellows as by the supporting community worldwide. The AF community members all wanted to be a part of something meaningful and bigger than themselves.

As the program leader for the first eight years of its life, for me the litmus test of the Fellowship community specificity was always the first round of video conferences and web seminars that launched each program cycle. One typical video conference says it all: during the 2010 launching of the AF cycle, for example, 67 Afghan Fellows and Resource Persons, 30 international and local Mentors, and three UNITAR Staff connected from nine countries, across nine time zones, overcoming language, cultural, and tremendous technological challenges, to kick off the program cycle and connect with each other professionally and personally. There were Mentors who joined in the middle of the night, like Prof. David Eaton at University of Texas at Austin, and Howard and Sue Lamb in Washington DC who travelled to a video-conferencing facility to be able to join. Our Mentor teams from the University of Calgary with Dr. Lorne Jaques would get to the VC facility through snowstorms. Even more amazing were the Afghans themselves, who would determinedly connect over phones or computers from the middle of the legendary Kabul traffic jams or make it to their offices in spite of bombings or attacks en route, to ensure their participation in the program launch. It is significant to note that all Mentors, international and Afghan, and all faculty members were volunteers.

When I tried to describe my experience of this phenomenon to another faculty member and friend of the program – Dr. Duffie Van Balkom – he immediately understood what I wanted to express and introduced me to a book – *The Power of Meaning* by Emily Esfahani Smith.

Dr. Smith's premise is that the pursuit of meaning is a more sustaining pursuit than the pursuit of happiness. She suggests that there are four pillars of a meaningful life (Belonging, Purpose, Transcendence, and Meaning). And we can each create lives of meaning by building some or all these pillars in our lives. I would like to submit that the Fellowship for Afghanistan, throughout its existence, delivered the power of meaning by giving the 500-plus community members a sense of true Belonging, joint Purpose, and Transcendence to a higher reality which was life-changing for many, and helped the AF community develop a narrative about its time together.

From its first few cycles the Fellowship began to evolve organically, moving in the direction where the needs of the community seemed most compelling. The Fellowship in its final form was one of numerous iterations, adapting to how the Afghan professionals, and indeed Afghanistan itself, changed over the years. However, it is important to note that the AF Community from day one was very conscious of the "fierce urgency of now" — the opening that post 9/11 presented, and the important role the Fellows and their partners around the world could play. As the core team at UNITAR, we too constantly reminded all players that this program will be as good as they made it. The community responded with a genuine sense of ownership. As Mr. Sayed Maqbool, Fellow 2009 AF Cycle, said, "How can we ensure that the Fellowship mindset is shared and believed in by other Afghans in the country?" This question spoke to the belief that from the start all AF players felt the Fellowship needed to be shared with as many Afghans as possible.

My mentor and boss, Nassrine Azimi, once commented to me — and I am paraphrasing here — "What's history? It's all geography!" Never does this ring as true as when you look at the history of Afghanistan.

Afghanistan's greatest strength has been that it sits at a major crossroads of the world. But this has been its greatest vulnerability as well. Every nation that invaded Afghanistan disrupted the country, on its way to get somewhere else.

These disruptions, cultural exposures, brushes with some of the world's most momentous moments shaped the people of Afghanistan to be warriors, artists, poets, and most importantly survivors. They also left Afghanistan in perpetual states of war, divided loyalties and always in the eye of the storm.

When I come down from the macro to the micro however – people to people (Afghanistan to Japan) and everything in between, moments that flash across my mind are — more that makes us the same, rather than different —

- Trying new foods in Hiroshima, Kabul, Dehradun, Singapore, Abu Dhabi .... Flashes from 2003 with Afghans bringing their own roti with them to Hiroshima

- Japanese interns and Afghan female participants shopping together

- Afghan fascination and wonderment with aquariums in Osaka because coming from a landlocked country, sea-life was never a norm

- Running joke in the program that UNITAR's signature Afghan Fellowship was being managed by an Iranian, a Pakistani, and a Kazakh, all women ... it must have initially not filled the Afghans with much confidence!!

- Common words between Farsi, Dari, and Urdu entertainingly meaning very different things — the Afghan/Farsi word jaan (for respect or affection) vs. the Urdu word jaan (beloved, my life)....

- Emotional outpouring and connection with loss and grief when meeting the hibakusha in Hiroshima, and sharing traumatic memories...some of it very raw and recent on the Afghan side

- Emotional moments of telling stories in class, so unusual for the more reserved community members such as Singaporean and Japanese colleagues ... and then so normal for everybody just a few months down the road

- Afghans singing all night in Hiroshima in the hotel lobby as a send-off for friends such as Michael Fors, Duffie Van Balkom, and I, and the hotel staff letting it happen contrary to the norms of the hotel. Oh, those beautiful voices, one after the other

- Having all-girls' evenings with Fellows, Mentors and Faculty at the hotel

- Eating dinner with Afghan, American, Canadian, and Japanese colleagues at a Persian restaurant all the way in Singapore!

- Having audio/video conferences all night across multiple time zones, from multiple locations
- Traveling from Hiroshima to Tokyo with the whole group of 80 plus people on the Shinkansen!
- Starbucks offering caffeine to the addicted at every corner of Hiroshima
- The sea being warm like pea soup in Abu Dhabi
- Musical nights at each workshop where one and all were pulled in to participate, the Afghans offering Dari and Pashto songs, sometimes Urdu songs, Singaporean interns contributing with their national anthems, our Indian members offering beautiful Bollywood songs (alas UNITAR team members Berin and Sokout only offering renditions of nursery rhymes!)
- Meetings with coaches and faculty every morning to take stock of the day, and plan the next
- Animated meetings with mentors and coaches to plan next year sessions
- Passionate arguments among the Afghans, when Afghan case studies were presented in class; hearty laughter during role playing and simulation exercises
- Watching Obama's victory announcement in Hiroshima in 2008 with all of us — Afghan, Japanese, Canadian, Singaporean, Australian, New Zealander, Indian, Kazakh, Russian, Pakistani, and American, one and all stunned with the wonder of it all, moved by the universality and yet uniqueness of that historical moment, and of democracy
- Having discussions on faith and spirituality while standing near the Itsukushima Shrine, on Miyajima Island

All that makes us the same, rather than different....

The People and Their Story .... From the people of Afghanistan to the people of Hiroshima

As in any narrative the cast of characters has to be inspiring and gripping and the Fellowship Community had no shortage of stories, and players who played larger than life roles.

The Afghans – Owning the change they want to bring

> "I think anybody who had any contact with any of the Fellows could sense the commitment, resilience, and dedication to bring their country to a different position. Everybody was touched by that. Everybody then wanted to contribute in their ways."
>
> Sue Lamb, AF Core Faculty Member

In the pages that follow, much will be said by the Afghans and other players of the community about the Fellowship story. Post-August 2021 a lot of this will feel bittersweet. But none of the achievements – personal or professional – become any less real. In fact, the story becomes even more compelling as it demonstrates what the Afghans are capable of, what they accomplished when given the opportunity, respect and empowerment.

Since the early days of the Fellowship (2003) till the last cycle (2018) in every discussion that we had with the Afghans, we kept emphasizing the urgency of seizing this opportunity, and maximizing the benefits while the world was focused on them, and while there was funding and good will. It was obvious that we were preaching to the choir. All Afghans we worked with had rushed back from wherever they were with one goal: to rebuild their country. They recognized the importance of this moment in time, wanted to access in droves every educational and training opportunity possible, and literally devour every paper/book in their areas of interest.

Within the Fellowship itself, we had the best of the best applying themselves, to overcome language barriers, cultural barriers, technological barriers... to fully participate in the program. To meet the Fellowship requirements while working multiple jobs, they worked hard on the demanding assignments and training events. One such example was the AF alumni Dr. Gul Afghan Saleh, Ph.D. While participating in the Fellowship, he was working on massive infrastructure projects with the development community, and working towards completing his Ph.D. The Fellows travelled miles, sometimes through treacherous circumstances to get to training venues, sometimes just for an hour-long session with their international mentors at centers with available internet connections. Some had to raise funds themselves, to ensure their participation in the program. The Coaches and Afghan Resource persons from among the alumni worked pro-bono as did the international faculty and Mentors to help Fellows in each new cycle. The Coaches helped run the program in Kabul and at workshop venues. Where needed the Alumni stepped in to arrange for training venues in Kabul, transportation, visas, even funding from agencies that they worked for, for projects proposed by their class fellows. They kept pushing us to do more – "why don't we have longer workshops? More materials and handouts? More seminars? Why don't we convert this program into a degree program?"

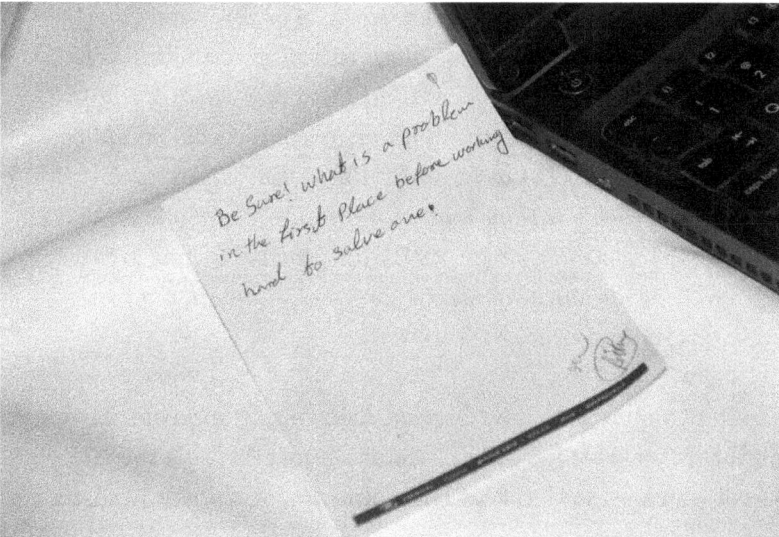

People cared about what they were doing. They took ownership.

This book also tells the story of the global close-knit partnership within the AF community, a partnership of mutual respect, driven by Afghan ideas and passion, and the Hiroshima context – quite unique among the initiatives on the ground in Afghanistan during the last 20 years.

Nassrine Azimi – Social Entrepreneur with Vision

> "A social entrepreneur is a person who pursues novel applications that have the potential to solve community-based problems. These individuals are willing to take on the risk and effort to create positive changes in society through their initiatives."[5]

> "Much has rightfully been made of the need for a clear and compelling vision in any endeavor. A vision can set direction, mobilize followers, align activities, and galvanize the will required by an individual or team to accomplish something significant. Without a compelling image of the future, and — as importantly — clear steps to achieving it, organizations will drift and quite likely fail. Any winning strategy begins with an aspiration that articulates what winning means for an individual, organization, or endeavor."[6]

These two quotes define Nassrine Azimi's role and contribution to all the projects we have collaborated on together, the most important of which is the UNITAR Hiroshima Fellowship for Afghanistan.

---

[5] *Social Entrepreneur* - Adam Hayes; Investopedia.com; Apr 24, 2021 (Social Entrepreneur Definition (investopedia.com)

[6] *How Social Entrepreneurs Make Change Happens?* Roger L. Martin and Sally R. Osberg, Harvard Business Review, 2014

One afternoon in July 2003, in between her preparations to move to an entirely different country (Japan), to set up a UNITAR office from scratch, Nassrine, my boss since 1996, called for a meeting. As was her habit she set a challenge for me: this time to develop a plan for a Fellowship for Afghanistan. It never occurred to me for a second to say no, primarily for three compelling reasons that she threw on the table: 1) the chance to work for Afghanistan itself and its pressing needs, 2) the chance to go on another under-funded, over-ambitious development adventure with her which was always fun; and 3) the incredible opportunity to work in a region we both came from and connected to by unbreakable cultural, familial, and historical bonds. What seemed like at most a five-year project, has become a lifetime commitment to not just Afghanistan but the AF Community at large.

From the beginning Nassrine was clear about her vision: the Fellowship had to be needs-based, offering training in any tools of management and development that the Fellows identified as a priority at that moment in time. But above all, with the training at its core, the Fellowship had to provide a community — one that was internationally connected, offered long-term support to its members and empowered the fellows to seek transformative change in their spheres of influence. Nassrine ensured that the Fellows, the Afghan and international mentors and faculty, and the Hiroshima Office team all saw each other as partners and fellow travelers working towards the same goals. More importantly she made believers of all of us, helping us put our work in the larger historical and global context. In later cycles, the Fellows sometimes only got to meet Nassrine a few times, but no one ever forgot or failed to be convinced on hearing her that they were there for an important purpose greater than themselves, and therefore the sense of responsibility for and ownership of the Fellowship was a must — as the Fellows called it "the Fellowship mindset." Of course, it also helped that she communicated all this in Farsi, English, French, and Japanese!

David Eaton – Making it happen

The first time Nassrine and I met David was when he flew in the from University of Texas at Austin (UTA) in 1996, to attend the re-opening of the UNITAR New York Office. Since that day David has been a stalwart pillar and supporter of the UNITAR mission, spearheading the involvement of UTA in the effort. It was this same commitment that made the backbone of David's involvement in the Fellowship for Afghanistan from 2003 to 2018 as a core faculty member and advisor. I always explained to new Fellows/Mentees or colleagues to the program that David was the ultimate example of the perpetually over-extended, but always invested, brilliant Professor. One half-hour of focused review and advice from David was worth many hours with anyone less effective (something which many Fellows found to be true by the end of the program). So when charged by Nassrine to start working on the first design for the Fellowship, my obvious next step was to take the program design to David for one afternoon of extensive brainstorming and review, of what became the first blueprint of many iterations for the program's design and curriculum. It was one of the best invested $300 airline tickets to Austin Texas by the program.

During our time working together, David never said no to any new or ambitious idea, he would simply listen, and come back with practical ways of making it happen. If we asked him to go to Kabul, he accepted, sometimes even going alone without any support staff, to deliver workshops when needed. When the Fellows asked UNITAR to offer university credits for completing the Fellowship, David immediately stepped in and worked with our team and UTA to establish the mechanisms for the curriculum to be recognized by the university. When the program needed Mentors with similar experiences and jobs as the Fellows, David brought in many UTA alumni working in the Texas government who could relate to the challenges of our young Afghan civil servants. Some of the AF Fellows' best and long-term relationships were formed with UTA mentors such as Jennifer Fox, Steven Polunsky, Meredith Melecki, and John Barton. One of David's most practical contributions to each cycle was his session with each team on their project proposals. At the beginning of the session dejectedly the Fellows felt as if he was pulling their proposals apart by identifying holes in the narrative, methodology or funding, but by the end everything would fall back into a better place and make more sense. Painful to watch but gratifying in the end!

Howard and Sue Lamb – Consolidating the Community Framework

The story of Howard and Sue's contribution to the program design and philosophy has many chapters and aspects, but the one which became the cornerstone of the program in the way it strengthened Afghan ownership was selecting the best graduates from each class to become coaches for the next. Nassrine had already envisioned and directed me to incorporate matching Mentors around the world with the AF participants as a key aspect of the program design, but at the end of the first cycle when reviewing and planning for the next year – Howard and Sue asked us the one question which changed everything – "What are you planning to do to avoid losing this group of professionals that you have just trained?" Thanks to their vision and recommendations we incorporated Alumni Coaches and then subsequently, Alumni as Resource Persons, Mentors and even Faculty Members.

Michael Fors – Leading and Inspiring the Community to Achieve its "Bolero"

Among the many lessons that Michael taught us in the AF Community on leadership, coaching, team development, project management and implementation, and social entrepreneurship, the recurring theme was how to work together to achieve performance. He always used the case of Zubin Mehta and his Los Angeles Philharmonic Orchestra. The Orchestra, like any team, had to go through different stages of team development to finally come together to perform Ravel's Bolero. With this example Michael not only tapped into the universal power of a beautiful piece of musical work, but most importantly he inspired every team in the room to slog through the challenges of working together with people from different ethnicities, cultures, work styles, and agendas to eventually deliver the perfect pitched performance, every team's Bolero!

Years of working with Michael (1997 to-date) makes one appreciate the incredible positivity, generosity, and professionalism that he brings to everything he does. While teaching servant leadership he himself was its best exemplar. Unusual for many international executive coaches, Michael brought all of himself to the Fellowship, without any reservations. When speaking in a session he would always say this is what WE want to do for Afghanistan, this is what WE hope for Afghanistan and he meant we – the Afghan Fellows, the AF Community and himself. Afghanistan stopped being "the other" for him very early in the program, and each of us are the richer for it.

Lorne Jaques – Transformational Change through Social Capital

If David facilitated the academic infrastructure to support AF, Howard and Sue helped build the pillars of its community, and Michael showed us how to perform as one well-tuned team, then Lorne made us ask and strive to answer, time and again, the very important question – Why does it all matter? He kept reminding us that we have to lead the projects we undertake, and not let the projects lead us. Lorne brought to the program his years of development experience, his faith in the social capital within the community as a powerful resource, and most importantly a rare (in international development circles) and sincere belief that the development process is a two-way street, where listening to the local partner as the primary expert on what's needed is the only way to hope for any shared ownership or impact.

> "You can only do transformational development in an organization and ... the organization can only transform itself; if, it has the most important qualities of a community...the most important of those qualities .... is: Social Capital. And the weaker its social capital ...the more vulnerable are its members, and the weaker its performance potential."

Lorne Jaques

The lessons we all learned from Lorne were not easy, passive exercises. Every one of us, from the Afghans to the international community members had to actively reset minds, apply these principles and own the end results, to complete the AF experience.

Sharapiya Kakimova – The Firm but Empathetic Shepherd

Sharapiya Kakimova, my seamless partner-in-crime during the first six years of the Fellowship's life (and then a key Mentor for many years), a fearless and passionate warrior once she adopted you or your cause, was also – I am told by the Fellows from various cycles – a scary Kazakh who they felt compelled to entrust their fates to during an AF Cycle. The AF being a new and important program in the UNITAR portfolio, in the early years Nassrine, Sharapiya and I strategized together over even the smallest of mechanisms – details such as the sequence of events, logistical requirements, expectations, and in addition to the core curriculum aspects to convey and emphasize, such as connections to Hiroshima and emphasis on building a self-supporting AF community. All of which was firmly implemented by Sharapiya, a true tiger-mom for the Fellows, believing in tough love tempered with much laughter, often even keeping Nassrine and I on the straight and narrow! Thanks to Sharapiya's persistence, the foundations of the AF community culture and traditions were established along the lines that we had envisioned early on, and it lasted throughout the program's duration.

Sabahuddin Sokout – Servant Leadership

When Michael Fors introduced the concept of servant leadership in the Fellowship, the example he immediately identified within the AF community was Sokout. And to a person, all 60 people in the room completely agreed with him! Sokout wore many hats in the Fellowship. He experienced the program from the perspective of an Afghan, as well as that of UNITAR. If anyone needed help with the content of the program, Sokout was their man. If Mentors or UNITAR needed first-hand review of the dynamics or conflict in one of the Fellowship groups, or the political or security situation on the ground, Sokout was the fair, reliable observer as well as peacemaker. If the female participants had any concerns about group members or the program logistics – they knew to turn to Sokout. Sokout intervened and resolved issues without judgment and with honesty. He was always the bridge between the Afghanistan-based and the international members of the community. If there was a professional milestone to celebrate, a personal tragedy to share ....

Sokout ensured that the whole community stayed connected and invested in each other.

> *"...servant-leaders have the humility, courage, and insight to admit that they can benefit from the expertise of others who have less power than them. They actively seek the ideas and unique contributions of the people (employees) that they serve. This is how servant leaders create a culture of learning, and an atmosphere that encourages followers to become the very best they can."*[7]

Sokout represents the best of the AF – he has been Fellow, Coach, Resource Person, Mentor, Faculty Member, fund-raiser, UNITAR Representative in Afghanistan, colleague and partner for managing the program, a visa expert for multiple countries, and an impressive ambassador for the best that his country has to offer. However, over and above all this, he is to-date an Afghan who is always, always, serving his fellow countrymen/women in the best way possible.

Faculty, Mentors and Coaches – Arteries bringing the community to life

As has been mentioned before, through the fifteen-year duration of the Fellowship for Afghanistan, the Faculty, the Mentors and the Coaches, Afghan or International, all worked pro-bono to contribute to the program and its mission. AF could not function without any of them, but with them it also became alive with memorable interactions, cultural missteps, and laughter, and above all a rich exchange of knowledge and experience. Remember this

---

[7] *How Humble Leadership really works?* Dan Cable, Harvard Business Review, 2018

all started in early 2000s, without digital distance learning as a norm, or even much available as basic infrastructure. Also, where there were so many distances to overcome (physical or otherwise) meaningful and productive digital communication really happened if you got to meet each other in person at least once. In that context, UNITAR encouraged the Mentors to join the Fellows for on-site workshops when possible, and the majority of the Mentors made it to at least one or two of the in-person workshops, often funding their trip through personal contributions, institutional support or even travel miles collected. Once they met their groups and the AF community as a whole, the quality of understanding and communication was electrifying. As one of our Mentors – Dr. Roger Galbraith – exclaimed after his first experience in one of these workshop sessions (on the performance of the Afghan utility company – a subject on which every Afghan had an opinion!) – "Nothing compares to this, the energy in the room is just jumping off the walls!"

The role of the coaches evolved and expanded with every cycle. They became the first line of support to the Fellows with their assignments. They interpreted the Fellowship to the new cohorts who often struggled in the beginning to understand its unusual structure and expectations. The Coaches became Sokout's core team in each cycle when moving a 40 to 60 strong group from milestone to milestone and physically from place to place and event to event. The Coaches and Afghan Resource Persons also started taking upon themselves the development and delivery of Afghan-specific case studies, and facilitated training in Afghanistan and abroad with other Faculty Members. But above all, they modeled all that we hoped a UNITAR AF Fellow would become, and the Fellows wanted to be them in the next cycle.

One example of the many workshops where the community had large and memorable gatherings was a 10-day training event held in Abu Dhabi in July 2011. The 60 Fellows of the 2011 Cycle were joined by a dream team of 12 Coaches and Resource Persons, around eight Mentors, four Faculty Members and the UNITAR team. For ten days, we rolled up our sleeves and packed each day with learning, problem-solving, and meetings. We fought, we complained, we had breakthroughs and tried to maximize the opportunity for face-to-face interaction in every way possible. These are the experiences which delivered the power of meaning by giving the community members a sense of true Belonging, joint Purpose, Transcendence to a higher reality which was life-changing for many and helped the AF community develop a narrative about its time together.

The UNITAR team and the Donors – the Enablers

The interesting thing about the UNITAR Hiroshima Office (HO) team was that everybody had to be "all-hands on deck" for every program the office managed. This was the culture facilitated by Nassrine's vision and leadership style, and became one of HO's unique characteristics. It was not just about the logistics of the training, but staff became substantively invested also in the mission, the final product of all the programs the office was implementing. In the case of the Fellowship as the association of the Fellows with UNITAR lasted multiple years, deeper relationships were formed, the whole team stayed engaged, and the AF became the centerpiece of the Hiroshima Office's portfolio. The Hiroshima Office team to-date has always been young but extremely well-qualified and resourceful. We liked to call ourselves the Lean and Mean team, who aimed for high impacts with limited resources serving a large corner of the world with many needs. The team over the life of the Fellowship was enriched with the commitment, sensibilities, and experiences of many mentioned here alphabetically (and some not listed.) Many in this group ably steered the program after both Nassrine and I were no longer directly involved, keeping true to the spirit of the Fellowship and making it even stronger .... I name them here in alphabetical order — Johanna Diwa, Nigel Gan, Rachel Krause, Mihoko Kumamoto, Berin McKenzie, Alex Mejia, Chris Moore, Hiroko Nakayama, Gaston Nishiwaki, Kaori Okabe, Sergei Shapashnikov, Shamsul Hadi Shams, Junko Shimazu, James Short, Alissa Tukkimaki, Brandon Turner and Atsushi Yasui. Berin, and then Nigel took over the leadership of the program once I left, and did a remarkable job maintaining both continuity and change. Thanks to Alex's efforts as head of the office, the program expanded its reach by doubling the number of Fellows, and consequently its impact and community, while Mihoko focused on broadening the strategic reach of UNITAR's work in Afghanistan to new areas, notably women's training and sports.

The Hiroshima Prefectural Government, the main donor of the AF, provided that rarity in international development assistance: continuity. The funding it earmarked for the Fellowship continued throughout the lifespan of the program. Just as importantly, the donor did not impose any rigid expectations, leaving UNITAR the flexibility to adapt to the evolving needs of the Fellowship. In the same spirit the Fellowship was supported by many other financial and in-kind supporters throughout its duration, such as the City of Hiroshima, Singapore International Foundation (SIF), Microsoft, University of Texas at Austin, University of Calgary, Ministries in the Afghan Government, the Agha Khan Foundation of Afghanistan, and others.

Was it all a Waste?

In the wake of August 2021 and the shock of the Afghan government's unravelling many around the world have been debating similar interventions and development projects. For the most part this has become tired and cynical. Why did the Afghans not defend their hard-achieved gains? What did the Afghans or the international community do, or not do, over 20 years.

The Fellowship showcases the global community partnership that came into existence as a unique outcome. Ideas and passion came from the Afghans and their projects. They decided what they wanted to do, whatever fired them. Sometimes it was about small projects, which eliminated bottlenecks in their work. Sometimes far larger and ambitious projects, which solved one community need at a time, slowly building on a workable macro solution. Everybody respected the ideas, supported the projects, shared their experiences and expertise to fine tune the outcome.

It was a unique relationship, driven by a pursuit of shared goals. Indeed except for the UNITAR secretariat staff supporting the program all faculty members contributed in-kind or pro-bono. In contrast currently the takeaway by the world-at-large is that the Afghan intervention was just a lot of money spent, people going along for the ride, with no productive strategy or goals. In the Fellowship this was certainly not the case, it was **personal investments** by people, equal and mutual. It was an exchange. Relationships mattered. Even now the social capital of the community is in play, everybody is reaching out to each other with offers of help. The suffering of our Afghan community members feels like a calamity in the family, with members reaching out to commiserate and help/reassure. This is the humanity that development projects need to tap into – in the end this is what will last and sustain. Therefore, we believe that this book can upend the current discourse – namely "Was it all a waste?", an important question to answer for Afghanistan, and also for future development and humanitarian initiatives. In a way this book's timing maybe apt, because the Fellowship for Afghanistan has become more of a model that we must and can share, rather than being only the beautiful story that it will always remain.

Spring is Here

*For all of us from this region, generations have lived through disappointments and betrayals by our leaders, by our fates, by ourselves. Yet each time there is a glimmer of hope, we say **Spring is here** and open a new chapter ...... This is the resilience which will ensure the survival of the Afghan people, of Afghanistan.*

بہار آئی

بہار آئی

کہ جیسے یک بار لوٹ آئے ہیں پھر عدم سے

وہ خواب سارے شباب سارے

جو تیرے ہونٹوں پہ مٹ مٹے تھے

جو مٹ کے ہر بار پھر جیے تھے

نکھر گئے ہیں گلاب سارے

جو تیری یادوں سے مشک بو ہیں

جو تیرے عشاق کا لہو ہیں

ابل پڑے ہیں عذاب سارے

ملال احوال دوستاں بھی

خمار آغوش مہوشاں بھی

غبار خاطر کے باب سارے

ترے ہمارے سوال سارے جواب سارے

بہار آئی تو کھل گئے ہیں

نئے سرے سے حساب سارے

فیض احمد فیض

Spring is here

By Faiz Ahmad Faiz

translated from Urdu by Mustansir Dalvi

Spring is here, and it is as if the full flush of youth, every forgotten dream is back from the abyss.

The longing that died for a touch of your lips was annihilated and then resurrected each time.

All those roses are back in bloom brimming with the musk of remembrance, blazing red with the hue of your many loves.

Every torment boils over—the perpetual regret of losing friends, the euphoria of losing myself in the moon-rise of your glory, the wisp of memories and all they bring to you and to me all the questions and all the answers.

All that is accrued, all that is called to account stands freshly renewed, now spring is here.

Faiz Ahmad Faiz MBE NI was a Pakistani poet, author and activist in Urdu and Punjabi language. He was one of the most celebrated writers of the Urdu language in Pakistan

A Short Primer on History
Sabahuddin Sokout[8]

In 1921 British India recognized Afghanistan as a fully independent country, but still the Treaty of Rawalpindi limited Afghanistan's foreign policy. Socioeconomic reform initiated by Amir Amanullah Khan were to help Afghanistan not fall behind other countries, but British deception continued influencing people and minds to doubt and counter Amir and his reforms and actions as anti-Islamic acts. In 1924, and again in 1928, rebels, supported by foreign countries at Afghan borders (i.e., British India), forced Amir to end the reforms and finally leave the country.

In 1972, once again Afghanistan tried to rise as an independent country connected to the world. President Sardar Daud Khan instituted reforms and an economic growth plan, but the Cold War, the competition between the Soviet Union and the United States, changed Afghanistan into a battlefield. The alignment of Afghan political parties (Khalq and Parcham) with the Soviet Union caused Afghanistan to be invaded again by another superpower. A new government assisted by the Soviet Union came to power at the cost of life to President Daud Khan, who was killed along with all his family members inside the Presidential Palace.

After the withdrawal of Soviet troops from Afghanistan in 1989, new reforms caused economic growth, and Afghan businessmen

---

[8] UNITAR Afghanistan Program Coordinator, AF Fellow, Coach, Afghan Resource Person, and Faculty Member

were again counted among the successful traders in region. Still, the conflict continued, and finally, the UN established the Office of the Secretary-General in Afghanistan and Pakistan (OSGAP) on October 17, 1990, in order to help Afghanistan with its political transition. However, interference from other countries caused Dr. Najibullah to flee and reside inside the UN office in Kabul. He was later executed by the Taliban.

The defeat of the Taliban in 2000 and the invasion of Afghanistan by the US started a new era in the 21st century. The steady improvement of Afghanistan's economy by 2019 notwithstanding, once again conflict and instability, and the lack of a clear policy by the Americans, plunged the country into uncertain times. The reset button has been reset. The change of regime in Afghanistan means to start everything from the scratch — constitution, laws, development policies, and the national strategy.

Afghanistan, Conflict, Reconstruction
Jonathan Moore[9]

Editors' Note:

In September 2002, one year after the September 11 attacks in the United States, Jonathan Moore, Akio Inoue[10] and Nassrine Azimi went to Kabul, to research what shape a training program out of Hiroshima should take. More than 30 interviews later — with Afghans from all walks of life and backgrounds as well as non-Afghans with international organizations, diplomatic and humanitarian missions, and grass-roots NGOs — the foundations and philosophy for the UNITAR Hiroshima Fellowship was born.

The notes below by Ambassador Moore were drafted during a second visit, in October 2006, when he and a few other members of the Hiroshima Fellowship community accompanied the UNITAR team to Afghanistan for a fact-finding mission[11]. They have been slightly edited for clarity.

---

[9] Former United States Ambassador at Large for Refugee Affairs and Ambassador to the United Nations; Former Senior Special Fellow, UNITAR Hiroshima Office. (1932-2017 RIP)

[10] Akio Inoue, Professor, Tenri University, Tenri, Japan

[11] In addition to Jonathan Moore, Nassrine Azimi and Sharapiya Kakimova the mission included Ismail Sudderuddin, Jobaid Kabir and Hideaki Shinoda

"Looking to a future containing promise, hope, danger and uncertainty, the key resources of Afghanistan nation-building lie in the willingness of its people to be forbearing, persistent, unified, and resilient. This social psychology is essential, as in any prodigious human endeavor...... continuing to do what can be done as well as possible, not being intimidated by the imposing difficulties, and respecting the need for time. Capacity-building, training, at different levels and in a variety of formats and focuses, and where Afghans and internationals collaborate, is a critical component, helping to develop both the competence and confidence to be able to continue to move forward."

Jonathan Moore, in "Post-Conflict Reconstruction in Afghanistan," Notes prepared in the context of the Hiroshima Fellowship assessment, October 2006.

Post-Conflict Reconstruction in Afghanistan
Jonathan Moore (written in October 2006)

It is exceedingly difficult to understand, let alone write about, the status of "post-conflict reconstruction in Afghanistan," particularly if the author is an outsider and when some of the readers, who are not, have particular experience and insight which make them better informed. The whole process of nation-building is fiendishly complicated and also constantly changing, its different moving parts impacting each other intimately and ruthlessly, and difficult to comprehend at any given moment. But perhaps individual interpretations can be useful in contributing to a better sense of what's going on – as long as they are taken as incomplete and imperfect and if they are combined with other accounts and independent reflection.

Afghanistan is currently experiencing a particularly problematic phase in its process of nation-building, considering the progress and lack thereof in several major categories of effort. Given the prodigious ambitions and obstacles which are inherent and the history of similar undertakings in other countries, this is to be expected. Delays, setbacks, and erratic progress are part of the reality, along with the extended time required before a sustainable viability can be reached. The insecurity and the prevalence of violence in Afghanistan is the biggest single drawback to progress; it is currently increasing and in some areas of the country is intense. This of course contributes to everything bad, most prominently endangering civilian populations, preventing programs of social and economic development, diverting local popular support for such programs, and challenging central government authority and solidarity. Widespread security is the sine qua non of development, and in order to achieve it there needs to be adequately trained and equipped military forces, both Afghan and international, deployed in sufficient numbers. So far, that capability and quantity has not materialized in the face of Taliban resurgence and the persistence of recalcitrant warlords, independent militias and banditry. The requirements for success here are more commitment and more perseverance, in bringing force to bear against the insurgents and in concerted help to the people in reconstruction and basic services. A higher priority, more effectively implemented, is needed for many more police, trained, led, deployed and supported by the government and the populace and which will have a hugely salutary effect when accomplished. More pressure is needed from international diplomacy and from Pakistan in order to prevent the flow of opposition fighters and supplies from there back and forth into Afghanistan. The international provincial reconstruction teams deployed to many regions of the country must enhance their efforts to determine how best to pursue security, development and mutually supporting relationships with local communities at the same time.

It is generally understood that meaningful social and economic development cannot take place without security having been established, but development, starting with humanitarian action, includes a multitude of different initiatives some of which have got to be undertaken at the same time as security is being established, without waiting for it to be fully reached. (And security cannot be sustained without significant development having been achieved.) In Afghanistan, more has got to be done than has been effectively undertaken thus far to get the activity and the benefits of early development – e.g., agricultural support, infrastructure upgrading, basic utilities and services delivery, strengthening of local governance, employment, education – into the countryside, at the grass roots, where the largest and neediest population lives. As is the case with everything else under the nation-building aegis, this is easy to say and awfully difficult to do, and major efforts have been devoted to this end, but they have fallen short and better undertakings must be found.

Truly remarkable progress has been made in Afghanistan toward building a legitimate, representative, and accountable central government. This should not be obscured by its shortcomings and reversals, which are to be expected in the messiness of transitional politics, but the momentum seized to advance the commitment to national unity and coherence against the various tendencies of factionalism and separatism. Corruption is having a corrosive and multiplying effect at all levels of Afghan society, but it has not produced a death grip and can be reduced and not merely by punitive action. A system of effective legal institutions and protections is growing painfully and fitfully, but must be accompanied by a higher commitment to efforts bolstering the life of the poor and vulnerable populations in the provinces.

The phenomenon of narcotics, of opium production, is crucial for Afghanistan's recovery and growth for several reasons. It is growing. It is the livelihood for large numbers of Afghan farmers. It dramatically aids the multiplication of insurgency and violence, corruption, and general disorder. The international community is growing aggravated and weary about the problem. And there is presently no operative strategy which has proved capable of dealing effectively with it. Again, integrated action is needed on multiple fronts: police, stronger incentives for alternative crops, reconstruction funds, support of local government, more military forces, and greater sophistication in the attitude of the international community. The intimate relationship of interdiction, alternative livelihoods and eradication must be better calculated, in priority and sequencing. Alternative livelihoods must be advanced, without marginalizing the poor, as part of long-term agricultural sustainability rather than as a short-term fix merely to wipe out poppies. Proposals to permit Afghan farmers to sell opium to pharmaceutical companies, for legal painkilling medicines, should be adopted. In all categories, much greater resources are required.

A huge, imponderable factor in assessing the evolution of Afghanistan post-conflict reconstruction is the seriousness and the staying power of those members of the international community who are most involved and care the most about Afghanistan's independent and viable future – seriousness and staying power in personnel and resources, in security assurance and development assistance, above all, in time. How well things are going on the ground will influence this, but the answer is also subject to a number of variable forces beyond the reach of the domestic actors. This issue has come into vivid focus right now, and it is obviously a healthy and reassuring sign that the current discourse emphasizes staying and investing more rather than leveling off or leaving.

Ultimately, looking to a future containing promise, hope, danger and uncertainty, the key resources of Afghanistan nation-building lie in the willingness of its people to be forbearing, persistent, unified, and resilient. The social psychology is essential, as in any prodigious human endeavor – slogging it out, continuing to do what can be done as well as possible, not being intimidated by the impos- ing difficulties, and respecting the need for time. Capacity-building, training, at different levels and in a variety of formats and focuses, and where Afghans and internationals collaborate, is a critical component, helping to develop both the competence and confidence to be able to continue to move forward. [12]

Editors' Postscript:

As a follow-up to the above-mentioned 2006 Mission, University of Calgary's Fellow to UNITAR in 2011, Alisa Tukkimaki, conducted a survey to capture the unfiltered voices of Afghans on Afghanistan and its future. The survey is included as Appendix A

---

[12] ANNEX: BROAD NATION-BUILDING PRINCIPLES

Jonathan Moore October 2006

The current phase of Afghanistan post-conflict reconstruction exhibits several broad principles which are common to experience in other countries undergoing nation-building, and which it is useful to keep in mind. Among them are:

1. Security must be present for significant reconstruction and development to take place.
2. Nation-building takes a long, long time and requires steadfastness and patience without a certain outcome; progress will not occur steadily but in fits and starts, forward and backwards, and forcing components of it too fast will founder.
3. The whole enterprise is made up of many variable factors which are interdependent and interactive, and can reinforce or hamper each other; both prioritization and simultaneous action are necessary.
4. Efforts to advance sustainable development are the most complex and difficult challenge, and are often relegated to an inferior status and delayed for too long.
5. The structure and processes through which the international community mobilizes and implements its contributions to nation-building, and the resulting relationships with the national actors, are terribly difficult to manage well and inevitably become part of the problem as well as the solution.
6. The capacity and quality of performance of local assets is paramount, and the achievement of coherence and collaborative action out of diverse interests and factions for the nation's common good is enormously problematical.
7. Concerted efforts from the bottom up are necessary to join productively with the expected actions from the top down for progress to be achieved.

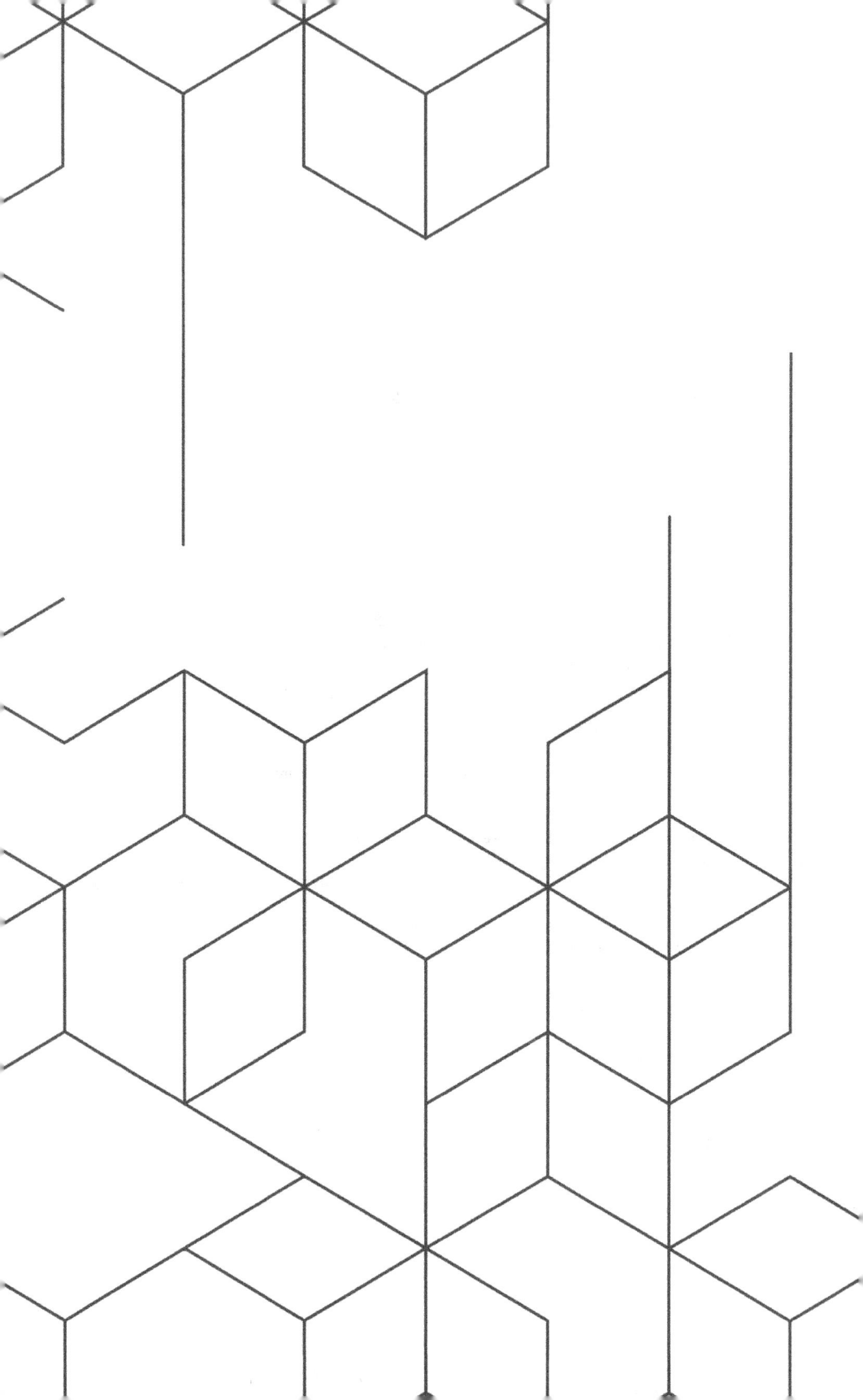

PART II
THE FELLOWSHIP—FROM VISION TO REALITY

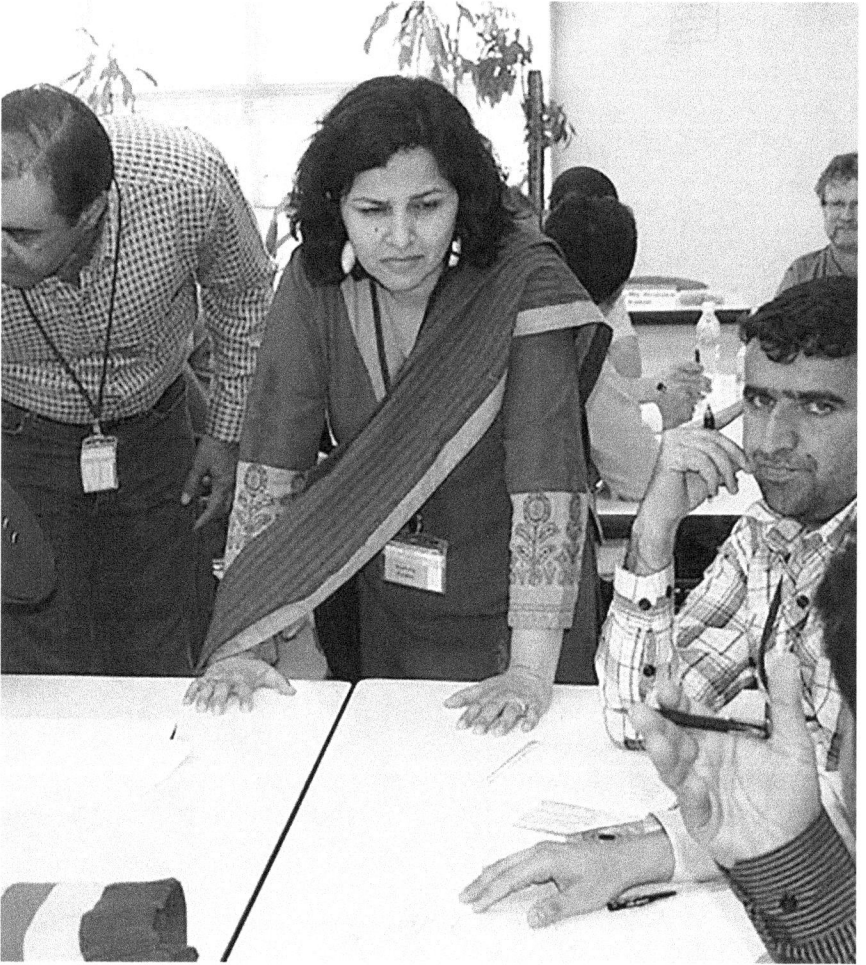

A LOW-COST, HIGH-IMPACT PROGRAM:
The UNITAR Hiroshima Fellowship for Afghanistan –
Curriculum and Program Evolution

Humaira Khan-Kamal

As all of us who worked on the Fellowship from its inception till the last cycle will tell you, the hardest question to answer about the UNITAR Fellowship for Afghanistan was "Please describe the Fellowship, and the training methodologies used in the program."

A few immediate answers come to my mind:

1. The program evolved each year;
2. It was different and unique for its time;
3. It had multiple players, roles and moving parts;
4. It was need-based and learner-driven -- within the overall structure all parts and roles were adapted to the needs of the Fellows, responsive to feedback of the AF community and the changing financial and political environments;
5. It was a blended-learning program.

We could find fingerprints of every community member on the curriculum — the Fellowship became richer for it. It is also significantly telling of the commitment of the AF Community to the mission of the program that the number of partners in the program increased from two to 29 partners over the 15 cycles. Of these, by the last cycle,

40% were Afghan Institutions and ministries, a fact which speaks to Afghan commitment to, and ownership of the program.

Maybe one of the more succinct and pertinent descriptions of the Fellowship was by a World Bank colleague, who called it "a low cost, high impact program". All those involved continued to have a strong commitment to the mission, by staying focused on the individuals in the program, and staying with them over the long-term. We were quite convinced that we did not want to train our Fellows for a few weeks and then lose them in a vacuum. The program mission as well as the training methodology had to proceed as building blocks. This approach can be traced in:

- the organic evolution of the Fellows to empowered professionals in their workspace,
- the transformation of Afghans and international faculty and mentors into one single community of like-minded professionals working for and with Afghanistan,
- the structure of the program from the selection process to the final presentations on learning and projects to peers and supervisors in Afghanistan, and
- very noticeably in the development of Fellowship projects from organizational needs assessments to implementation.

Here I will attempt to explain the goals, structure, and methodology of the program in the simplest way possible, to give the reader some context to all our stories going forward.

The Core Principles of the Fellowship in response to Afghan needs and Requirements:

a. The enrollment of highly qualified and experienced participants from a variety of disciplines, organizations, geographical and ethnic representations, public/non-profit/academic representations -

(all critical to the constant Afghan need to identify common goals and purpose as well as richness of resources and skills in the diversity);

b. Training participants while they continued with their jobs *(This ensured training to be targeted and specific to the job that needed to be done, be it million-dollar infrastructure projects, or small but targeted projects critical to streamline work processes -- such as building capacities in a six people team to use digital tools for reporting between provinces and head office)*;

c. A mentorship-based learning process, which sought to address the specific individual needs of each Fellow *(This principle recognized that Afghan expertise and skill levels were uneven based on accessibility of past learning resources, as well as lack of capacity to absorb development assistance in the early years because a whole generation of Afghan professionals and adults had been lost in the wars. All their learning had to be managed in real time, in the face of monumental and urgent requirements for reconstruction and management of projects)*;

d. An effective combination of various training methods, on-site workshops and distance learning mechanisms *(There was a critical need for flexibility in learning platforms for Afghanistan, given the challenges of security, costs, IT infrastructure and the absolute commitment to connecting the best with the best to get the job done)*;

e. Building professional networks within the country and between Afghanistan and the rest of the world—with capacities to contribute to the reconstruction of the country and its institutions *(This was considered the most important goal to sustain and protect the legacy of the program once resources, support and attention spans of international assistance dissipated)*.

AF Evolution Timeline

CYCLE	STATS & NEW DEVELOPMENTS	CURRICULUM DEVELOPMENTS, WEBINARS & ROUNDTABLES (RT)
2002	Fact-finding Mission to Kabul, Afghanistan. More than 30 interviews conducted with Afghans from all walks of life and backgrounds, as well as non-Afghans with international organizations, diplomatic and humanitarian missions, and grass-roots NGOs. Findings of this mission (N. AZIMI (NA)/A. INOUE/J. MOORE (JM)) to form foundations/philosophy for the UNITAR Hiroshima Fellowship;	
2003-04	1. Due to limited English language and business IT abilities and infrastructure, language lessons and computer classes had to be added and infrastructure support provided; 2. Element of Coaches: at the end of cycle H. LAMB (HL) and S. LAMB (SL) suggested selecting Alumni from previous cycle as Coaches to invest back the capacities created;	Pilot year, blended learning, Individual projects (projects become most important vehicle of on-the job learning), Personal Development Plans (PDPs), themes directly related to Fellows' work, extracted from Toolbox of capacity building, leadership and management; (H.KAMAL(HK) /NA/D. EATON (DE)) Training of Trainers (TOT) modules desired to ensure development of core group of experts who could train others within Afghanistan.

CYCLE	STATS & NEW DEVELOPMENTS	CURRICULUM DEVELOPMENTS, WEBINARS & ROUNDTABLES (RT)
2005	1. NUMBERS: Fellows 23, Coaches 6, # Events: 3 onsite workshops - Final WS in Hiroshima, VCs 6; 2. FEATURES- Flexibility, Fellow ownership, selection process to include screening for language skills and computer literacy levels; 3. AF FOCAL POINT required in Kabul; 4. COACHES added; 5. TORs for Mentors, Coaches and Fellows developed and required (HK); 6. INTERACTIVE BULLETIN BOARD created on UNITAR AF Webpage to support Distance Learning; 7. ROUNDTABLES on Macro topics related to Afghanistan introduced; 8. STUDY TRIPS to organizations in Japan introduced; 9. CULTURAL EXCHANGE and interaction activities introduced.	1. ADDITIONAL TOPICS COVERED: Project Management in Public service, TOT, Stratrgic Planning Process and Skills, Result-based Accountability; 2. TECHNICAL AND PROFESSIONAL WORD Glossaries for different English terminology to be developed in Dari and Pushto by Alumni; 3. PRESENTATION SKILLS to be taught; 4. AFTER-ACTION REVIEW BY COACHES introduced in each training session; 5. MENTORS INVITED and encouraged to attend at least one in-person WS, to facilitate Mentor- Fellow communication and relationships; 6. Cultural Briefings on Japan were added in the Hiroshima WS (NA /S. KAKIMOVA (SK)); 7. LAPTOPS FOR FELLOWS - Presented by UNITAR to support the Distance Learning process NA/SK); 8. Small STIPENDS awarded to Fellows and Coaches for travel to Kabul for VCs every month (NA); 9. HIROSHIMA Round Tables with AFGHAN Ambassador to Tokyo Haroon AMIN - Afghan National; Strategy for Post-Bonn Period.

CYCLE	STATS & NEW DEVELOPMENTS	CURRICULUM DEVELOPMENTS, WEBINARS & ROUNDTABLES (RT)
2006	IMPORTANT YEAR — Fellowship starts getting closer to its final shape/format 1. NUMBERS: Fellows 22, Mentors 14, Coaches 6; # of Events: 3 workshops, 4 VCs, 5 Audio-conferences and 8 project work sessions were conducted; 2. GOAL - AF seeks to ensure sustainable learning in the workplace; 3. UTA CREDITS - offered for the first time (D. E/UTA); 4. U of Calgary DISTANCE LEARNING PLATFORM offered (L. JAQUES (LJ)/UofC) - paid for by University of Calgary; 5. Introduction of Audio-web conferences and local project work sessions in addition to the video-conferences to increase opportunity for work within teams with Mentors; 6. MS PROJECT SOFTWARE donated by Michael Fors (MF)/ Microsoft for all Fellows and Coaches; 7. Wildlife Institute of India (WII) Dehradun host a workshop in India; 8. Increased reliance on ORGANIZATION & TRAINING NEEDS ASSESSMENTS as introduced by HL & SL; 9. Involvement of Fellowship Alumni in SELECTION OF PARTICIPANTS for the new cycle.	1. ADDITIONAL TOPICS COVERED: Organizational Needs Assessment, Capacity building and project mgmt, i.e. Tools from the Management Tool Box per the current needs of Afghan Professionals - such as project design & proposal writing (DE), report writing, TOT (Duffie VanBalkom (DVB)/LJ), Accounting and budgeting, project management and reporting, team building and team work (M. FORS (MF)), Communication skills, Leading organizational development; 2. UTA Credits offered for the first time; 3. TEAM PROJECTS not individual project, Each project was required to have a small capacity building component (NA/HK/SK); 4. Increased reliance on organizational needs-assessment for development of projects; 5. KABUL: RT with Nancy HATCH-DUPREY on the Importance of Preservation of Afghan Culture and History through decades of Conflict.

CYCLE	STATS & NEW DEVELOPMENTS	CURRICULUM DEVELOPMENTS, WEBINARS & ROUNDTABLES (RT)
2007	1. NUMBERS: Fellows 23, Coaches 6, Mentors 18, Afghan Resource Person (ARPs) - 2; EVENTS: 3 workshops, 4 VCs, 4 AWCs, 8 PWS; 2. UNITAR Official Representative in Afghanistan - AF Alum - Sabahuddin SOKOUT (SS); 3. Module on Coaching for Coaches given by MF & HK; 4. Three assignments as Project Architecture Milestones through the cycle developed by MF, HL, SL, HK; 5. Offering Access to MIT Open-CourseWare to AF Alumni and Kabul University (NA); 6. Formation of AF Alumni Community organization - ACTRA (Afghan Consultancy, Training and Research Association) which becomes a partner in conduct of events in Afghanistan (SS and Abdul Rashid Janbaz).	1. ADDITIONAL TOPICS COVERED: Organizational culture and change process; development of team projects; tools for project scheduling, monitoring and evaluation, budgeting and reporting; proposal writing and the use of tools such as MS Project software; 2. "Voices of Afghanistan – Lessons, Challenges and Hopes," attended by H.E. Mr. H. AMIN, Ambassador of Afghanistan to Japan.

CYCLE	STATS & NEW DEVELOPMENTS	CURRICULUM DEVELOPMENTS, WEBINARS & ROUNDTABLES (RT)
2008	1. NUMBERS: Fellows 24, Coaches 6, ARPs 2, Mentors and Faculty 17; Workshops 4, Webinars 5, AWCs 6, Project Work Sessions 6; 2. New 5 Web seminar module on HRD&HRM for Fellows and Alumni Community 3. Training for Afghan Resource Persons (HK/MF); 4. Expansion of module on Coaching for Coaches to 9 sessions and facilitation activities plus After-Action Review (AAR) sessions at each workshop; 5. Use of DISC and Team development exercises and simulations by MF; 6. Introduction to Social Capital by LJ; 7. Group/team project in the area of Gender, Ethics and Social Issues; 8. Partnering with Alumni Association (ACTRA) to jointly host and facilitate the module on HRM&HRD (SS).	1. ADDITIONAL TOPICS: Followship, Result-based Mgmt, Presentation of Afghan Cases written and presented by ARPs; 2. Five WEB SEMINAR SERIES on Human Resource Development and Management (HRD&HRM): I. "Leading people, an organization's greatest asset: An introduction to human resources management and development" - DVB; II. "Motivation, Communication and Conflict Resolution" -- Y. UESUGI (YU); III. "Practical Tools for Effective Performance Management" - CHIN. H. Y (CHY), P. LOW (PL) E. LEE (EL); IV. "Developing Training as a Capacity Building Tool" -- J. HATFIELD (JH); V. "Basic Communication Skills for Improved HRM "; 3. ROUNDTABLE HIROSHIMA - Afghanistan's Reconstruction – Challenges and Commitments," organized in partnership with the Embassy of Afghanistan in Japan.

CYCLE	STATS & NEW DEVELOPMENTS	CURRICULUM DEVELOPMENTS, WEBINARS & ROUNDTABLES (RT)
2009	1. NUMBERS: Fellows 25, Coaches 6, ARPs 2, Mentors and Faculty 27; Workshops 4, Webinars 5, AWCs 6, Project Work Sessions 6; 2. New 5 Web seminar module on HRD&HRM for Fellows and Alumni Community; 3. Training for ARPs; 4. Expansion of module on Coaching for Coaches to 10 sessions and facilitation activities plus AAR sessions at each workshop; 5. Partnering with Alumni Association (ACTRA) to jointly host the four-day Orientation Workshop, managed, conducted and evaluated by Fellowship Coaches and ARPs; 6. Singapore International Foundation (SIF) expanding support for the program by hosting the Study-trip to Singapore and workshops I and II; 7. Partnering with ACTRA and local sponsors to jointly host the Cycle AAR Seminar in Kabul conducted by Coaches and ARPs; 8. Group/team project in the area of community development; 9. U of C and UTA expand their involvement with Fellowship by increasing the number of Mentors in their mentoring teams; 10. Performance of the AF network as a resource for Fellows and the program on multiple fronts	1. ADDITIONAL TOPICS: Curriculum Emphasis on Leadership and Mentoring; Five WEB SEMINAR SERIES on Human Resource Development and Management (HRD&HRM): "Organizational Needs Assessment" HL & SL; "Result-Based Management" P. COX; 2. ROUNDTABLE HIROSHIMA - Importance of history and culture in post-conflict reconstruction - Reflections from Hiroshima to Afghanistan; 3. END OF CYCLE SEMINAR IN KABUL - 2009 Fellowship After-Action Review, and Lessons Learned" in partnership with ACTRA

CYCLE	STATS & NEW DEVELOPMENTS	CURRICULUM DEVELOPMENTS, WEBINARS & ROUNDTABLES (RT)
2010	1. NUMBERS: Fellows 55, Coaches 10, ARPs 5, Mentors and Faculty 24; Workshops 5, Webinars 6, AWCs 6, Project Work Sessions 6; 2. Afghan Case Studies developed and Presented by ARPs; 3. Two Workshops and study trips to Dubai and Abu Dhabi; 4. Expansion of Program to double the number of participants (A. MEJIA (AM), Afghan Civil Service Institute-USAID, SS).	1. ADDITIONAL TOPICS: Management of Productive Meetings, Introduction to distance learning tools, Motivation and delegation, Performance Maximization, Transformational Change, Conflict resolution; 2. ROUNDTABLE HIROSHIMA - Why is it important for Japan to continue to invest in Afghanistan's Reconstruction -- The Anatomy of the Japanese Policy of Engagement (JICA); 3. END OF CYCLE SEMINAR IN KABUL - 2010 Fellowship; After-Action Review, and Lessons Learned" in partnership with ACTRA.
2011	1. NUMBERS: Fellows 58, Coaches 10, ARPs 5, Mentors and Faculty 24; Workshops 5, Webinars 6, AWCs 6, Project Work Sessions 6; 2. Afghan Case Studies developed and Presented by ARPs; 3. Two Workshops and study trip to Abu Dhabi; 4. Introduction of new topic - Self-efficacy (LJ).	ADDITIONAL TOPICS: Self-Efficacy, Monitoring and Evaluation
2012	1. NUMBERS: Fellows 54, Coaches 10, ARPs 5, Mentors and Faculty 24; Workshops 4, Webinars 5, AWCs 6, Project Work Sessions 6; 2. ARP MODULE expanded to include Social Entrepreneurship (MF / B. MCKENZIE (BM))	1. ADDITIONAL TOPICS: Inclusion of Social Entrepreneurship in the ARP Module; 2. WEB SEMINAR on Leadership, Projects and Development - LJ;

CYCLE	STATS & NEW DEVELOPMENTS	CURRICULUM DEVELOPMENTS, WEBINARS & ROUNDTABLES (RT)
2013	1. NUMBERS: Fellows 59, Coaches 10, ARPs 5, Mentors and Faculty 24; Workshops 4, Webinars 5, AWCs 6, Project Work Sessions 6; 2. NEW Expanded and Customized ARP module for ARPs as Facilitators of Change with 4 new session in addition to the CforC sessions (HK).	1. ADDITIONAL TOPICS: NEW ARP MODULE - Community Mobilization to Harness Social Capital in Networks -Session I: Social Capital, The Interaction of Government and Social Capital and the nexus between Social Capital and Social Entrepreneurship; Session II: Community Mobilization; Session III: Peer to Peer Mentoring Networks; Session IV: Leadership and Social Entrepreneurship; 2. WEB SEMINARS: • Risk Identification and Mitigation • Results Based Management; 3. HIROSHIMA ROUNDTABLE : Post-2014 Afghanistan and the Role of Japan
2014	1. NUMBERS: Number of new Fellows was reduced to a class around 30 (M.KUMAMO-TO(MK)/BM/SS) ; 2. Web Seminar on Gender Issues at Work was added as a topic in HRM &HRD Module (W.LOW)	WEB SEMINARS: • Understanding Qualitative Data; • Gender at Work;
2015	AF Alumni invited to be Mentors in the Fellowships for South Sudan and Iraq, allowing the Alumni to become resources and apply learned capacities to assist others, and engage in the global community (MK/Nigel GAN (NG))	
2018	Final Cycle of the Programme	

Roles of Different Players in the Fellowship

The Fellowship utilized several layers of enhanced and continued learning, allowing for the development of an indigenous community able to contextualize/adapt the themes of the program to changes in Afghanistan. These mutually reinforcing layers included:

Fellows: First time participants in the program, the Fellows were the main beneficiaries of the cycle, divided into groups at the beginning of the Fellowship.

Coaches:

1. Selected from highest performing Fellows of previous cycles, and tasked with providing unity and guidance to the group;

2. were also responsible to be main contact between Mentors and the groups as a whole; and

3. received additional "Coaching-for-Coaches" training so they could continue their professional development while being equipped with the skills to coach their group.

COACHING FOR COACHES MODULE

The Coaching for Coaches Module offered eight web-based sessions and two on-site working sessions through each cycle year. The on-site working sessions also included fellows and mentors, ensuring that all players developed a better understanding of their roles and what was expected of them. To provide an element of continuity, coaches for each future cycle were selected from fellows who had already participated in these working sessions. The aim of the on-site sessions was to help coaches widen their focus from individual development, to planning for the fellowship and Afghanistan's capacity-building.

Afghan Resource Persons (ARPS)

1. Selected from the highest performing Coaches of previous cycles, ARPs acted as apprentice faculty members, working alongside international resource persons to contextualize and adapt the training being offered to the changing realities in Afghanistan;

2. ARPs were also offered further training in a module specifically designed for them, examining community mobilization to harness social capital.

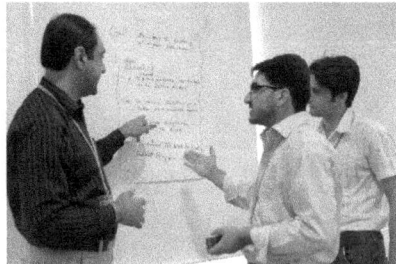

ARP MODULE - VISION AND CURRICULUM

In the Long-term - ARPs to develop into facilitators and leaders of change. Within the Fellowship - Facilitating/training to build capacities among Fellows; Be Mentors to Coaches and work with them to reinforce the Coaching for Coaches module and requirements; Be responsible for organization of Fellowship Community and highlighting the social capital available to Alumni when needed - activities and documentation; Developing concepts for social entrepreneurship projects cashing in on social capital networks within and outside the Fellowship.

  MODULE I: Training as Trainers/Facilitators

  MODULE II: Community Mobilization to Harness Social Capital in Networks (Interaction of Govt. and Social Capital, Community Mobilization, Peer to Peer Mentoring Networks.

  MODULE III: Leadership and Social Entrepreneurship

Mentors:

1. were experts, practitioners or academics in various disciplines;

2. from numerous countries including Afghanistan, willing and able to volunteer and share their knowledge and time, to guide and advise when requested, and at ease in a two-way learning relationship;

3. Mentors/Mentor teams, together with the Coaches were asked to commit to overseeing at least one group of five to six 'mentees' for the duration of each cycle;

4. sometimes also acted as Faculty/Resource Persons.

Faculty/Resource Persons: were involved in the core curriculum development, and facilitation and presentation at workshops and seminars, either in-person or electronically.

Process
Team Project Work

ASSIGNMENT I:

    a. Each Fellow undertook an organization/needs assessment in her/his workplace for one of the following purposes:

b. To determine the needs and service requirements of a population or customer group served by the Fellow's organization;

3. To determine the capacities and priority needs of the Fellow's organization in order to more effectively support the organization's mission; or

4. To determine the capacities and priority development needs of a particular group of employees within the organization (e.g., supervisors, engineers, scientists, teachers, secretaries, etc.)

In the weeks in between Workshops I and II, Fellows were offered guidance by UNITAR's team of Mentors, Coaches and Afghan

Resource Persons. Following individual presentation of the findings of Assignment One at Workshop II, each team then used the results of the organization needs assessments to decide on a team project.

Assignment II tasked teams with developing a concept paper in the form of a high-level Project Plan. Elements of the Fellowship covered in Workshop II contributed greatly to the development of Assignment II. This process was also the focus of the Coaches, ARPs and Mentors, and discussed at length during Audio Conferences.

Assignment III called for the development of a team project plan for organizational development or change projects for Afghanistan. Through a formal presentation involving all group members, a report was made upon the development of a detailed project plan for the team's organizational development or change project as developed through Assignments I and II.

Training Tools
Combination of Different Training Methods. The Fellowship undertook a combination of different training methods with a series of skill-building activities, including:

- On-site workshops
- Study-trips
- Mentor/ARP/Coach/Fellow communication
- Team projects
- Distance learning activities.

For the Coaches and ARP, in addition to specific training, learning was also offered through hands-on responsibilities and roles in the program including facilitation, training, case writing, coordination, logistical management, dispute resolution etc.

Holistically individual development was also made possible through study trips and exposure to post conflict reconstruction efforts and legacies, like Hiroshima's revival and peace messages, and stories of resilience of the Hibakusha[13]. The Fellowship events in countries outside of Afghanistan also included two-way cultural exchange activities, with the Afghans taking ownership of representing the many sides of their people and country, as well as intellectual exchanges through Roundtables with experts on topics of interest to both Afghans and their hosts in Japan, Singapore, India and the Emirates.

Throughout the Fellowship process, participants utilized the training offered in a number of assignments and projects, which were both peer- and Mentor-reviewed. This served to reinforce the themes of the Fellowship, and instilled from the beginning a learning-by-doing element into the training architecture.

---

[13] A-Bomb survivors

The Fellowship offered four workshops held throughout the process, typically two in Kabul, one in Hiroshima and one alternatively in Abu Dhabi, Singapore or Dehradun.

Curriculum Emphasis on Leadership and Mentoring
Endeavoring to widen the impact of the Fellowship, UNITAR placed special emphasis on methodology and skills development related to leadership and mentoring. The objective was to develop the capacity of each Fellow to be a facilitator able to contribute to organizational and human resource development within his/her respective ministry or organization.

The outcomes of the projects undertaken by most of the teams indicated that this objective was met with considerable success. Special efforts were also made to ensure the Fellows' team projects focused on management of change and organizational development, and the necessary skills and knowledge to support the process were included as the recurring themes throughout the Cycle curriculum.

In addition, AF Alumni were invited to serve as Mentors in other UNITAR post-conflict training programs, in Iraq and South Sudan, which further emphasized the resources and experiences that each brought to the community at large.

Video Seminars

Throughout the Fellowship, video seminars linked Fellows, as a group, to AF Faculty around the globe. Presentations delivered during such events corresponded to the phase in the Fellowship at which the Fellows were starting to formulate their vision and work. It included:

1. Tools For Maximizing Performance
2. Training as A Capacity Development Tool
3. Conflict Resolution skills
4. Leadership Development
5. Risk Identification and Mitigation
6. Results Based Management

Audio Conferences

All groups connected via various digital platforms, Skype in later years, to both UNITAR and their Mentors monthly, so that the project and Fellowship process could be discussed. Standing as milestones in the program, these video conferences were augmented by ad-hoc discussions between group members, Coaches, ARPs and Mentors.

Snapshot of a typical AF Cycle (2010):
60% Government, 36% NGOs and Pvt Sector, 4% Academia, 28% Women

Fellows: 52
Coaches: 10

Mentors and Resource Persons (international): 27
Hiroshima University, Japan (1), Tokyo University, Japan (1), UNITAR Hiroshima Office, Japan (1), University of Texas at Austin, USA (7), University of Calgary, Canada (10), Singapore International Foundation (4), Lamb and Lamb Associates, USA (2), and Microsoft Corporation, USA (1).

Afghan Resource Persons (Fellowship Alumni): 5 **Activities: Five Workshops and two study trips to Singapore and Japan respectively:**
Workshop – Cycle Launch: Orientation Workshop
Workshop I - "Leadership & Organizational Development for Performance and Results"

Workshop II - "Project Planning & Proposal Writing"
Workshop III - "Leading Change in Organizations – Change strategies, project implementation and team management"
Workshop IV: Cycle After-Action Review and Lessons Learned

Five Seminar Series on Human Resource Development and Management (HRD&HRM):

I. Introduction to human resources management and development

II. Organizational Needs Assessment

III. Tools for Performance Maximization

IV. Result-Based Management

V. Tools for Conflict Resolution

High-level Roundtable in Hiroshima on Post-conflict Reconstruction
Topic: *"The importance of history and culture in post-conflict reconstruction – Reflections from Hiroshima to Afghanistan".*

Distance learning: regular e-mail communication with Mentors, videoconferences, and a minimum of twelve scheduled audio-web conferences and project-work sessions for each group

Coaching for Coaches Module: Coaches and Afghan Resource Persons were trained through web conferences and on-site sessions.

New elements:

- Partnering with Alumni Association (ACTRA) to jointly host the four-day Orientation Workshop, managed, conducted and evaluated by Fellowship Coaches and ARPs

- Singapore International Foundation (SIF) expanding support for the program
- Partnering with ACTRA and local sponsors to jointly host the Cycle After-Action Review Seminar in Kabul conducted by Coaches and ARPs
- Expanded roles of Coaches and ARPs in content and mentoring of Fellows and Coaches respectively.
- Expansion of module on *Coaching for Coaches* given by Microsoft Corp
- Group/team project in community development
- U of C and UTA expanding their involvement with the Fellowship by increasing the number of Mentors in their mentoring teams

A visual snapshot of the Fellowship Activities (2010 Cycle)

	Month 1	Month 2	Month 3	Month 4	Month 5	Month 6	Month 7
	Orientation Workshop	Web-seminar 1	Workshop 1	Workshop 2	Web-seminar 3	Web-seminar 5	Workshop 3
	Introduction to the Fellowship: Concepts of Coaching, Mentoring, e-learning, and learner-driven learning	An introduction to human resources management and development.	Understanding leadership and organizational development as tools for maximizing performance within organizations. Understanding the performance model, social capital, stakeholder analysis, problem mapping; change projects with transformational abilities; intro to result-based management	Project planning: Needs identification, identification of solution, scope, stakeholders, sponsors, methodology, resources, evaluation and monitoring, next steps	Tools for Performance Maximization: Training and development, Performance appraisal, Coaching/giving feedback, Balanced scorecard, Benchmarking	Tools for Conflict Resolution: Conflict mapping, ABC triangle, Win-win solutions	Leadership and Change in Organizations: Leadership theory, Leadership as influence for change, Understanding and managing the change processes, Lewin Model, Reframing organizations
	Additional tools: How to contract out roles between players in the Fellowship context: between the Coaches, Mentors, Fellows and Mentors. Communication tools for Professionals: verbal and written	Web-seminar 2: Organizational Needs Assessment	*Additional tools: Skills in coaching/facilitation, Individual workstyles; and team development*	*Additional tools: Skills in proposal writing; fundraising; friendraisig*	Web-seminar 4: Result-based Management: detailed briefing and exercises		*Additional tools: Leading project implementation and evaluating team performance*
		Assignment 1		Assignment 2		Assignment 3	
		Conduct an Organization Needs Assessment within your organization (Individual assignment)		Team project: Development of a Change project concept paper/high level plan		Team Assignment: Development of a detailed project plan with fundraising proposal	

Academic Credits Offered Through University of Texas at Austin[14]
As early as Cycle I, till the last Cycle in 2018, the Fellows were persistent in their request for internationally recognized credits/certification for participation in the Fellowship. This spoke to the following three beliefs –

a. AF Alumni were convinced of the value of the work they did within the Fellowship framework and wanted recognition for it.

b. They also insisted on the accreditation to ensure that they could use this training as a steppingstone to pursue further learning and personal development

c. Being part of a global professional and knowledge community mattered to each and every one of them. Not one Afghan wanted to choose to exist in isolated darkness.

Recognizing these aspirations, David Eaton upon request of the AF team, took upon himself to help us meet this goal and started negotiations with the University of Texas at Austin (UTA). Not only did UTA agree to offer the requested accreditation but also helped with the financial costs of the process. This process also allowed the Fellowship to streamline the curriculum and structure description, which was required to be submitted for the UTA approval and catalogue each year.

---

[14] AF Syllabus listed in UTA 2010 catalogue is included in Annex B

Core Partner Institutions

Hiroshima Prefecture; City of Hiroshima; Government of Afghanistan; Office of the President, Afghanistan; Ministry of Foreign Affairs, Afghanistan; University of Texas at Austin, USA; University of Calgary, Canada; Hiroshima University, Japan; Singapore International Foundation; Agha Khan Foundation of Afghanistan; Microsoft Corp.; JICA.

The Early Evolution – Creativity in the Face of Challenge
Conversations with Sue Lamb

Interview by Humaira Khan-Kamal and Jenny Xin Luan[15]

Sue Ries Lamb has over 40 years of experience in national and international organization development and change management. Her areas of specialization include: organization development and change management; work process redesign; executive and managerial coaching; women in management; team building. In recent years, she has been focusing on developing and facilitating a series of dialogue sessions that help people think about, discuss, and take action against racism at the individual, interpersonal and institutional levels.

Sue and her husband and partner Howard were deeply involved in the Fellowship's design and curriculum development for about six years. In this conversation, we have tried to capture those memories, and takeaway points from the experience.

Memories from the program

Humaira Khan-Kamal: As a core member of the AF design team, one of the things that you were very good at was remembering people and the small things happening in the background. When you think back to your involvement with the Fellowship over the years what are a few moments/encounters which stand out in your memory?

[15] Jenny Xin Luan, Editorial Research Assistant for the Afghan Fellowship Legacy Project; Former Shansi Fellow at the United Nations for Training and Research Hiroshima Office
Interview conducted on February 9, 2021

Sue Lamb: Well, the first one that always comes to mind is from 2003, the first year of the program. We were in Hiroshima. I had never met anybody from Afghanistan before. I was absolutely intrigued with the friendliness and the engaged way that so many of the Afghans had in terms of being so much themselves. There was something about both the Afghans and the Pakistanis I worked with. I remember how we used to talk about the Renaissance people – they so impressed me with the breadth and scope of all their interests and knowledge — in their poetry, their music, their economic background. I mean, they could talk about any topic with you. But I remember most of them – if any – had never really worked with the Internet before. I remember one of the professors from Kabul Polytechnic University taught biology. We had a speaker who was helping them understand how to use the internet (I believe it was you). Everybody was just staring at the screen. I was sort of standing next to this gentleman and I said, "why don't you ask a question?" He was a little bit intimidated, but then I asked, "what are you interested in?" Then he said, "The origins of biology." I suggested he ask, so he asked the question. I will never forget his face when he saw page after page after page of resources that were now accessible to him. Up until that time, he had never had resources other than old Russian textbooks and lectures. This entire new world was open for him. That was one of the exciting things.

Humaira: I remember this instance and one of the fascinating things about the computer and internet accessibility was that among the cohort, many of the fellows were computer engineers who were familiar with engineering software. However, because the country had been closed to the outside world, internet was just this mind-blowing opportunity.

Sue: It really was. It made me appreciate the resources we have so much more, seeing it through their eyes. So that was one of the first things.

That same year, one of the things that so impacted me was going to the Hiroshima Peace Museum. Being with the Afghans during that experience, and understanding that here was Japan and its ability to totally rise again after all the devastation. And I think that had a particular impact, a positive one, on the Afghans who were just getting over three decades of war and devastation. There was a hopefulness around that.

Then, when we went to Kabul the second year, I was so excited because by this time we had some connections and so many of them were now our friends. Many said they wanted us to come visit and see them. However, when we got there, of course we were very restrained, because this was at the time when, I think, it had been one year after two UN people had been killed on Chicken Street. So my impressions of Kabul were very limited. We lived in a guarded compound with wires on the top of the walls. We really didn't get to go much of any place. It was such an impact on me to see how dusty, drought-ridden, and bullet-marked the whole city was. I had been expecting something so different. It was a bit disappointing but there was also this sense of, Oh my, I'm here. In Kabul. One of the biggest things of my overall impressions was the privilege of being able to work so closely and have such intimate relationships with people from the other side of the world.

Humaira: Your account gives us a sense of the two-way sentiments of people reaching out and trying to understand each other. I think that's one of the things which framed the Fellowship.

Sue: Another thing to mention, Humaira, is the Fellow's projects. The whole sense that every Afghan Fellow committed to a project year by year. For Howard and me, there was a sense of remotely having a role in helping to revitalize a country. The diversity of the projects was just amazing.

Humaira: Could we also talk about the phase of starting the Fellowship? There were so many elements pulling us into different directions. It all started in Hiroshima, our host city. The major donor of the program was the Hiroshima Prefecture. I was wondering if you could talk a little bit about how you got involved in this program and describe your first visit to Hiroshima.

Sue: As you well know, the reason that Howard and I got involved was our connection with you and your family. We had taught a three-week program for change agents in Pakistan under the USAID agency for education aid (formerly USAED). One of the things you said to me in our first call was "my boss and I are looking for some trainers who are not glitzy." (laughs) I knew exactly what you meant. You did not want can-trainers with very sophisticated kinds of technology and that certainly sounded like a fit. Also, we had already made such a connection with you while we were in Pakistan so the idea of being able to work together again was very exciting for us. Certainly, we were going to honor that. Your dad was a very special student of ours.

Humaira: Then, you agreed, and of course we pulled you in completely (laughs). You came to the launch of the program where everything was still a question mark amidst much uncertainty in Afghanistan. It was a new kind of program. Could you talk about what it was like in the beginning, working with Afghans, Japanese, and UNITAR, and some challenges?

Sue: The first thing I want to say was it felt so collaborative working with you and Nassrine. There was a sense that whatever our experience and suggestions, everything was so appreciated. It was very motivational to have that experience. And then, neither of us had ever been to Japan before, so it was transformative being in that beautiful country. That impression on many Afghan fellows was very eye-opening.

Some of the challenges – number one, not knowing anything about the Afghan culture, except what we could read up to that point. As a woman, I really had a lot of questions too about gender relations and the first cohort was mainly men with only two ladies. I was feeling my way through the simplest of interactions, like eye contact and physical distance. There was a lot of challenge around that because I have found from other travels that what I had read, from our State Department for example, was very outdated. (laughs) It was the sense of really feeling my way but with wonderful support from people at the hotel and of the program. As I said earlier, I think my most impactful experience was probably going to the Hiroshima Peace Museum.

Pedagogical challenges of training – simultaneous translation story

Humaira: In terms of the training itself, what were some of the pedagogical challenges?

Sue: Simultaneous translation – not knowing what is being said, hoping the translation is accurate, then waiting for the translation to come back, and again not really knowing the culture. We tried hard not to use idiomatic language and to explain things very simply. Also, we did not have any background about who the people were. We had respect for them, but we really did not know anything about who it was we were involved with until later in the program.

Humaira: That is true. At that time, in 2003, UNITAR did not have any foothold in Kabul to screen the participants themselves. We had to rely on other partner agencies. We met our Fellows for the first time when they came to Hiroshima.

Jenny: What was the challenge with simultaneous translation like? What were the fellows' English abilities like? How was the process of delivering your training materials?

Sue: It was very uneven, Jenny. Some people understood and spoke quite good English. Many others did not. In some senses, that made it even more challenging. If everybody was at one level, you could move with the appropriate pace. However, in this case, there were probably times when it was a little bit tedious for some fellows to have them sit through all the translations – from the instructors to the interpreters and back. In one sense, we could say they learned it very well. (laughs)

Humaira: One Fellow who was very helpful in that first Cycle was Mr. Hakim Gul Ahmadi. Most people spoke many languages in the group, but not everybody spoke fluent English. Hakim did. And the poor guy, he was very generous because he was there to learn himself, but he volunteered to be the translator while Howard and Sue were talking. He was not a professional interpreter. I think what was quite significant was the commitment of the trainers and the trainees to make this happen. The interpretation was tedious because all the training sessions became double the time.

Sue: One personal note of admiration around Hakim was what he did after the Fellowship. He built and opened several schools for women around Afghanistan.

Humaira: That was one of his projects, wasn't it?

Sue: Yes. I still hear from him almost every year and we exchange greetings.

Humaira: One follow-up question, how do you think the connection to Hiroshima impacted the overall philosophy of the fellowship? There was a reason why the city and the prefecture got involved. They had the motivation themselves and there is this context. How would the Afghan Fellows receive the message? How do you think that impacted the way the fellowship unfolded and its message?

Sue: As I said earlier, the whole sense of Japan rising from the war's devastation and becoming the country it is had both an overt and a subliminal message for the Afghans, in terms of hopefulness and optimism. It was like "we could do, you can do the same" type of impact.

Humaira: On the curriculum and the development of the design of the fellowship, for me, it was always, as you said, an organic process of collaboration that we all kind of "stumbled" upon but actively pursued.

Sue: Wait, wait, I'm not going to let you say we actually stumbled on it. I think that you and Nassrine had a lot to do with creating that collaboration. (laughs)

Humaira: Right, and that was our goal, but I think everybody who got involved and got into the spirit – it didn't have to be explained to anybody, the Fellows or the international community members. Everybody was suddenly on the same page and that was I think the Fellowship's magic. Of course, it came with its challenges. But one of the things I wanted to ask you was – you know, you and Howard made some very specific contributions to the curriculum design and I'm curious to know your philosophy behind the emphasis on some elements. One of them was about organizational needs assessment and organizational development but also the concept of re-tapping the resources created within the program - the coaching and not letting the community unravel after the training was done. Would you talk a little bit about your philosophy behind it and how they impacted the Fellowship?

Sue: Howard's and my background is as organization development consultants. We brought to AF a set of values in philosophy: one would be that it is important to develop the system that you were working with as opposed to just offering "expert help" of some kind. We were aware that, for the personal projects, some Fellows were just deciding what they should do as a project with a particular system, as opposed to getting input from the system itself as to what was needed. That was the first thing we thought about – the importance to ask those people at different levels in the system what they think was needed for the organization. Since we have an opportunity to do a project now, it does not mean that the organization always knows what is needed. You certainly want to get the input in a collaborative way instead of the mentality of "I'm here and going to fix this or that." That was a major philosophical approach we brought.

Additionally, what we call "experiential learning" is very key as opposed to "didactic learning". We were always very conscious of how we got people to DO their learning, rather than teaching concepts in abstract. There was a lot of experimentation and exploration: using your own wisdom to guide you as opposed to thinking only the expert has things to feed you. That was a piece of it. With the "coaches", for example, we knew we had to build a kind of internal capability, or the program would die because it was certainly not going to be funded forever. So it was having that whole notion of how do we help the system develop its own means of survival? The Fellows also developed specific enthusiasm to keep the program running like developing the glossary of terms in Dari, a resource that they did not have before. We were very excited about how many creative ideas and ways people in the program had when they were encouraged to develop it for themselves and for those who were going to come after them, as opposed to the "expert" coming in and helping them.

Humaira: With reference to the glossary, I want to add that you involved the Fellows in developing some of the handouts on Afghanistan during the program. The wonderful thing was they really felt they owned it and they kept updating them over the years, which was actually a very useful tool to get people more invested.

Sue: Yes, one other thing I would mention is that I remember when we got involved in the projects, I remember feeling the time pressure. I would have to slow myself down and remember to ask the fellows questions about what it is they think they need to do. They were Howard's and my clients too. We needed to do the same thing with them that we were encouraging them to do with their organizational clients.

Humaira: In terms of mentoring, I know you have experiences with many organizations. What are some of the strategies to approach mentoring over distance, time, and language? Also, as you said, the fellows had very diverse needs in the group. How did you manage that?

Sue: Some of the strategies I have already mentioned are asking questions and getting them to think about their own learning needs as opposed to being dependent on someone else. There were times when I remember just being dismayed because I knew a particular individual knew what they wanted to do but could not write it. For me, one of the most personal challenges was finding when it was appropriate to help them with their English and doing some of the writing and when to just back off and let them struggle with it. So, it was very much of an individualized approach. We both mentioned Hakim earlier. He could write as well as I could write.

Another thing was when the fellows were divided into project teams. That was hard because there were times when there were four people in the team and three of them were working really hard and one was not. That was another challenge: how to ensure that each member would pull his or her weight.

I remember once Howard and I were on one mentoring call in our monthly sessions. There were people from 10 different countries 15 time zones on the call. Just think of the amount of coordination.

Humaira: Even the Afghans were in different places. Somebody would be in the capital and somebody else would be in one of the provinces.

Sue: I think that in 2003 when we started there were just five cell phone towers in the whole country!

Humaira: You're right, soon after cell phones took over everything and they hardly used landlines. Moving back to the blended learning methods, one of the signature features of the Fellowship was that it was actually 70% distance learning and 30% on site. At the time (2003), there were not a lot of distance learning options around and certainly less in Afghanistan. Even in the US. Skype came out much later. To do video conferencing, all parties had to be on a particular device platform, so we had to travel physically to places which offered that hardware. I was just wondering if you had any thoughts especially when you compare it to the current environment – where we are only on Zoom! (laughs)

Sue: Yes, when we started, we were going to the World Bank in Washington DC, about a half an hour drive. We had to be there by 5:30 in the morning. Half the time the arrangements for letting us into the building were not quite up to par. There was one gentleman at the World Bank Global Development Learning Network (GDLN) who was wonderful about working with us, Mr. Nayyer Iqbal. That was a journey. The whole process leaving from and returning home—it would take three hours. Now, we hit a button and we are on anywhere in the world. So, that was one difficult aspect of it.

Humaira: Yes! Especially for the Afghans as well. Many people traveled from other cities and provinces to Kabul to participate in those sessions. Sometimes, there were traffic jams or bomb blasts on the way, but they still made it.

Sue: I remember a lot of people traveled through very difficult, challenging, unsafe journeys to get there and be on the calls.

Humaira: For blended learning, it definitely helps if you have met with each other at least once in person which was not always possible in the AF. Hats off to people's commitment to the process because it is hard to stay engaged with each other when you do not see each other sometimes for a month or the whole cycle. Efforts were made to make the human connections in addition to the knowledge connections.

Sue: This is a question for you. I've always assumed that when we went to project teams, did that create more communication and coordination in between sessions? Was that in itself a good intervention?

Humaira: Yes, you are right. We scheduled local sessions for the Fellow teams as well as audio sessions with international mentors. Every month, they were required to meet with each other at least once, so they could do their homework, be ready for the session with the mentors.

Sue: While we're on that, a fun memory just came up. We already said that most of them had never done anything with the internet. For at least the first few years, most of them had not done PowerPoint presentations at the beginning. But I remember one project team was bowling Howard and me over with their PowerPoint presentation, by the end of their first year. I think that happened for a lot of folks.

Humaira: A side note on what you always mentioned and what I hope we recognize is that even when the World Bank stopped being able to support the video conferencing for the program, colleagues in the Bank made it happen on their own. They would just say, "just come, we'll make it happen." I think that was quite amazing: the good will the program managed to garner.

Sue: I think anybody who had any contact with any of the fellows could sense the commitment, resilience, and dedication to bring their country to a different position. Everybody was touched by that. Everybody then wanted to contribute in their ways.

Humaira: To wrap up, I was just wondering if you have some final thoughts from the whole experience and the relationships that you formed with the fellows and others? What were Howard's and your takeaways?

Sue: For both of us, it was truly one of the very top experiences of our lives. It was so far-reaching to begin with. Then, it was the depth of the connections we made and knowing that these people were making such incredible progress. It was a sense of, in just the smallest ways, being able to support something so much bigger than what we were. Every year, Howard and I tried, while we were physically, mentally, and emotionally capable, to have at least one pro bono project that was local and one that was international. Being with the Afghan fellows, we were able to do something that was important to us and see the incredible progress being made right before our eyes, every year. The gratitude and appreciation went in both ways between us and the fellows. There was so much growing of all kinds. You know, I don't get to talk about the experience that much, but whenever I do get to mention it I get the sense of, wow I was there, it really takes me back.

Humaira: You were very important to the Fellowship, informing it, and moving it along. And of course, you left an impact on so many people's lives. Was there anything you would have done differently?

Not just how you did your role, but in general thinking about the whole development program.

What could have been done differently? Build the network earlier.
Sue: One thing we have not mentioned much is the building of the critical mass from one year to another. I think that was a huge piece of the success of the program. However, it could have been a bit more deliberate to build that from the very start. Who are the people we are noticing in the peer program? Who would we like to particularly see as part of the alumni network in different roles? We did find the roles of "coaches" and "mentors" eventually but that could have been done sooner. By adding roles like "researchers" and even "administrators", we could have created an even more sophisticated and comprehensive network. This is one of things that I would try from the start.

Humaira: Yes, I think the most significant thing in this program was the process. Next time we would and should be much more deliberate about it. You will be happy to know that UNITAR has used the model in other programs, especially the Hiroshima Office, for Iraq and South Sudan for example. They have tried to implement those elements, so we have learned from it.

Sue: Oh, that's wonderful to hear!

COACHING FELLOWS TO LEADERS
Michael Fors[16]

Introduction

In this chapter, I will explore the origins of the Afghan Fellowship by looking at its original design and objectives. The Fellowship began as a way to teach program management, strategy, and leadership skills. Its objective was to teach Afghan leaders how to design programs that would solve social problems and have positive impact. If the leaders could learn to do this systematically, and then could have success in their role and get promoted faster, they could take on increasing levels of responsibility that allow them to have greater impact on their post-conflict nation, the region, and the world. The design took a page from Intel's management development programs, working in teams and applying the learning to a joint live case study. It also added facilitators, mentors, and Afghan Resources Persons as coaches, which allowed for coaching and mentoring, creating a strong alumni network. Women leaders were a particular focus, as many research studies have shown that developing women's professional skills is a way to accelerate development in post conflict countries.

I will also focus on several important themes laced throughout the program. A particular focus was the concept of servant leadership. Participants were carefully recruited and selected due to their

---

[16] Michael Fors is currently Leader of Corporate Division Development in Boeing's Leadership, Learning & Organizational Capability (LLOC) Team. Has been a core faculty for the Fellowship through its 15 years, and was a lead resource person till its final cycle.

leadership potential. They were taught about servant leadership and that they needed to be in it for the right reasons, to helps others, rather than lining their pockets. They also needed to use their leadership gifts wisely, assuming their responsibility to give back. They were reminded many times that enlightened people in the world have found that the greatest thing we can do as humans is to give to others. By giving, you get much more in return. They also were told that they have more potential than they realize, and can do more than they think they can.

A component of social entrepreneurism was added to the program. This element taught them how to develop an innovation and start-up mentality, and use it to solve social issues. The idea is to grow a business that solves a social cause — and re-invest profits to scale and therefore solve the social issues on a much broader scale. Afghans created many ideas for social entrepreneurism, and businesses actually grew from this focus to help Afghanistan.

The chapter will include memorable and touching human moments from across all years of the Afghan program and its expansion to Iraq and South Sudan, from the perspective of an individual who was consistently involved throughout nearly all cycles of the Fellowship. From the early years of teaching an older Afghan generation who returned to government after fighting wars at the front, to the ambitions of a younger generation, to dancing after the Obama elections, to reactions to the Atomic Bomb Museum and survivors, to stories of corruption in Afghanistan, to stories about travels to various countries around the world to deliver the program, and to a lack of security in Kabul. Through it all, the Afghans remained resilient, humble, and humorous. Through it all, they showed a deep devotion and caring for their country, desiring peace and stability. They greatly respected all who helped them, treating all of us who were leading the program with reverence, gratitude, and as members of their family.

The Magic of a Successful International Development Program
In the realm of international development, very few programs have impact or staying power. Many are launched haphazardly in an attempt to make a quick difference. Most are overwhelmed by the number of linkages required locally to be successful. There is little persistence to ensure the programs are designed effectively, are having the desired impact, and can not only continue over time, but scale to make a positive difference to a country or region. Entities are also haphazardly involved, from multi-nationals, to NGOs, to national and local governments, and to the private sector. Historically, this has been the situation in international development globally. Afghanistan has been no different, as an alliance of international countries have attempted to develop this post-conflict country that had been at war for over 40 years.

The intervention in Afghanistan by the U.S. and an alliance of international countries beginning in 2001 was largely a military and police intervention. The goal was to train and make Afghanistan's military and police forces independent, so that they can stop terrorism within their borders, and therefore stop terrorism from happening around the world. It is debatable if any positive impact was made in this 20-year effort, particularly now with a U.S. pullout of troops and the Taliban moving back into Kabul to take greater control. As was learned in the past, when a leadership void is created in a country, it may be filled by other, less positive forces. This happened in Afghanistan's past, when U.S. policies created a void in that country prior to 9/11. History indeed repeats itself.

So, what more can be done to stabilize a country beyond the training of military and police forces? Civil development is often neglected, as entities are at a loss to know how to comprehensively develop a nation. Given that many international development initiatives fail, and Afghanistan has been largely a military and police intervention, it is worth looking at any programs that may have had staying power to provide civil development. One that was deemed by the Afghan Civil Service Institute as the longest running program in Afghanistan is the UNITAR Hiroshima Fellowship for Afghanistan Program. It persisted for over 15 years, training about 500 Afghan civil servants in leadership, strategy, and program management. Due to its success, it was scaled to other post-conflict countries, such as Iraq and South Sudan. It is worth examining why this particular program was so successful, to determine if it can serve as a model for other civil service international development programs.

The Afghan Fellows Program was successful for a number of reasons. This chapter will examine six critical factors that made the program magical: The Program design; the UN staff; the alumni serving as coaches and Afghan Resource Persons; the international mentors; the Afghan participants themselves; and the program's strong themes with a call to action.

1. Program Design
In 2001-2002, several academics and private sector experts teamed with the UNITAR staff to design a program, anchored at the then nascent UNTAR Hiroshima Office, that could leverage best practices from around the world. Partnerships were formed with the Afghan Civil Service Commission, Ambassadors to the UN, and to Afghanistan, and leaders in Afghan government ministries. Members of leading universities and professionals from the private sector were enlisted as team members to design, develop, and lead the program, named the Hiroshima Fellowship for Afghanistan.

As a leadership development effort, the goal was to ensure the program was practical, focusing on real world problems the Afghans were experiencing. In essence, by attending the program, the Afghans would receive help in solving problems, grow in leadership, and learn valuable processes and tools to apply to other problem scenarios. Following adult learning principles, the idea was to present to the Afghans standards of excellence in strategic planning, team development, program management, and leadership; help them apply these skills to their situation, and then have them receive coaching from each other as participants, coaches, mentors, and past alumni. A virtual village was assembled to support these leaders in their quest to solve a real-life problem, and grow skills that will make each participant a much stronger leader for the rest of their careers. The program design leveraged highly successful leadership development programs from Fortune 50 companies, such as the First Line Leader Program at Intel Corporation, which had been successful for many years in teaching individual contributors to become strong leaders of people and organizations.

Over time, as UNITAR developed its networks in Afghanistan, participants went through a rigorous process to be selected for the program. These high potential leaders were viewed as leaders who could take on greater levels of responsibility in the future, and were in key positions at the time.

Specifically, the design of the program was powerful due to certain variables. Once selected, participants were tasked with identifying a problem they as leaders were experiencing in developing Afghanistan from within their division of government (ministry). Early workshops in Kabul and online helped the leaders with skills and tools to get started in the Fellowship program. In this case, a workshop on conducting a needs assessment helped them identify root cause issues of a problem, and to scope and shape it. The needs assessment workshop provided an opportunity for participants to practice consistently approaching problems similarly, asking a set of questions that allow them to figure out how best to solve the problem. Participants enlisted other leaders and members of their ministry to complete the assessment, thereby enrolling their government in owning the problem as a top priority.

A second step in the program involved the formation of teams, so that Fellowship participants could work together on a problem, facilitating learning, program management skills, and leadership development, each also presenting their problem and needs assessment. After the presentations, the team decided whose problem they would all take on as a focus for the rest of the program. This was the team's first experience in making a decision, and was often a challenge, as naturally every person was advocating for their own problem to be solved!

Soon, however, the teams rallied around their chosen, singular problem and became invested in solving it, not only for the selected participant, but for Afghanistan. The problem was meant to be addressed not just with a plan, but actual implementation as their program ended. Individual problems not selected by the team were also kept alive through an individual action plan, and as the teams solved their chosen common problem, the learning taken away from the team effort could be applied to the individual problems as well. In this way, many problems in Afghanistan were being assessed, scoped, and solved as a result of the program.

In a major workshop, midway through the program, the teams came together in-person to work on their live case study. They learned how to create program management plans that fully defined the solutions to their problem. Elements included a clear problem statement, solution, deliverables, timeline, assumptions, communication plan, and change management plan. These standards are used worldwide by governments, non-profits, and Fortune 50 companies.[17] The goal was to teach participants how to create a plan that consistently drives effective program implementation. A strong

---

[17] Elements of the plans were aligned to world class standards by the Project Management Institute

theme was that as they grow to become leaders, they will use this methodology at an organizational level, ensuring all programs driven within an organization have strong program management. With such consistency, they become better leaders, but also there is a greater likelihood that problems would be solved in Afghanistan.

Also, in this workshop, the teams were put through rigorous team development exercises, that taught them how to build high performing teams. This set of exercises operationalized a world class Tuckman Model for Team Development. While the Tuckman stages of Forming, Storming, Norming and Performing are known around the world, the Afghan Fellows Program operationalized how to form and develop teams to be high performing, with concrete steps to move a team through the stages. Hands-on team development exercises set very tough challenges for the teams, and they learned through failure and success in accomplishing these challenges. The lessons directly translated to their teamwork in driving their chosen program, including lessons in clear leadership, deliverables, roles, utilization of resources, timelines, decision making, handling of conflict, and the optimization of workstyles within the team. These lessons, similar to project management, were meant to provide the leaders a formula for systematically developing teams as they gain greater levels of responsibilities in larger organizations.

Due to security reasons after the first few cycles, this workshop was held in various countries that were near Afghanistan, to keep costs low. Participants over the years traveled to Dubai, Dehradun, Singapore, and Abu Dhabi. There was wide variation in the level of support provided by countries where the program was held. Some countries embraced the UNITAR program and welcomed the participants with open arms. Other countries, surprisingly, even ignored the fact that the Fellowship was happening within their borders.

Additional workshops helped the Fellows to flesh out their plan, adding details and practicing pitching the plan to other stake-holders, sponsors, and leaders. Pitching to peer colleagues in the program was a way to practice refining of their ideas. One sign of success was that after a while, we couldn't tell who owned the original idea picked by the team, as every team member could speak to the problem being solved as if it were their own. Coaches constantly asked key questions to help teams think about how to improve their plans, and work better together as a team. Mentors from around the world reviewed the work, providing feedback and also asking key questions.

The Fellowship culminated with a trip to Hiroshima. This was by design, so that Japan could host the participants (the Hiroshima Prefecture as the key donor, but also Hiroshima City and other local partners were always fantastic hosts). Participants were able to learn how Japan was reconstructed after World War II and engage with its current culture and people. Importantly, the program and graduation ceremony happened in Hiroshima. The teams would present their final plan for solving the problem they had selected. We were always impressed by the level of team performance in these presentations. A panel of judges rated the final presentations, determining which presentations and solutions were ready to be implemented, needed more work, or were not ready at all. The panelists acted like funders, and would hold up green, yellow, or red devices to cast their vote after each team presentation. By far the majority of presentations were given green ratings, meaning they were ready to be funded and implemented now (approximately >75% of presentations). A much smaller percentage were yellow (roughly 20%, meaning the plans needed more work), and it was rare to see one that was red (approximately <5% of all presentations, meaning the plans needed much more work).

There was a certain euphoria among participants after their final presentations, once they achieved the high standard of excellence. They were celebrated, and encouraged to implement their own projects as well as the team projects. Feedback and evaluation data showed that it was the best program participants had attended. It was transformational, they said, not only in the skills they learned, but the high performing level of teamwork they achieved. Many teams stayed together as they returned to Afghanistan, implementing their team project for the good of Afghanistan. The special combination of ingredients in the design worked consistently at every cycle, helping to make for a magical experience for participants over 14 years.

Because the Fellowship was deemed to be the longest running civil servant development program in Afghanistan, as mentioned, people took notice. The Civil Service Commission, the Finance Ministry, and other ministries sent many participants, knowing it was transformational for change in Afghanistan, and had such a solid substantive track record. As alumni grew in the ministries, word of mouth spread throughout Kabul about the Fellowship, and into the provinces. Numerous participants applied and joined, knowing they may be traveling in dangerous circumstances to Kabul for workshops, and to return to their families in outer provinces. NGOs and the private sector also wanted people to attend the program. Most notably was the Aga Khan Foundation, who saw the program as foundational leadership development training for their leaders and high potential, up-and-coming leaders.

Expansion of the Program
The program was perceived to be effective and successful in conflict or post-conflict assistance, so much so that it was modeled and expanded by UNITAR to include versions that served other post-conflict nations, such as Iraq and South Sudan.

Memorable Mission to South Sudan – Another Legacy of the Afghan Fellowship

Defying U.S. State Department wishes, several of us traveled to South Sudan during their Civil War to replicate and adapt the Fellowship. As the youngest democracy in the world, South Sudan had held elections, but the President and Vice President, coming from two of the majority tribes, declared civil war on each other. The recommendation was to have U.S. $2000 strapped to my body at all times, in case things got dangerous, and I needed to find my way out of the country quickly. Leaving two little kids at home, and taking out a special very expensive life insurance, the journey commenced. Landing in Juba was quite the experience, with UN workers, NGO relief workers, and armed military surrounding the runway.

Francis Scopas, our UNDP rep who was supporting this UNITAR program, greeted me and helped me find my suitcase in a chaotic jumble of bags thrown off the plane. It was unclear who anyone was at the airport – security, military, civilians all seemed to be together with little to no FAA type security. Francis gave my passport and my $500 cash to someone. It disappeared behind a wall for about an hour. We moved along the length of the tiny building through a throng of people, stepping over suitcases the entire way.

Just when I had lost all hope, my passport reappeared with a stamp that said I could enter the country. The drive to the hotel followed winding dirt roads through villages of huts. The people were curious about our UN truck, but kids playing in the street knew to step aside so we could make our way. The hotel was surrounded by armed guards and rolled barbed wire fencing.

For one week, we remained in that hotel and never left it, as did the South Sudan government officials.

The rooms had mosquito netting, but were riddled with torn holes. At night, the floor of the hotel room crawled with insects, until a light was turned on, and they would scurry into the corners and cracks in the wall. Even though we were on heightened alert due to the civil war and fighting in the city, the program continued. Most of the officials were young, career government officials. Smart and ambitious, they wanted to learn, to be the best leaders they could be, regardless of who was president. I had lunch with Francis every day, who had three small children living in neighboring Uganda. It was too dangerous to have them with him in South Sudan. He was dedicated to serving his country and making it a better place for them to grow up. The program had been a success in South Sudan, proving that the design and execution could work its magic outside of Afghanistan.

Sadly, part of the prologue was less than happy. As I was departing, I left my older dress shoes at the hotel on purpose. My reward to myself for surviving South Sudan was to go on a safari in Kenya, and my plan all along was to shed baggage weight. Francis contacted me right away via email, and said he had the dress shoes in his UN locker, and I could collect them next year when I returned to run a second version of the program. He looked forward to our lunches together, and was excited to further stabilize South Sudan by helping to host this program annually.

Several weeks later, Francis was killed in Juba as he commuted home through the civil war, and our farewell photo together at the hotel was the last chance I had to see him and talk about how together we would make the world a better place. His death was devastating and heartbreaking

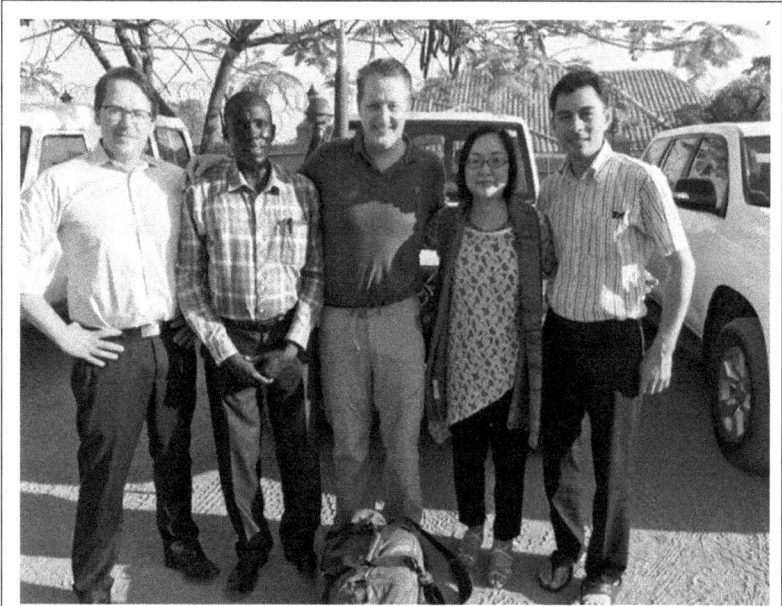

Leaving South Sudan after the program. From left to right: Berin McKenzie, Francis Scopas, Michael Fors, Mihoko Kumamoto, and Shamsul Hadi Shams.

2. The UN Staff

The program design was only one factor that helped to create magic in the program. The UNITAR Staff contributed greatly to its success. It began at the top with the Executive Directors. Nassrine Azimi was the person who was responsible for the vision of the Fellowship. She deserves full credit for its establishment and success. After leading UNITAR's New York Office, she spearheaded the opening of the UNITAR Hiroshima Office, becoming its founding director and setting the stage for the Fellowship. Nassrine was dedicated to helping the Afghans. Many times through the years she would exclaim, "these people!" She meant she was always incredulous that no matter how much adversity the Afghan people experienced, they responded with resilience, grace, ambition, perseverance, and a sense of deprecating humor. Another favorite phrase of Nassrine's, that will never be forgotten, is the phrase "hope springs eternal." It signifies that there is always hope for humans to do what is right and make the world a better place. Her optimism, drive and determination made this program successful in the early years. The Fellowship would have never started or survived without Nassrine's passion and intelligence. Nassrine stepped down from leading the Hiroshima UNITAR office, to focus on the highly successful Green Legacy Hiroshima campaign, where seeds from trees that survived Hiroshima's nuclear bomb are sent around the world to remind everyone of what happened in Hiroshima, to not have it happen again, and to promote peace. The saplings from the Hiroshima nuclear bomb surviving trees now exist in hundreds of sites around the world. Nassrine continues this legacy, while also starting up a new initiative, enlisting our Afghan alumni to build botanical gardens to preserve local species. Many places in the world, including Afghanistan, do not have botanical gardens to preserve local plants and trees, and plant more greenery to offset global climate change. Nassrine is on it, working all of these issues with our alumni.

Nassrine and Humaira

As Nassrine left, the UNITAR office went through a few leadership changes, but they kept the program going. Then, Mihoko Kumamoto stepped in to lead the UNITAR Hiroshima Office. With every change of leadership, there were questions about which strategies and programs would continue, and which will stop. Mihoko did not allow the Fellowship to skip a beat, ensuring funding, and it continued forward with funding from several sources. Since Mihoko had been in the UN system and is Japanese, she was able to solidify and continue the relationship with the Japanese government, Hiroshima prefecture, and the city of Hiroshima to keep the program alive. Mihoko showed a grace under pressure, a logical strategic mind, and a dedication to her staff and program participants. Under her leadership, the Afghan program flourished, as well as the many new programs that have blossomed to serve the world. Now, she leads the UNITAR Division of Prosperity, expanding her scope beyond the Hiroshima Office, to global programs impacting individuals worldwide.

UNITAR Program leaders also played a key role in ensuring success. For the Fellowship one of the most indispensable was surely Humaira Khan-Kamal, the first program leader, who had worked with Nassrine and I at the New York Office. With her strategic mind, passion, persistence, and sense of humor she created a fantastic program and environment. Of Pakistani background, Humaira could relate to the Afghans in unique cultural ways, and she was constantly driven to ensure it was a wonderful experience for participants. She could work on details and logistics as easily as she could pop up to a much higher altitude to improve the overall program design and support from the ministries. She was incessant in her teasing of the Afghans, and they responded in kind. She also kept pushing the Fellowship to greater and greater heights always, such as partnering to add coaches, mentors and resource persons in the early years. Because Afghan culture has a loose sense of time (read:

it is OK to be late and not on time for a program session!), Humaira was always chiding participants who were late or not working hard enough. The result was that as programs progressed, the Afghans were on time and knew to take advantage of this great life opportunity they had in this program. They began working much harder, thanks to Humaira.

Humaira and I leading a program session

As Humaira stepped back from the Fellowship, Berin McKenzie entered the fold. Berin ensured that we had sound instructional design in modules, and also aligned the models we were using to other models that were common within in the UN. He brought an intellect, sense of humor, and sense of showmanship that the Afghans really liked. However, he was also still very focused on the substance and outcomes of the Fellowship. Nigel Gan and Shamsul Hadi Shams also provided great support for the Afghans, and were also very involved as the program expanded to Iraq and South Sudan. Both brought strong organization, passion, and desire to have the program succeed and proliferate.

One of the stalwarts of the program, responsible for much of the magic, was Sabahuddin Sokout. Sokout was the person on the ground in Afghanistan, creating relationships with the Civil Service division, and each ministry. He was responsible for promoting the program, raising funds, recruiting participants, and interviewing them to ensure they qualified for selection. He also served as manager and tour guide for all trips that the Afghans took, helping them with passports, visas, crossing borders, and even shopping! But beyond that, he was a coach and mentor to each and every participant who ever went through the Fellowship. Sokout was there from the start, doing it all, the backbone of the program. Over time he became the quiet, strong, guiding servant leader behind the scenes. I have called him for years the epitome of a true servant leader. He resolved so many hairy issues behind the scenes, all the while ensuring the participants could be in the best possible position to learn and perform. Robert Greenleaf, the founder of Servant Leadership, once wrote:

«Can you be both a servant and a leader? If so, can you be effective in the real world? I think the answer to both questions is yes. The idea of The Servant as Leader came to me as a result of reading a book by Herman Hesse, Journey to the East. It is the story of a band of men on a mythical journey. The key person in the story is Leo. He is a servant who does chores for the travelers, but he also lifts their morale with his positive spirit and his singing. He is the glue that holds the group together. The travelers all sense Leo's extraordinary presence. The journey goes well until one day when Leo disappears. Without Leo, the group falls apart, and the journey has to be abandoned. They simply can't continue. The traveler who tells the story goes looking for Leo, and after some years of wandering, he finds Leo. He discovers that Leo, whom he had known first as servant, was in fact the titular head of the Order that sponsored the journey. Leo is its guiding spirit, a great and noble leader. You can imagine what Hesse was trying to say when he wrote this story. To me, this story clearly says that the great leader is seen as servant first, and that simple fact is the key to his greatness. Leo was actually the leader all of the time, but he was servant first because that was what he was, deep down inside."

Sokout, too, embodies servant leadership. It was a concept we taught to all the Afghans. It is a subtle and powerful concept, and it took the Afghans some time to understand it, because they had grown accustomed to authoritarian leaders. Seeing Sokout role model it, brought the magic of servant leadership to life for them. The bond between Sokout and I grew strong, and over the years he became the brother I never had.

Sokout and others associated with the program needed to make ends meet on the home front. Sokout had to take extra jobs, because the UN could only pay him a set contract amount during the year. He once told a story of taking a role managing a construction project on the outskirts of the city. Kabul was never safe or secure, and the Taliban were always threatening to take back neighborhoods. Sokout mentioned that the Taliban heard the work crew were supporting the new president and the U.S. led involvement in Afghanistan. Sokout arrived to work one day, only to find American soldiers' heads on spikes in the construction zone. The message stated was clear: You will leave the heads on the sticks as a warning to all others for seven consecutive days, and work among them. Or, your heads will be on the sticks next. The Taliban were making it clear that supporting the president and the new leader is a very dangerous undertaking for any individual. To this day, they are still very much in charge on the outskirts of the city and ready to regain territory and power as international forces leave.

Sokout at an Afghan Cultural Celebration

Through the years, we had a fantastic support staff in Hiroshima, providing logistics, media, and financial support. This cannot be underestimated, because a program like this is a year-long effort of recruiting, finances, interviewing, workshops in Kabul, a working trip to another location outside of the country, and then the final culminating trip to Hiroshima. Along the way, a village of people were involved, from all over the world. The coordination of materials and notes alone was a staggering endeavor, but the small Hiroshima UNITAR staff, often supported by interns who were simultaneously supporting the Fellowship, and learning from it for the first time, never missed a beat. They definitely added to the magic of the program with their unwavering support for the participants and the resource persons leading the programs.

3. Alumni Serving as Coaches and Afghan Resource Persons
Upon graduation, participants joined an alumni network that kept them connected to the program and continuing to learn from each

other. Many would continue to implement their chosen program. Others would lean on each other for advice in their professional lives. The bonds from the Fellowship, the networks created, and, in particular, the teamwork were strong, and it was seen over many iterations of the program that people would remain in touch. It didn't hurt that Sokout was a true ringleader in getting people together and having the learning continue. Several alumni stepped up over the years to help Sokout with the alumni network, but they tended to fade away, while Sokout remained the rock — solid, stable, constant.

Top performing participants were invited back to be coaches for the following year. These hand-picked individuals showed great leadership potential, and the thought was they could themselves further develop stronger coaching and facilitation skills working with teams. The coaches went through a number of training sessions with Humaira and me. They were taught that a coach's role is to ask questions of the team, to have them stop and think about what they are doing and why they are doing it. The teams owned their own solutions, coaches were never meant to step in and lead them. Each team needed to identify its own leaders and make its own decisions. This was a new concept for Afghans, who embraced it each year wholeheartedly. It created a climate where teams needed to form, storm, norm, and perform on their own, supported by good questions provided by their coach. Coaches asked questions at key times to have a team think about how they were performing. They asked questions about what the team was accomplishing (deliverables, roles, interdependencies), but also how it was performing, asking about a range of issues — leadership, decision making, conflict, and even effective meetings.

Top performing coaches were invited back for their third year with the program, and they added to the magic of the program. They helped train and coach the coaches, but also taught particular subject matters with leaders of the program and me. In this way, they continued to develop their leadership skills, and gained subject matter expertise in leadership, program management, change management, and other important subjects being taught to the Fellowship's first year participants. They added expertise and experience, but again supported the participants in finding their own way and making their own decisions in the program. The Afghan Resources Persons (ARPs) were very valuable in another regard, however, in that they put a stamp of approval on the program, having seen and supported it for three years. Their thirst for knowledge was palpable, and it rubbed off on the participants, who saw senior alumni continuously wanting to learn more. In return, they not only taught and gained subject matter expertise, but they also received special advanced learning being piloted for the Afghan program. They were the first to receive special sessions on Advanced Leadership and Social Business, for example. Their feedback and insights helped shape the subjects that would become a part of the mainstream Afghan program. It is interesting, because as the program itself was winding down, these subject areas that were tested have emerged as full programs on their own for Afghanistan, Iraq, other countries in the Middle East, and countries in Africa.

Graduates of the Fellowship served as important alumni. Upon graduation, they joined an alumni network that kept them connected to the program and continuing to learn from each other. Many would continue to implement projects they had identified during the Fellowship. Others would lean on each other for advice in their professional lives. The bonds from the Fellowship, the networks created, and in particular the teamwork were strong, and it was seen over many cycles of the program that people would remain in touch. They would support the program in Kabul, and also meet to share professional best practices. The goal was to have them apply the skills they were learning, talk about it, and share how they could best use what they had learned. The beauty of this was that they came from many different ministries, and also the private sector and NGOs. The network remained loosely intact, as it was difficult with professional and personal lives to always get together consistently with scheduling and the security situation in Afghanistan. As always, Sokout was the leader in keeping all the people together and having the learning continue. I found we were always brainstorming how to even further leverage this great alumni base. Years later, however, we remain in contact. An excellent success story involves a handful of our alumni applying their skills to help create botanical gardens in Afghanistan, since none of these exist in the country, and there is a danger of losing native plants and trees. So they get to apply the skills they learned to a new program, but also get to contribute to addressing global warming and biodiversity loss.

4. International Mentors

Mentors were selected to also support the teams. These were professional experts from universities, NGOs, and the private sector around the world. Each team would have at least two mentors and at important milestones, as participants were working through their projects, they would present what they had accomplished to their two mentors virtually, mentors then providing valuable feedback to shape the projects. While the mentors sometimes struggled to understand the context of the work being accomplished, they generally got up to speed and performed admirably, giving feedback that participants deemed valuable. Sometimes two mentors would disagree on their feedback, giving the Afghan participant team a dilemma. That was perfect, as often times in the real-world stakeholders do not say the same thing, and come at things from different perspectives, leaving a working team to sort through the feedback and make the best decisions possible. This dynamic further added to the magic of the program. Many mentors traveled, paying their own way, to see their teams of Afghan participants present their final project plans and graduate from the Fellowship.

The Afghans Themselves

By far the greatest magic in the program was created by the Afghans themselves. They have had war for over 40 years, and yet they retained their optimism, humor, and dedication to bettering themselves. They proved their discipline, humility, and resilience as a people, wanting to rise from war, to give better lives for their families and their nation. They were also very gracious, showing tremendous gratitude for anyone who helped them learn. They persevered through many security issues, dangerous situations, and even risked leaving loved ones behind in order to attend our program. They were always a true inspiration, and developed nations around the world can learn from their determination to make the world a better place. Many had suffered hardships in their own lives, growing up for decades in refugee camps due to the war. These tent camps were freezing cold in winter, muddy in the rainy season, filled with disease, and fraught with a lack of food, clean water, and sanitation. Every Afghan knew many relatives and friends who were killed as a result of decades of fighting in their country. They were forced to live through it all as innocent civilian victims, not by their own choosing, but by virtue of being born in this time and place. Yet, it may have been this very suffering that made them who they are, a resilient people who can teach the rest of the world that it is not about material possessions and spending time playing video games, it is about thinking about your fellow humans, and fighting to give them better lives, better health, a job, and a chance at happiness.

These magical Afghan participants always stepped up to perform extraordinarily well in the Fellowship, absorbing learning and lessons, and applying it to real life problems. Several stories stand out to place an exclamation point on their virtues as a people. In the early years (around 2004), many participants who were in senior government positions, were fresh off the battlefield, having fought the Taliban for years. They spoke little English, and virtually none

of them had a great deal of education. The former university structures had not returned yet, and most participants did not have
bachelor's or any advanced degrees. The minimum requirement
for Afghan Fellows was English, and an undergraduate degree.
English was very challenging, in the first three cycles particularly.
The older Fellows in many cases had received their education
in Russia, so they were fluent in Russian but not English. Many
younger ones spoke languages of active international NGOs from
Europe, such as French and German. They also knew Persian and
Urdu, but were not as fluent in English. In terms of education levels, the older Fellows had post-graduate degrees, but material was
sometimes outdated, sometimes from the Soviet era. The middle
generation had been in many cases lost in wars. The really young
ones were just young enough to have finished their BA(s). Some
of the most qualified and brightest Fellows were the medical doctors and the engineers. That being said, sometimes it was hard to
know if any of the young attendees were knowledgeable, because
of formal education or simply a life experience an outsider could
not even fathom.

I remember teaching one class at that time and wondering if I
was getting through to them about leadership, strategic planning,
team development and our other concepts. As they neared the end
of the program, I was on pins and needles, to see if they could
perform the cumulative challenge, presenting their program plan
to all participants and our panel of judges. Thankfully, they performed admirably, proving they had heard, absorbed, and applied
the lessons. As all teams finished, I saw one of the participants
marching right at me. He was a big, burly older gentleman with a
long thick beard who had spent a great deal of time on the battle-
fields of Afghanistan. Not sure what he was doing, I tried to step
back to make room for him to pass. Not to be denied, he sped up,
wrapped his arms around me, and lifted me into the air. Granted,
I am 6 feet 2 inches tall and 200 pounds. My eyes bulged as he

bear-hugged me (I was facing the audience and they could see my face blushing). The audience shouted in surprise and burst out laughing. He turned his head and gave me a giant, bearded hairy kiss on my cheek while continuing to lift me off the ground. He was overcome with a feeling of joy for the success of their presentation and the learning they had gained and that was his way of thanking me in front of all participants. If I was unsure we had gotten through to them with the lessons in this program, that instant erased all doubts.

Women in the program were treated specially, as Afghanistan looked to grow women leaders for the future. We only had three to four women in any given program, and we were determined to always push for more, while not opting for facile and superficial selections, as some international development programs were apt to do. Our goal was to have at least 10% of women in any given program year, but women had not been permitted to go to school by the Taliban regime, and girls were just starting to attend schools for the first time in the early years of our program. Many were educated in schools in neighboring countries when living there as refugees. Others in Afghanistan went to underground schools for girls, risking their lives. Women who wanted to make it in government needed professional degrees, and engineering and medicine were the two paths to achieve such success. Yet to make it in school and obtain those degrees required many things to go right for a woman, including a great deal of support from their fathers and other men in their lives. Many older generation Afghan men did not think women should go to school, have careers, or be in government. We were always paying special attention to the women in our program, to watch the dynamics with other participants, and ensure they were treated equitably. In one Fellowship cycle, we had an all-women team (2008), the first and only time we had a team comprised exclusively of women. At the end of the program, all teams were making their final presentations to the judging panel and participants. The lady-only team presented last and did a great job of applying the lessons and demonstrating a strong program to solve a key issue in Afghanistan. When finished, they received positive feedback from judges, and we could all see how happy they were with the huge amount of work they had poured into their project and the presentation. From the audience, an older gentleman, a participant, stood up. He said, "just a moment" in a rather gruff voice. We all paused, and turned to him, and he waited until he had the attention of everyone in the room. He said, "I need to say what I really think about this all women team, and everyone in the room is thinking the same thing." We all gasped. Then his tone softened and changed. He went on to say, "this team of all women presented a really complete program plan. It is by far the best presentation of any team in the room, and each of you ladies deserve a giant basket of flowers!" The room erupted in cheers and applause. What a giant step forward that moment was for Afghanistan, and we were able to be a part of it!

Another surreal moment came in Hiroshima in 2008. While having lunch at a café/lunchroom at the base of the UNITAR building, an announcement came out about the U.S. presidential elections. Afghans had believed the U.S. invaded Iraq in error, and felt as if their country was not getting the support it needed to stabilize and secure it. They knew that the roots of 9/11 had emanated from their country, not Iraq. They wanted peace and happiness, and justice to be served for 9/11. More than anything, they wanted the war to end, and a chance for the stability in Afghanistan that had eluded them for more than 40 years. A TV screen suddenly turned on, announcing that it was official: Barack Obama had won the United States presidential elections. Immediately, the Afghans leapt to their feet and began shouting, jumping up and down. To my amazement, they grabbed me by the hands, and sat me in the middle of the room. As leader of the program, they viewed me as a world citizen who was there to help them. Yet they also knew of my American roots. I was not the only American involved with the Fellowship at the time, but certainly the only American in the UNITAR building at that time. Loud music started from somewhere, and approximately 40 Afghans formed a giant circle and began dancing around me, dancing in hopeful joy that there would be better days ahead for their country, now that Obama was President of the United States. All I could do was to sit in my chair in the center of their circle, smiling and incredulously staring at them all.

In Hiroshima, the participants were welcomed everywhere as celebrities. A contingent of them would always get to visit the governor and the mayor, both important supporters of the Fellowship, alongside other donors including the Japanese government. While in Hiroshima, we would also visit the Hiroshima Peace Memorial Museum. Afghans learned that the Japanese had a phrase for the dropping of the bomb on Japanese civilians that killed over 300,000 people, "forgive but do not forget." They learned that the city was dedicated to peace and nuclear disarmament. At the museum, they would hear a survivor of the nuclear bomb, known as a *Hibakusha*, tell grim and heart rendering stories of the aftermath of the bomb and its impact on the local civilians. The Afghans took it all in, with empathy and grace. When asked about their thoughts, they were aware of the magnitude and horrors of what happened with a nuclear weapon, and the implications. One consistent theme for them was to share with their hosts that their country too had had war for 40 years. They always wanted everyone to know how much Afghans had suffered and faced many a tragedy, for a length of time that is beginning to span generations.

A contingent of the Afghan Fellows visiting Hidehiko Yuzaki,
the Governor of Hiroshima, who was offered
an Afghan robe and hat

It was always interesting to lead a program in a different country. Once, we held a 2009 program in Dehradun, India. A giant banner covered the front of the hotel, stating the UNITAR Afghan Fellowship was being held in its premises. During that same week, the Indian Embassy in Kabul was attacked, blown up, and on fire — 17 people were killed, and 63 were injured. Perpetrators looked to be local Afghans, perhaps with ties to the Taliban. We were on heightened alert instantly, as you can imagine local Indians may want revenge against Afghans for their embassy being destroyed. Yet, the Indians were savvy enough to know that these Afghan leaders were not involved or at fault. Similarly, the Afghans did not flinch at the bombing, knowing that their host country's embassy had been attacked back in their homeland. They continued being the gracious diplomats that they are, polite to the hotel staff and locals that they encountered.

Several times we had glimpses into their personal lives. One of the most senior ministers who attended the program admitted to having two wives, allowed under his religion. When another participant asked him why he didn't have more, he began to admit why. He said that they often argued with each other, and both spent most of the time mad at him. The result was that he ended up sleeping in the hallway of his house on the floor most nights. He exclaimed at one point, "I can't make it with two, can you imagine how much more complex and painful it may be for me and them if I had more than two!? Why would I want that?!"

Every program had an Afghan culture night toward the end. Afghans would bring traditional dress from their provinces and also amazing local food. Many of these cultural events were open to locals, whether it was Dubai, Singapore, India, or Hiroshima. The goal was to showcase Afghan culture and cuisine, so that people locally could get to know them better. They were great cultural ambassadors, explaining to their hosts the wonderful dried fruits, nuts, and other delightful dishes that they had packed in their suitcases from Afghanistan. The event always ended with the national dance, where the men dance in small circles, while in a larger circle. It looks simple enough, but as the music speeds up, one realizes this takes stamina, finesse, and athletic ability. One by one the men drop out of the larger circle until only the strongest remain. It is artistic, athletic, and a thing of beauty all at the same time. The Afghans would reward their instructors and the UNITAR staff with gifts, from handicraft and jewelry, to hats and robes. It was always great fun to receive a new set of clothes from the Afghans, wear it immediately, and have them tell me about the province it represents, and the stories behind the colors and patterns. I have a Hamid Karzai colored and patterned long robe (green, with golden vertical stripes) that I wear from time to time.

Our alumni would let us know how the situation in Afghanistan was progressing. One such participant, who also served as a long-standing coach and resource person, was visiting provinces regularly as a medical doctor. Because the Taliban kept lists of people who were "serving the current government," he suspected he was on "the List," so he would go out to the provinces each week, kissing his wife and children goodbye as if it were the last time he would see them. As this medical doctor transitioned to a well-known NGO in the region, the danger became even more real. As he took the executive leader from the NGO and a journalist on a tour of the Afghan provinces' medical facilities, their small party was stopped. The executive leader and journalist were taken hostage, and our alumni was pistol whipped. He was given 24 hours to come up with a large sum of money (~$1M). Rushing to donors who he thought could help, he asked for money but begged them not to involve the police or military. As he met the bandits the next day, offering the cash, he was pleased to find his boss and the journalist appearing unharmed. As the transaction was taking place, however, police swarmed in to capture the bandits. A donor had to tell the police about what was unfolding. The awkward part of the story comes as our alumni, his boss, and the journalist fly back to Kabul. On the same plane were the police with the arrested bandits. Knowing who he was, he had to get out of the country immediately. He was taken out of Afghanistan without his wife and children, finding refuge in Canada. It would take years before his wife and children could reunite with him in Canada.

Perhaps the story that symbolized the Afghan resiliency best occurred while I was teaching a coaching session, prior to the full event. It was done virtually and as we began the session, one of our coaches was missing. About 20 minutes later, he joined. I wanted to bring him into the discussion and coaching session, asking if he was OK and letting him know what we were covering. His surprising answer shocked me. He said "not really, I am not OK. I was in the city center and there was a car bombing. I couldn't drive any further, so I got out and walked the rest of the way to join this call. I am so sorry I am late, please accept my apologies." I said, "what? Are you OK?" He said, "Yes, but my car is not. It was damaged badly in the bombing and can't go anymore." I said, "Aren't you shaken? Don't you want to contact your family, go and be with them, or take care of your car?" I frantically googled «car bombing Kabul." Sure enough, the media was reporting a massive car bombing in the city center with many people killed. His response was, "Dr. Fors, you are doing something here for the future of our country...for my kids and grandkids...to try to make it safe for all...and a place people can be happy in their lives. That is so much more important than my car or my fear. Let's carry on with this meeting."

Program Themes

In sum, the program had many magical elements that made it successful. Some important design elements, too, were key to that magic. It was practical, experiential, and followed modern adult learning practices. It created a team challenge for participants, setting a standard of excellence for them to achieve, while still ensuring individual learning and action planning. A weaving of program themes provided magic from a content standpoint, and included program management, leadership, strategy, servant leadership, and social entrepreneurship. The team supporting the program was key to its success, including coaches, mentors, the UNITAR program leaders and staff, stakeholders, donors, and sponsors. Resource persons and mentors from around the world helped with the magic. We expected the Afghans to implement the programs created to solve social issues, and wanted to hear about the impact they were having. Many teams did implement the program that served as their team project. They also implemented their own individual program if it was not chosen as the overall team project. They would follow up on email or LinkedIn, beaming about the fact that their project had been implemented and was having great success. Indeed, the Afghans themselves made the program over the years very magical.

Indicators of success included promotion velocity, as we wanted alumni to take on greater levels of responsibility so they could widen their impact on Afghanistan, the region, and the world. We tracked their promotion velocity, and Sokout in particular tracked where alumni landed in critical roles. Leaders in the Aga Khan Foundation, The National Procurement Agency, The President's Office, foreign embassies in Kabul, and numerous non-profit and government agencies outside of Kabul were some of the places our alumni found leadership roles.

We expect them to continue learning, growing, and having an impact. At the end of each program, we would set expectations with them. They were told that leadership was a gift, and they had it or they wouldn't be in the program. We told them we wanted them to use it for good, to help others in Afghanistan and the world; not to be corrupt and line their pockets by abusing the power. We expected them to keep growing and learning, making their leadership exponential. They were encouraged to create organizational systems that leverage the learning they had systematically. That meant consistently driving world class program management, a system for developing teams to make them all high performing, and an ability to create consistently high performing organizations as a leader. They started a leadership legacy in which they determined how they wanted to be remembered as leaders in this world. The strong emphasis was on being a "servant leader" where they exist to serve the organization, teams, and individuals that are supporting them, helping them to achieve the vision that will make Afghanistan a better place to live for all. They were encouraged to continue their education (most did), and to know that they can do and accomplish more than they

realize. They were left with the following poem, which was my part-
ing gift to them, and a wish for them:

> *You have lived a beautiful life*
> *And have left a beautiful field,*
> *You have sacrificed the hour*
> *To give service for all time,*
> *You have entered the company of the great*
> *And with them you will be remembered forever.*

Anonymous

Overall, while I gave to the Fellowship over the years, I got way more
in return. I was awarded a UN Partner Award for my involvement in
the program. That was very nice of UNITAR. But, the greatest gift
I received was my interactions with the Afghans, the staff, and the
other leaders involved in the program. It is the friendships, connections, and memories that we shared that live in my heart and mind.
It inspires me to do more for Afghans and others around the world,
and I wish that many more people can see how many great things
come from being in a position to help others like the Hiroshima
Fellowship for Afghanistan did.

Receiving a UN Partner Award for involvement in the program

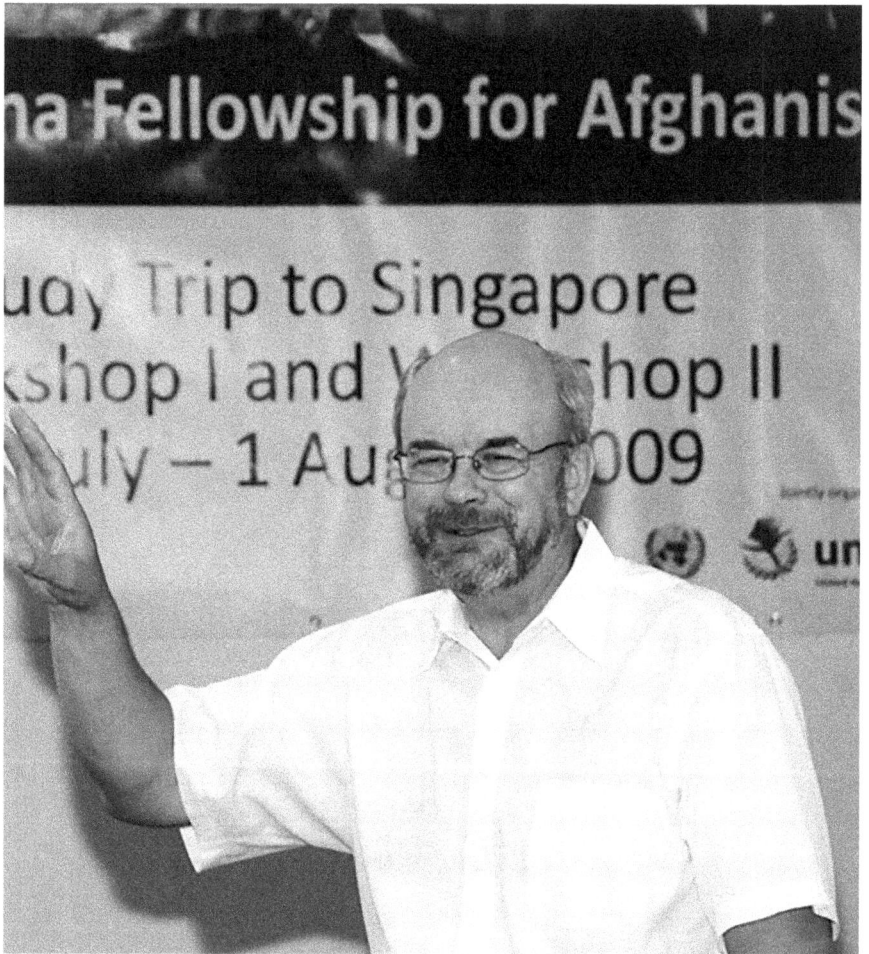

Empathy, community, social capital

Lorne Jaques[18]

A story first,

> In every session I did with the Fellows, I would place a chair on
> a table and gather the whole group around it in a chaotic mob.
> I think everyone was happy to get out of their own chairs, but
> they were also curious about what we were going to do with a
> silly chair perched on top of a table. What was the relevance in
> a workshop about leadership and participation?

I was always a little nervous about the exercise, but it always
seemed to be popular and generated lots of conversation,
energy, and speculation. Above the din of chatter and laughter
I'd shout out, "What is it?" leading to a few puzzled expressions and glances in my direction. Even to those whose English
vocabulary was still limited it was pretty obvious that it was a
"chair" or "a place to sit" or "metal & plastic" or maybe "wood"
depending upon where we were. I repeated the question several
times, "Yes, but what IS it????" until even the polite Afghani
curiosity started to turn to exasperation.

Of the many times we repeated this exercise, one occasion
impressed me the most as an effective way of generating reflection and deeper contemplation. That time I was the specta-
tor, which of course led me to reflections and contemplation

[18] Lorne Jaques served as Professor at the University of Calgary, and Chief of UNITAR's New York
Office from 2002 to 2004. He was a member of the core faculty of the Fellowship for Afghanistan
and advisor to the program through its 15-year span.

of my own. We were conducting my session virtually as the Fellows could not travel that year. They were in Kabul, I was in Calgary, Canada. It was mid-morning for them, it was midnight for me. Many of them were delayed in arrival at their classroom because of a bombing in the city. I was in my university office where I had a strong internet bandwidth staring at my computer. Still the 10,000 km distance resulted in some latency and poor-quality video and audio.

When it came time to put the chair on a table in that very crowded room half a world away, I muted my microphone and watched while the remarkable Sokout, the Coaches and Afghan Resource Persons, who had all survived one or more of these sessions in earlier workshops, plunked the chair on a table and shouted out, "What is this?" Or at least I think they did because they spoke in Dari or Pashtun, or both. The laughter was raucous, the participation broad and passionate. The outcomes of the follow-up conversation were completely lost on me as they were comfortably conducted in their own language.

Over the computer I was asked to summarize the meaning of the exercise in relation to the purpose of my session. Why were we spending time philosophizing about a chair?

Simply put, the hope is that we might recognize that even a common chair is the culmination of a highly complex process; one that involves many people in many places whose collaboration has led to this functional piece of furniture being in our room. Further, again with oversimplification, the chair only came to be because people learned how to manage the process of its design, construction, and transportation to our room through managing their relationships with one another. That potential chaos of producing a chair with so many relationships can be resolved with contracts, coercion, or extra cash. But smaller teams and communities produce their "chairs," or whatever their collective goals might be, by creating trust. Trust reduces the time and cost of managing inter-personal relationships. The "chairs" or other outcomes come quicker, cheaper and are more likely to fit the needs of the community when relationships within the team/community function of the basis of trust.

My own experience, and future as a contributor to the Fellowship, was deeply enriched by the opportunity to watch while others who were more linguistically and culturally qualified than me made the exercise work. Even then it was never clear that the original intention of the exercise was more effectively made or even more clearly relevant on that occasion. It did however change _me_.

Reflections of a Resource Person

Early in my career working with marginalized communities a friend and mentor, emphasized that my own transformation was as critical as anything that we might hope for the community. He said my changes needed to precede, and then accompany, that of others if I were to be an effective and legitimate ally.

My experience with the Afghan Fellowship (AF) demonstrated like no other that personal change and growth happens simultaneously and inevitably when you share the path with a community, walk the same detours and scenery.

There is an element of colonialism and elitism that threatens any relationship where there is power and privilege disparity. This is certainly true in training, teaching and facilitation settings. In those places the resource person, professor, and "leader" sets the agenda. We control the timing, the content and demand performance even if we express it as participation and apply our best professional judgement with legitimate good intentions.

Through my many years and diverse ways of involvement with the AF I developed a deep affection and respect for our Afghan colleagues. It is deeply humbling recognizing now many years later that I failed them in so many ways. That is not to say that we did not share many enlightening moments. I still think our time together left us feeling like we took something useful back to our "other" lives.

No, I think unrealized ambitions for more learning gold were tied to my deficiencies. That is not humility, I was learning.

There was an unfortunate lack of time in the early stages to understand context. One must immerse in the reality of those for whom the learning needs to be relevant. So many factors influence the outcome of knowledge sharing and creation including: the selection and priority of content; the style of teaching, and the space in which it happens. A fundamental understanding of the circumstances is necessary to achieve engagement of participants; the way all of those things are verified, and adaptations made.

We all succumbed to the typical conditions of most international education/training, in fact most other international development initiatives. Specific outcomes, costs, timelines, and countless logistical details need to addressed long before meaningful face-to-face encounters take place between resource people and the communities in which they intend to work.

The roots of poverty, insecurity, and deficiency are imbedded in decades, even centuries of circumstance that surround them. The change initiatives of well-meaning international partners are always limited by grossly inadequate time and resources relative to the history and breadth of the problems being addressed.

I know this. Almost everybody involved in the sector knows this. But we all eagerly entered the program because we were enchanted by the incredible collective and individual personalities of both the originators and then the Afghan Fellows who became our colleagues and friends.

Afghanistan's legacy of foreign invasions and internecine conflict was well known in the West. Indeed, there was no small amount of responsibility being felt in the West for the strife preceding the Fellowship. While this led to support for the initiation of the Fellowship, we all knew that it was going to be particularly complicated in Afghanistan.

There is such a strange paradox between the complex social and economic need and the urgency of rescue and development. We want to stretch our limited resources as well as avoid waste and redundancy in designing and delivering the best, most relevant program possible. We want results. We want them quickly because the need is urgent, or the money will go elsewhere. This was as true for the AF as it is for many similar projects.

The AF became very effective because the learning turned organic. Many Fellows became coaches and resource persons themselves. Organizers, external facilitators, and educators stayed with the project for many years leading to the kind of continuity that makes programs with good intentions into great projects with extraordinary achievements.

The unfailing passion of Nassrine Azimi and Humaira Kamal meant that the Fellowship got underway with literally a "hope and a dream." I did my first online session in 2003 at midnight from a strange little room in a fledgling startup in downtown Manhattan. They had boasted of flawless internet voice communications with anywhere in the world. I think there were maybe five Fellows in Afghanistan for that session who were subjected to my poorly designed content about leadership. At that point, as with many ambitious projects, the most important point was that we got started, we made something happen.

The Fellowship blossomed from there as Humaira and Nassrine worked their professional charm. The number of Fellows multiplied. Friends and colleagues were recruited from many places around the world and then the networks of contributors expanded exponentially. It was almost like a friendly virus. Money came from somewhere and was spent very carefully. Program content evolved gradually and with greater input from Afghanistan partners. My own participation ranged widely but included aspects of leadership, organizational and community development, stakeholder engagement and social capital.

While I drew upon my experiences from other parts of the world to speak of these things and draw illustrations, I was acutely conscious of my own shortcomings when it came to understanding the context of Afghanistan. I could draw upon my work in other post-conflict places, but Afghanistan did not align well with them as conflict seemed ongoing, unresolved, and highly complex. I had travelled to and worked directly with other communities where chronic poverty and disparities were rampant, but I had no opportunity to see them directly in Afghanistan. I had encountered many corrupt and ineffective officials in their offices abroad but the Fellows in our classrooms were passionate, wise, and deeply committed to their country rather than themselves.

Of the content themes that I was asked to share the one that led to my own greatest transformation was that of "leadership." A quick search today revealed over three billion hits on that general theme, just in English. The literature and expertise are rife with exploitation, speculation, and ambition.

Before the 2009 workshop I had decided to canvas the current and previous Fellows about the leaders in their life. We talked about it when we were together at the YMCA in Singapore. The results initially distressed me but ultimately inspired my own redress of the leadership idea.

I had the message pounded into my brain once again that the answers are always dependent on the question, and that power resides with the person asking. For my Afghan colleagues it was clear that leaders were role models that then shaped their own lives. It was not about the other, the leader... the one with the microphone, the one with wealth, the one who commanded their performance. It was with how they themselves chose to behave because of that interaction. To be able to subsequently emulate the person they admired. They could tell right away if that someone was worthy of their respect, and thus had created a willingness of the "follower" to contribute to a shared goal.

I thought a lot about this thanks to the Fellows. They came from government departments that had multiple levels of nominal leaders. For the purposes of the Fellowship our participants were placed in groups with a coach. They took instructions about their assigned tasks from all of us. They came from a fundamentally paternalistic, male-dominant culture. Roles and power were hardly new concepts. Aligning interest, recognizing individual strengths as well as recognizing there were always periods when and how anyone and everyone could take leadership in a team/unit/community became the new approach to this theme. Leadership became "Followship". (That isn't right either. We're open to a new label!) But it was transformational for me and was well received as a paradigm shift in the Fellowship.

The Challenge of Gender

I felt a distressing and unanswered tension about gender throughout the Fellowship. More specifically of course was the role and engagement of the women Fellows. I thought great efforts were made to solicit opportunities for women. More and more of them were recruited. At various times they were integrated into work groups with men in related fields. At other times they composed a group of their own. For the most part it looked to me that they were treated with respect by their colleagues. Resource people made explicit efforts to facilitate their engagement. Exclusions and poor behavior were confronted. Still, I felt that I lost an opportunity to expand the growth of the whole group by drawing more explicitly on the talent, feelings, and wisdom of the women. I lacked the skill and technique to do so and did not seek out the input of those who had appropriate skills and might have changed it. I think that I also hid behind my ignorance of Afghanistan, and indeed Islamic, culture in this respect. I wish that I had been a greater asset to the women, and in turn the entire Fellowship. There are no personal transformations to acknowledge.

I do not wish to conclude my humble reflections on the Fellowship on what could be perceived as a negative. Comprehension of gender, and specifically structural diminution of women, remains a universal challenge. As a father of two daughters, a husband, a mother's son, colleague, and friend to many more women than men, I accept my need to be constantly mindful of my behavior in this.

Personal Enrichment

I have worked in over forty countries and numerous cultures within each. I have been the benefactor of incredible learning and generosity. Without any doubt the Afghan Fellowship stands among the most personally rewarding. The magic of the Fellowship came from: the wondrous spirit of the Fellows through the years; the generosity of friends, colleagues and students who shared their time with the fellows; the camaraderie of the resource people, and; the remarkable facilitators of the necessary administration that comes with complex projects like this. My thanks to all who enabled my transformations.

Recollections of Dehradun Summer 2008 – updated May 5, 2020

I remember that trip well. The long grueling drive to the event site when we were stopped first on both the highway and then in the village which was part of the detour. A great pile of sand had been dumped on the only through-road. A dozen men standing around arguing for two hours about the best thing to do about that pile – should have asked a woman; we'd have been through in 20 minutes. What should only have been a 6-hour drive turned into 9. But it was extra time when friends and acquaintances found extra time to solve all of the world's most compelling problems – they just seem to come back in unique and challenging ways. Maybe another long car ride is in order? COVID wouldn't stand a chance!

Michael Fors who was on this trip with me has shared this unflattering photo which is unfortunately all too indicative of my state.

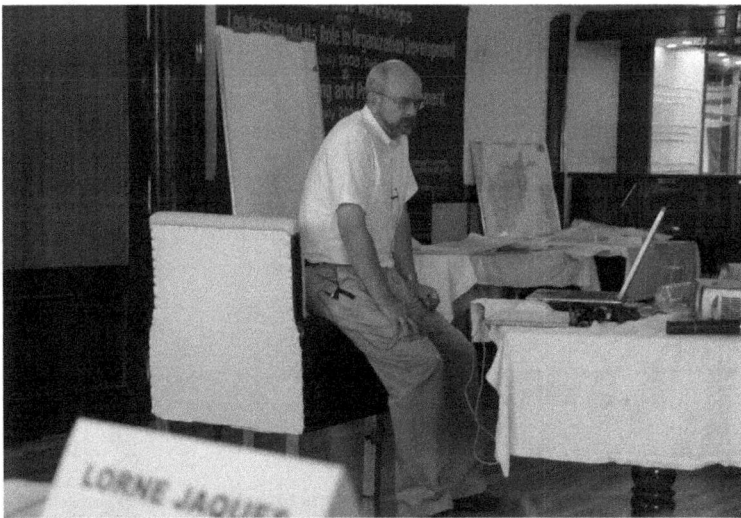

Unable to eat, sleep or concentrate. My colleagues, Afghan, Canadian, American, Singaporean, Japanese were all my source of the energy. I needed to struggle through the content we wanted to share. So much gratitude to all of you.

The story did not end in Dehradun though. I remember the knuckle-whitening trip with Michael in the small plane back to Delhi, the taxi driver who was completely lost driving through the city looking for my hotel (which we drove past at least three times) and, with a semblance of an appetite returning, my inability to locate a functioning ATM from which to draw even a few rupees to buy some rice.

I was struck so vividly walking through incredible crowds of locals. I was super conscious of both my whiteness and my privilege – a privilege I had inherited, not earned, from my own ethnicity and origins that made me a foot taller than everyone around me. I was the "other." Going to sleep hungry that night was also a privilege in those circumstances.

My fortune is my friends. Thanks for the reminder.

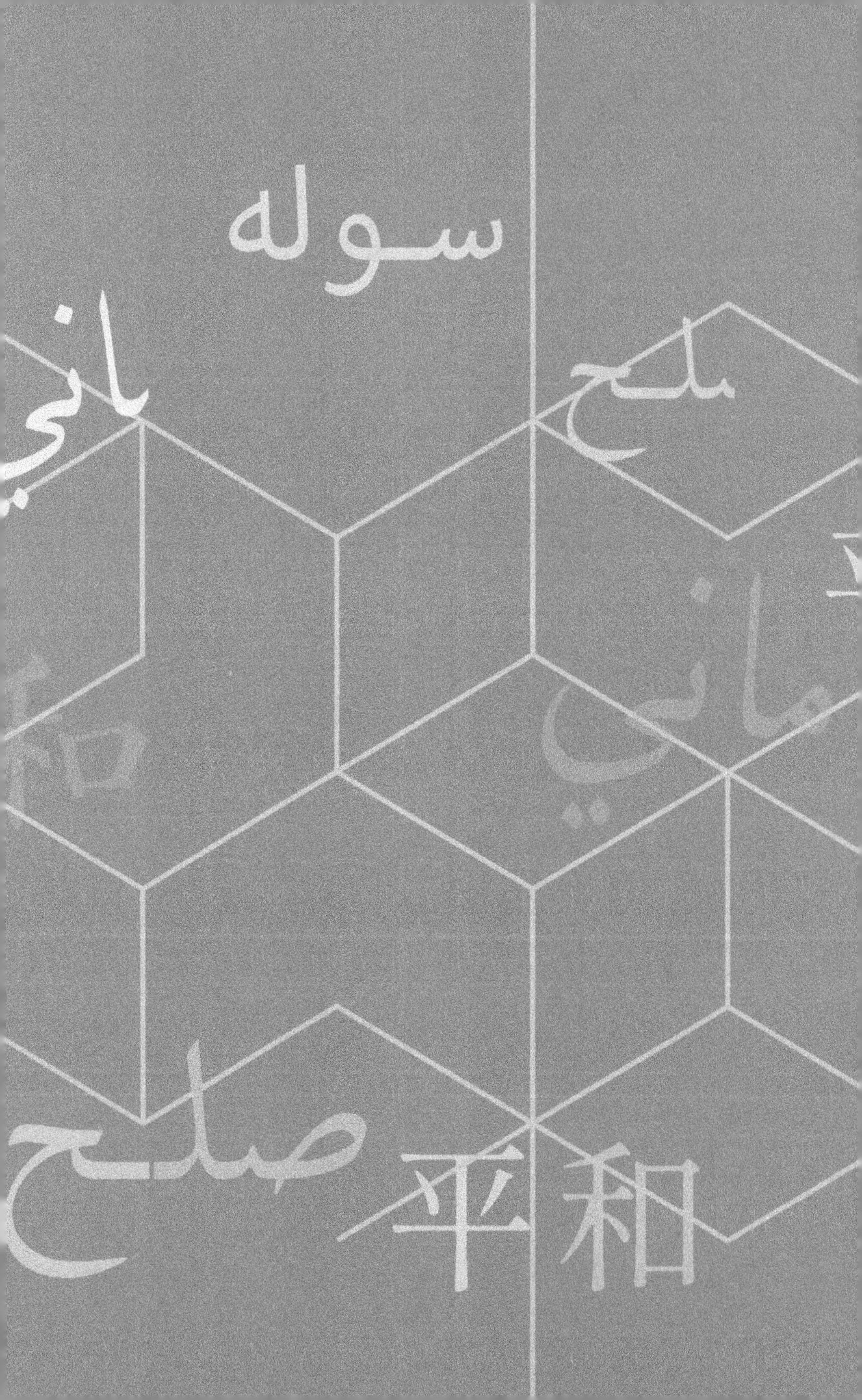
سوله
صلح
平和

AFTERTHOUGHTS POST-AUGUST 2021
November 17, 2021
Lorne Jaques

When I witness from afar what is happening as the Taliban swept through Afghanistan, I am distraught, angry, and worried for the Afghan friends I met during the AF. Indeed, I feel hopeless and helpless. I feel only a little better when I think about the AF in this way....

In trying to engage the curious about the complex needs and strategies for development I think about three different types of change: hard things, soft things, and messy things.

The hard things are defined literally.... They are buildings, roads, equipment. They are necessary, relatively easy to do and to photograph. They are almost always too expensive, are often sources of corruption and symbolic of power. Their relics, scattered over too many landscapes, prove that they are subject to deterioration and expensive maintenance sooner or later.

The AF focused on the softer (human) things and, indirectly, on the messy (complicated) things. The human things are about supporting the growth of individuals and teams to optimize their existing talents and entice them with exposure to other ways of thinking, listening, and sharing. Sometimes those come from other places and people who have developed an expertise in a related topic. Sometimes it comes from their colleagues across the table. We incorrectly label those things "training" or "education." Our Fellows were

153

already very well trained and educated.... The Fellowship created more intellectual space for them to enhance their skills, try out new ones and appreciate the wisdom found in others.

The strength of this softer human approach is that it leads to outcomes that endure and multiply as they are passed along to others. They are carried with people to new situations, locations and teammates. Most importantly they are organic and grow as people build upon them with their own accumulating experiences to guide them. They are very difficult to destroy and ironically become stronger under systemic oppression.

The messy kind of change comes from shifts in power, or more simply the way important decisions or choices are made. This was never an explicit objective of the AF. It is rarely an explicit goal in our desire to make things more fair, just, and equitable because it takes a long time and often involves setbacks. It is hard to find support for such projects because they take a very long time, the objectives are difficult to photograph, and they abound with risk. Local power holders come to believe such project threaten their status.

I think positive, messy, and complicated outcomes originate with stronger, wiser, and kinder humans. These are people who have benefited from new relationships, including with those who come from different origins ... distant and near. My hope for the Fellows, and Afghanistan, is restored when I think that the AF might have helped create some indestructible wisdom and commitment to the best values of humanity. That is true for all of us who shared the space that the Afghanistan Fellowship created over two decades.

Encounters with Afghanistan, the Afghans,
and the Afghan Fellowship
Sharapiya Kakimova[19]

The Fellowship was a great life school. It allowed me to learn many lessons which have helped me be more open, passionate, patient, flexible and better understand people from different cultures.

I grew up in the former Soviet Union and all I knew about Afghanistan was its endless wars and atrocities. When I went for studies to Hiroshima, Japan, I had a chance to be an intern at the conference on Post-Conflict Reconstruction, organized by UNITAR, Hiroshima University, and Hiroshima Prefecture. To tell the truth, I was not sure what to expect, but when it started, I discovered a completely new world of reconstruction and what could be done to make it work. With my engineering background, it was all new for me. Most speakers put people at the center of the process, and it all made sense. Therefore, when the following year UNITAR opened its office in Hiroshima, I was thrilled to become part of the UNITAR Hiroshima Fellowship for Afghanistan.

I will never forget my first encounter with the group of 25 Afghans, mostly men, in November 2003. My colleague and I had to meet the group at the airport in Tokyo and take them all by bus to Kyoto, where the rest of the UNITAR team was waiting. I had roughly

[19] Sharapiya Kakimova, is Coordinator of International Agreements within Chilean National Commission for Scientific and Technological Research (CONICYT). She was one of the founding team members of the AF and a Mentor in the program.

about USD $4000 in cash (an amount I had never held in cash before!) to use during the travel for food, parking, highway fees, etc. I was afraid not only of losing the cash but mostly of how 22 men with beards would treat me and whether they would listen to what I had to say or not. To my relief, I enjoyed every moment of the trip – the group made jokes, sang songs, talked about their country and most importantly, they all wanted to help me and to ease my responsibilities. When we arrived in Kyoto, I knew them all and I actually started to care for them. I guess that first trip with 25 Afghans was the beginning of my long, loving relationship with the Afghans, Afghanistan, and the Fellowship. It was my first life lesson from the Fellowship: no matter how hard our lives might be, we have to enjoy every opportunity it gives us, just like the Afghans enjoyed those very first days in Japan.

My care for those people and for their country got deeper when David Eaton, our Resource Person, and I visited Kabul for the first time in May 2004. The two of us represented UNITAR for the first time in Kabul, after the Fellowship's official launch. My sense of responsibility was overwhelming - I was in a country that had recently come out of the war, and I didn't have my mentors, Nassrine and Humaira, nearby to guide me... Truth be told I was a bit afraid, but, again, I found so much support around me that I forgot all my worries and that the country could still be danger- ous. That trip showed me other qualities of our Afghan colleagues – their warm hospitality and hunger for knowledge. They listened and asked questions again and again. It was another lesson for me – don't waste any opportunity to learn as it is the most valuable trea- sure someone can get.

The Fellowship evolved through the years, but our Fellows' eager- ness to learn did not change. Later, when I was teaching at a local university in Chile, I was disappointed with the students who did not appreciate their chance to learn. At that time, our Fellows were always in my mind – despite difficulties they faced every day (the situation in Afghanistan did not get better after my first visit, it actually got worse, forcing UNITAR to move workshops to other countries), our Afghan Fellows, Coaches and, later, Resource Persons retained a high level of responsibility and commitment. That accompanied with their eagerness to learn, developed in me great respect for these people, respect I carry inside me till today.

I also understood that every person from a different culture should be treated differently. I am a Kazakh who studied in Japan, so, although I knew Muslim culture, Japanese culture was embedded within me. I was especially strict about being on time. Once, when one of the Fellows came late to a bus for about 20 minutes without any particular reason, I was angry with him and scolded him in front of everyone. However, instead of being angry with the man, many were not happy with me. I felt very strange and at that moment understood that I had committed an error and had to fix it. I felt the urgent need to apologize to the man and did, first just to him and then in front of the whole group. I knew the man was not right, but I did not have right to expose him in such a way. When we got off the bus, Sokout, our irreplaceable representative on the ground, came close and expressed the group's appreciation for my apology. It was another lesson for me that I never forget – sometimes rules cannot fit everyone, even if you have been following them forever.

Not only had our Afghan colleagues taught me life lessons, all members of the UNITAR Hiroshima Fellowship Community have left a mark on me. The engines for the whole Fellowship, without any doubt, were Nassrine Azimi and Humaira Kamal. I learned so much from these two women throughout the years and feel so happy to know them and so grateful for all they have shared with me.

I also met people like David Eaton, Lorne Jacques, Michael Fors, Duffie van Balkom, Iqbal Khan, Sue and Howard Lamb, Ismail Sudderuddin, and many others, who were engaged in the process with their hearts, their souls, their time, and their dedication. I was so happy to be able to share the same process with all of them, with the people who believed in the Fellowship, believed in Afghanistan, and believed in peaceful solutions.

The most important lesson I learned from many when I think about the Fellowship and the community, was selflessness ... I think few people can say that they met such a wonderful group of people together in one spot and at one time – somehow the Fellowship gathered all the best qualities of very different people, and it is they who made it strong and long lasting. Without dedication, passion and energy put by many in the Fellowship, it would never have achieved what it did. I am so glad that all together, we built a strong Fellowship Community and I hope that the Community will stay together despite time and challenges.

UNITAR Hiroshima Fellowship for
Afghanistan 2010 Cycle

Launch and Orientation
Ceremony

A Complete Fellowship Experience
Interview with Sabahuddin Sokout[20]

On Wearing Different Hats

Tell us a bit about yourself — your childhood years in Afghanistan, your studies, the country's challenges.

I was born into a middle-class family and had the chance to join school at the age of 4. I was a well-behaved child, so my family enrolled me in school without noticing my age, they were just happy that I seemed focused on good choices! My childhood passed engrossed in studies, and like my older brother I was not able to make many friends in my neighborhood as I was never on the streets. I studied in Estiqlal High School, a very reputable school, where my father too had studied along with the sons of King Mohammad Zahir Shah. My father was my role model, and I have tried to follow his path. He was among the first six people to learn about the German Canton Plan, and he chose to study Economics. He was a senior accountant and worked in this capacity for 45 years. I also joined the Economics Faculty and graduated with a focus on National Economy and International Relations. I was able to continue my education and focus on Peace and Economy with my major on the role of SMEs in

[20] UNITAR AF 2005 Fellow, 2006 Coach, 2007Afghan Resource Person, Faculty/Mentor, and 2007-to-date UNITAR AF Representative in Afghanistan

building peace in Afghanistan. People may have heard about the problems of Afghanistan, but it is usually difficult for outsiders to imagine what we have seen or experienced. During the Cold War, the first problem caused by internal conflict in Kabul was the bombings. The first bomb exploded in a bakery in Shar-e-Now; I was among the first victims, I was coming home from school and got injured. The problems kept escalating, rocket shooting, and finally a civil war on every street of Kabul. Kabul was divided among eight unsavory factions, and it was a big challenge to supply food, still I needed to work and study to support my father and feed our family. Meanwhile as a teenager, with the war situation continuing in the background, I continued to focus on my studies, took English, computer and typewriting courses and studied at the university. While the Taliban were in power, I was able to find a job with one of the French NGOs (Pharmaciens Sans Frontières PSF) as a Radio Operator. When international organizations left, I chose to work in Jalalabad City to be away from the challenges in Kabul. Subsequently the Taliban left, and a new government was established. Based on what we had witnessed under the Mujaheddin rule in the 90s, we viewed the new government with fear and suspicion. The United States invaded, but committed the same mistakes as the Soviet Union, with unresolved ethnicity problems and the continued existence of unwanted parties struggling for power.

How did you encounter AF — what were your first impressions of the people, program and places it opened up for you?

My father-in-law was one of the Fellowship candidates and encouraged me to join the program. During the first day of the first Kabul workshop, I was late by 15 minutes.

I rushed into the class and sat in a chair as I did not want to disturb the participants. The Fellowship team's main representative Ms. Sharapiya Kakimova and workshop leader, Prof. David Eaton came and greeted me, giving me a sense of how important I was as a participant and as an academician, despite being late and expecting punishment. I found myself in a totally different and strange environment, where people cared about everyone as individual participants. I learned how and why one should be committed and dedicated to life and cultivate the energy to do something good. It was the first impression, and the five-minute exchange with these two people, which completely changed my attitude towards my life and relationships with others. In our workplace, anytime we participated in a program, we needed to provide a final report focusing on what we covered and experienced, but the Fellowship was totally different, we needed to commit ourselves and dedicate enough time to study, tackle assignments and report back to our Coach and Mentors. On the other hand, we were encouraged to transfer the gained knowledge to people around us, in our office and home; it was another positive point which impressed me the moment I joined the Fellowship.

Can you describe the various roles you have played, and continue to play, in the Fellowship through your 16-year association? What skills and strategies have you learned and used performing these many roles?

I have had many different positions, which entailed different responsibilities during the Fellowship. As a Coach, I was responsible for working with a group of Fellows, guiding them throughout the program to take lessons, tackle assignments, and meet deadlines. My coaching responsibilities also contained practical implementation of the projects proposed by the Fellows, and fortunately, during the four years of coaching, 90% of the proposed projects were implemented. As a Mentor, I was responsible for giving presentations, helping Resource Persons with their presentations contextualizing the topics to Afghanistan's professional environment, and engaging with the content and instructional design for the Fellowship. My main responsibilities in Afghanistan as the official UNITAR Representative were different and more complicated. This is because I had to deal with different people with different backgrounds, positions, and ethnic groups. I had to present to and get the buy-in of different authorities to nominate Fellows, pay the fees, and be directly engaged in the program. One of my responsibilities was to explain the real needs of Afghanistan along with the actual progress in terms of human resources to the Hiroshima Office to design the next cycle program as per those needs. On the other hand, people in key positions such as the Afghan Ministry HR Directors and the Foreign Affairs Directors were my first line of contact as one group came with the needs and the other with the partial funds required for the Fellowship. Over time some of the deputy ministers and ministers got directly engaged in the program as they witnessed the positive impacts of the Fellowship within their organizations. Facing people with different backgrounds and authorities required cautious actions in terms of behavior and communication. Besides the many strategies I learned during my work for the Fellowship, I found that a strong communication strategy to be the most useful at a practical level. Before approaching people or authorities, I collected information about the needs and ways in which those agencies could be better developed, and I also thought about the major topics of the Fellowship, that could be aligned with the objectives of those entities. I divided the resolutions into three parts: the "processes" in order to speed up delivery of services; the "relationship," i.e., how the entities could be better connected to the environment and the possible stakeholders, especially funding agencies and line ministries; and "staffing," which covered staff training and development to prevent brain drain from those authorities. I also shared with them related recent studies and technologies developed in international markets to equip my audience to navigate in different environments and look for the best opportunities to take them there. Based on my training, this was the level of my preparations as I approached these prospective partners, along with some AF alumni. My process was to give enough time to people to digest my points and allow them to respond with their proposals and needs. My plan was to offer multiple ways to our partners to achieve concrete goals, and this allowed me to set up the successful launch of each Fellowship cycle. Because the end proposal came from the target organizations themselves, those responsible felt ownership and were directly engaged in their employees' progress and development in the program.

On Servant Leadership

Your leadership style within the AF Community has often been described by your colleagues and Fellows as an example of a true Servant Leadership style. Do you think this is a fair description of what you hope to bring as your work ethic? What is your motivation?

I always tried to serve first. In our language (Dari) we say that "leadership is the means to serve people," it means it is important to be a servant before you are a leader. Leadership needs commitment and dedication as one needs to think about people first to help them dream, learn and finally do well. I was a Fellow before I became a UNITAR staff, I went through all the steps, knew what the obstacles were and how to learn to deliver my best. My country Afghanistan has been dependent on foreign aid, and often the magnitude of the external money donated to Afghanistan put it under more pressure and unduly influenced the internal policies and strategies of the country. Keeping in mind the high cost of the assistance we received, I have always tried to use the funds and opportunities in ways that produce the greatest impacts for our people and country.

I was also always trying to listen to people, to give them a sense of how important they were as human beings and as Afghans. To encourage them to learn and tackle their assignments, I always tried to encourage Fellows to propose realistic projects applicable in Afghanistan and come back to us with their stories. I tried to create opportunities and space for my compatriots to talk and present their ideas and never tried to impose my own ideas on them. I was inspired by the work of our AF mentors and Resources Persons who dedicated their time, energy, and knowledge to Afghans. I also tried to build trust among the Fellows to build a community of professionals, which could rely on each other's support and cooperation. My thoughts and efforts have always been for my people and country whether I am in or out of Afghanistan, and with this motivation I will continue to tackle my responsibilities and help my people.

AF Vision to the Individual Afghan Experience
Due to your multi-layered involvement in AF and deep understanding of the anatomy of the program from different perspectives, how do you think the AF vision has translated into actual outcomes for the AF Communities, individually and institutionally?

The Afghanistan Fellowship provided excellent opportunities for individuals and organization to develop capacities. A huge number of the graduates, who were promoted to higher positions and organizations, reformed their work process or teams through direct involvement. Director generals, deputy ministers, ministers, Member of Parliament, mustofies (MoF directors in provinces), provincial authorities directors, and so on are the positions the alumni possessed after their graduation from the Fellowship. Addressing problems of HR, procurement policies and even fraud in different ministries such as the Ministry of Finance and the National Procurement Authority have been due to the efforts of the Fellowship alumni. Provision of blended learning and initiation of short-term studies abroad are other examples some institutions have experienced using the Fellowship training (Rokyan Management Consultancy and Raqim Construction and Project Services). Supply chain management and SMEs roadmap within the Ministry of Commerce and Industries and railway management in the Railway Authority of Afghanistan have been tackled by the Fellowship alumni and Afghan Resource Persons and so on and so forth. The alumni emerged as social capital because they developed and fostered trust and civic engagement, they have been able to wear different hats and adapt their positions to society's needs, and this happened because of the Fellowship's sustainable impacts on their knowledge and experiences.

I feel that it is important to list below some of the projects that have been implemented at the national level:

Project Name	Funding Agency	Years	Remarks
Benchmark Survey for Irrigation Projects	LBG/USAID	2005	For Ministry of Power & Energy
Developing Afghanistan Encyclopedia	UNDP	2005	Academy of Science of Afghanistan
New Method of University Teaching	AICC	2006	For Kabul & Poly Technique University
Media Improvement System	Gov.	2006	For National TV of Afg.
Procurement System, Talent Management	Gov.	2007	For DABS & Election Committee
Hygiene Education Program	MoPH	2007	For MoPH
Hospital Management & Best Practices	MoPH	2008	For MoPH

Project Name	Funding Agency	Years	Remarks
Community Based Monitoring System	CIDA/AKF	2009	For MoPH
New Teaching Method in Universities, VC Facilities	Kansas University	2009	For Kabul University
Media & Publication Unit Improvements	MoPH	2009	For MoPH
Tax Payers Education Program	MoF	2010	For MoF
Reform & Capacity Building Program for the MoPW Staffs	MoPW	2011	For MoPW
Research Project for FMIC	FMIC	2013	For MFIC
Establishing an Innovation and Entrepreneurship Center (IEC)	Tabish University	2015	For Tabish
Enhancement of Reporting Mechanism through Implementation of Video Conference System	MAIL	2015	MAIL
Save Women, Save Society	BARAN Org.	2015	MoPH
Kabul Life Savers	MoPH	2015	MoPH
Empower Women, Empower Society	AKF	2015	AKF Bamyan
Development of Standard Operating Procedures to Upgrade NPA's Management Information System	National Procurement Authority	2015	NPA

The alumni learned to expand their mindset and to develop their skills and talents to change their attitudes towards their working environment. The alumni have stayed connected with each other and represented the professional community in all ministries and organizations.

AF Community
One of the most important AF goals was to create a sustainable, connected, and professionally diverse community as a resource for Afghanistan. As the lead representative of the AF, what strategies have you used on the ground to achieve this goal? What is needed to strengthen the Community further? What do you believe should be this Community's continued purpose and performance?

The Fellowship contributed to the professional environment of Afghanistan by presenting the best professionals into society. To help the alumni stay connected and deliver the services using their gained knowledge, I used to organize separate programs for different authorities as well as encourage the alumni, especially people in key positions to use the trained and practical resources to improve the capacity of their offices. The National Procurement Authority was always keen to use the UNITAR resource persons such as Sayed Ghiasuddin Sadat for different trainings they organized within this authority. I also tried to give chances to committed alumni to participate in different Fellowship programs as Coach, Mentor, and Resource Person, and share their knowledge and experience with other Fellows. One of the good strategies used during the Fellowship that I am still using is to connect alumni from inside and outside of Afghanistan to provide professional support for our trainees. Most of the alumni, who remain connected and act as resources for each other, are still providing virtual presentations and consultation to different entities. The first professional Think Tank, by the name of Capacity for Afghanistan (C4A) has been established by one of the UNITAR alumni, Mr. Imtiaz Sharifi, who was able to gather more than 3,000 educated members from different parts of Afghanistan. They asked me to join this Think Tank as an honorary member to contribute to its improvement.

The AF accredited trainings have been combined with the HR policy of different organizations such as the Ministry of Finance. For example, the HR Director of the MoF as a policy gave priority to graduates of the Fellowship within prospective candidates for entry to the Ministry or for promotion. Due to the stringent standards, during budget reviews within the Ministry of Finance, review teams made an effort to approve the budget for those entities, which had allocated funding for training often through the Fellowship or other UNITAR programs.

AF also established a pool of professionals connected to each other. In some of the entities such as the Ministry of Public Works, Ministry of Rural Rehabilitation and Development, Ministry of Public Health, President's Office, and the National Procurement Authorities, most of the key positions have been filled by the UNITAR alumni, who believed in each other's capacity and enjoyed mutual trust, built during the Fellowship, as they worked and delivered results together.

AF also introduced a pool of professionals from abroad, who continued their engagement with the alumni to support them beyond the Fellowship. For example, Dr. Michael Fors provided different presentations and supported the FMIC hospital with different policy development as per Dr. Bashir Sakhizada's request.

Finally, AF enriched the training resources of many organizations with its professional curriculum. Most of the HR directors of different organizations added the UNITAR curriculum within their staff's training pamphlet, to help them better tackle their responsibilities.

Many of the Fellowship resources are contributing to UNITAR's programs for different regions such as South Sudan, Iraq, and Sahil regions. The AF Alumni have been committed not only to help the Afghan people to grow and improve, but also to supporting people from different countries.

The situation in the country has changed recently, but the alumni and the Fellowship community are still connected with each other. Some of the alumni have left Afghanistan, but they support their friends from wherever they are. It is a critical need to keep the professional community alive, and we need strategies to keep them connected as the main aim and purpose have been for them to perform and enable other Afghans to experience a prosperous life. Connectedness and trust in people and institutions have been the strengths of the Fellowship alumni, and this needs to be further enhanced.

Final Reflections

What has been AF's long-term impact on the Afghan professionals over the last 18 years? How has it impacted you personally?

The AF offered a holistic experience, which allowed Afghans to also learn to observe different people with different backgrounds and culture during the study trips. Being raised in war and conflict situations, being economically and socially under pressure and living in a most insecure place, people forgot the higher goals of life. They had been compelled to only focus on basic struggles for food and safe haven. I have observed many Fellows in the early days of an AF Cycle, just sitting in class without much enthusiasm or effort to be closer to each other and work together. However, as the Fellowship continued, the experience and exposure to ordinary people in different localities away from Afghanistan made them sit together, listen to each other's stories, feel for each other, and establish a pool of professionals dedicated to their people and country.

Personally, in the past it was difficult for me to talk or give presentations, work with people with different cultures and ethnicities, and lead a program in a place with multiple challenges emerging daily. The Fellowship taught me to change my attitude, adapt to different environments, and serve people in a way that no one got left behind. I still do not know which of the Fellows was Pashtun, Tajik or Uzbek, I sat with each Fellow, gave them the opportunity to learn and grow and serve other Afghans. This was because the Fellowship taught me how to have the right heart and understand the full extent of my responsibilities.

The Fellowship also gifted me with a family, a very lovely family. All my directors, Ms. Nassrine Azimi, Mr. Alex Mejia, Mr. Brandon Turner, and Ms. Mihoko Kumamoto have been a great support; they made me believe in the importance of my role and understand how I can focus better on my life and work. My direct supervisors, Ms. Sharapiya Kakimova, Ms. Humaira Kamal, Mr. Berin McKenzie, and Mr. Nigel Gan have always been available for support. They eased the way to work and life. They connected my life with my working environment with strong ties.

My colleagues in the HO, all of them have been assets in my life for the past many years. Ms. Junko Shimazu, Mr. Shamsulhadi Shams, and Ms. Kaori Okabe have given me different kinds of support and helped me be a successful UNITAR family member. My mentors, the resources, Dr. Michael Fors, Prof. David Eaton, Prof. Howard and Sue Lamb, Prof. Lorne Jaques, Prof. Duffie VanBalkom, Dr. Henry Kwok, Ms. Patsian Law, Ms. Shona Welsh, Ms. Rama Kanan, and many others have been the means for me to change my attitudes towards my life, relationships, and work. With all these, I would like to confess that some names have been engraved in my heart, and they are unforgettable, thus I proudly mention the names of Dr. Michael Fors, Ms. Humaira Kamal, and Ms. Nassrine Azimi, a brother and sisters, who have been always thinking about me and my family in any situation, so I am always witnessing and feeling their love for my family and me.

What is next for you in your personal journey to serve Afghanistan (AFLP? Projects with the AF Community? With the Afghan government? With UNITAR? GLH?)

> There are ties between my country and me. I was born to work and serve my people. In the most critical situations, even when under pressure and concerned about my family, still I decided to continue serving my people. I will work in this country for its people, especially for those who have been marginalized, women and minorities. My hope is that UNITAR can continue and expand its support, organizing different training and educational programs in Afghanistan. I am trying to contribute to different programs that have been initiated by our alumni and friends in and for Afghanistan such as Green Legacy Hiroshima

and other initiatives to make a difference for the next generation. I am trying to replicate what we learned in the
Fellowship using the support of Alumni in Afghanistan
and sharing our gained knowledge with those, who might
not have opportunities to study elsewhere.

Finally, in spite of steep challenges facing the country, what is your
assessment of the current political and economic prospects for
Afghanistan, places where you see potential, opportunity or encouraging progress? And what are your hopes for the people and the
country's future?

Sometimes I find myself stuck in a puzzle; I cannot
believe what I have been observing. I have seen the rehabilitation and the progress but am witnessing the loss of
a lot of it now. Any political fortuity has been followed by
conditions imposed on Afghanistan, and this history has
been repeating even after one hundred years.

We never learn from our past; Afghanistan has been
dependent on foreign aid and therefore, subject to
the influences of donor countries. With all the positive
changes during the last decade, many Afghans are still
trapped, have failed, or are broken. Political leaders have
never been in favor of the country, but citizens must
trust each other, increase our civic engagement, respect,
and improve co-existence with our different ethnicities,
accept diversity, and eradicate differences and discrimination if we want to be a peaceful and prosperous nation.
Afghanistan is politically and economically dependent
despite decades of effort and rapid human resource development. The flight of intellectuals and the massive brain
drain from Afghanistan make the situation precarious.
However, leaving the country is not the logical solution,
for who can build this country if we all leave?

We must learn from the past; we must change our attitudes towards life and our relationships; and we must accept our responsibility to work for the country and its institutions rather than investing our loyalties in personalities and individuals. We as Afghans have a shared destiny and a common future; we can work and create common values; and we must learn how to share those values with each other. It is possible, if we trust each other and contribute to our country through social engagement, social inclusion, and social cohesion.

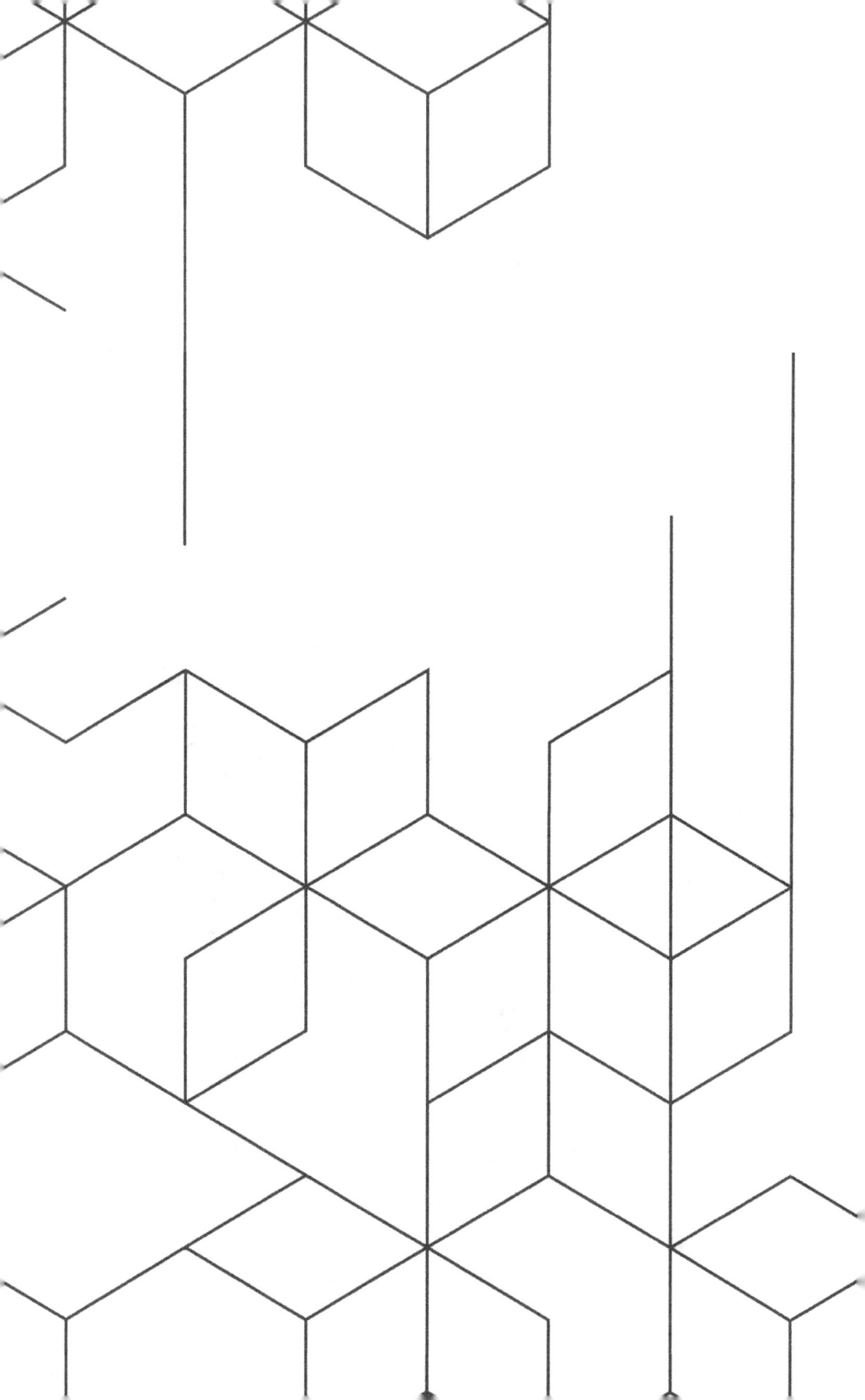

PART III

THE GLOBAL COMMUNITY — IT TOOK A VILLAGE

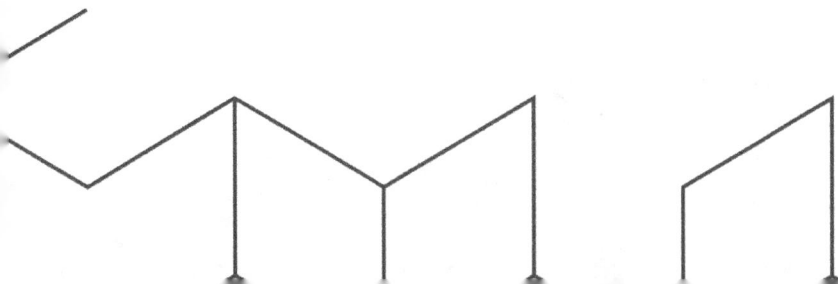

Power of Connections When Done Right –
On Distance and In-person Learning
Roger Galbraith[21]

I was a Mentor in the UNITAR Afghanistan Fellowship program for a dozen years. I've been involved in international programs since the mid-1970s and this was the most rewarding experience I have had. This is a little bit of a surprise since almost all of my involvement was at a distance rather than in-person. But the structure of the UNITAR Fellowship was so well designed that I felt it maximized the benefits.

Doubts
When I participated in my first video conferences, I wasn't sure whether a Mentor in Calgary, Canada could contribute much. I had taught in a variety of African, Middle Eastern, and Asian countries, but I had no direct experience or knowledge of Afghanistan. The level of challenges that they faced was made abundantly clear in one of our first sessions when I asked one participant to stretch beyond just looking at the obstacles her organization faced to look for the successes and bright spots. There was a long pause and some quiet conversation with the Fellows with her. She looked downcast and stated: "You don't understand. This is Afghanistan. There are no positives here." It's not easy to respond to something so heart-felt. And it doubled my feeling that the program was up against

---

[21] Roger Galbraith is a pediatrician and was an Associate Clinical Professor of Pediatrics at the University of Calgary. He has served as Mentor in the Fellowship for Afghanistan from 2006 to 2018

tremendous odds when the overall system was shackled by layers of obstacles that sucked the positivity out of talented people.

Connecting

My co-Mentor, Lorne Jaques, remained optimistic and the key leaders like Humaira Kamal had an infectious enthusiasm. As assignments came in, I provided what comments I could which were always graciously received. Our conversations and emails remained focused on the tasks of the Fellowship, and I didn't feel I learned a great deal about the Fellows' personal lives or struggles. Although I wanted to learn more about these, it seemed my contribution was better maintained on the Fellowship in hopes that what they could take from it that which would benefit them as individuals and Afghanistan as a country.

Over time I could see the Fellows become more positive. The projects they chose carried great meaning. For example, the development of a guideline for monitoring of community health services filled a real need in rural Afghanistan. Their passion and commitment for their work was inspiring.

Our initial video links required that all the mentors were all in the same location in Calgary and to use a special video call platform. We met at the University of Calgary – often very late in the evening while it was early morning in Kabul.

This seemed like a small hassle when I looked at international work I had done in the past. I lived in Nigeria in 1980-82 where I taught math in a secondary school in a small town. This was a time of prosperity and progress for the country, but infrastructure was still sadly lacking. Mail services to Canada took six weeks and letters often took longer than that or were lost. The nearest city I could make an international phone call was six hours away. The service was so unreliable that it could take several hours to connect on a call and the line would often be dropped. Most of us did not even try within the country, but would wait to travel to one of the French West African countries like Togo or Niger where better telephone services were available.

In the early 1990s, I was one of the charter members of medical care and education charity called Project Outreach International Child Health Society. Our initial teams focused on Vietnam which was still desperately short of medical supplies. Planning the trips was always extremely challenging as it was so difficult to be in communication with our Vietnamese colleagues. We would send a fax with our plans and specific questions, but the answers were often very delayed. Over time we realized that a big reason for the delay was that the cost of sending a fax was so expensive for them that they wanted to gather all their information together so they could only send a single fax.

Being able to have video calls meant we could see our fellows and coaches in Afghanistan and have conversations. Emails allowed a back-and-forth on assignments. Technology opened a dialogue that I could never have dreamed of in my work just 20 years previously! It wasn't as easy as Zoom meetings are now, but aside from some limits to the internet in Kabul some days the biggest issue seemed to be people getting to the video location – snowstorms in Calgary, traffic jams in Kabul. I was amazed how easily we could link together.

Face to Face – an Electrifying Experience
In 2010, I joined the Fellowship study session in Hiroshima. Seeing the Fellows, Coaches, Mentors, and Resource Persons in person was even more striking. Animated discussions. Enthusiastic participation in simulation games brought by Michael Fors. Nervous presentations by Fellows of their work. Camaraderie and respect between all. All were hallmarks of a highly engaged and high functioning Fellowship.

By that time my co-Mentors were Cheryl MacLeod and Lubna Baig, who were unfortunately unable to join me. More than anything I wished they could have experienced just how positive the atmosphere was in person rather than just via my descriptions.

The Fellowship matured and I was impressed by how the Coaches became more active in discussions and providing feedback on assignments. The evolution to having Afghan Mentors was also a sign of the progress the Fellowship was making. In both cases, I felt that their advice and guidance was of greater help than what I offered, but I tried to add pearls and vignettes to provide a different perspective. As a Pediatrician I was somewhat nervous when the health sector groups were stopped, but I found that new groups faced similar types of challenges and I enjoyed learning about projects that were not specifically health related.

Another highlight for me was attending the 2011 conference in Dubai. Again, it was great to see the enthusiasm of the Fellows and the leadership. I recall the presentation one articulate woman gave on a project to improve the delivery of secondary school final marks to students. It was a practical step to address bureaucratic issues that led to tremendous frustration for graduating students and was ripe for backdoor shortcuts to those willing to pay bribes. She had to convince others that this sort of change was possible and that it would make a difference. Progress in any country comes from practical solutions of what "can happen" as much as lofty ideals of what "should happen."

The Secret Ingredient – Long-term engagement and Meaningful Relationships

The biggest regret of my experience with the UNITAR Fellowship for Afghanistan was that I was not able to expand it to Yemen. I worked for many years to provide teaching in Clinical Care and on Leadership in Health Care there. As the security situation in Yemen deteriorated our trips there became increasingly difficult. And teaching there for two weeks without ongoing formal follow-up was limited in impact. The Fellowship seemed like an ideal way to take our teaching to the next level. UNITAR was supportive and encouraging, but I could not find a key individual or organization in Yemen that was willing to step forward and say they would act as a sponsor. Looking back at the disasters that have befallen Yemen I wish that we could have established a Fellowship there ... the war, famine and societal breakdown would have had devastating consequence, but maybe there would have been a few leaders in the country better equipped to deal with this devastation.

The structure of the Fellowship provided an opportunity for learning and growth over many months. Bringing back Fellows as Coaches ensured continuity from one year to the next. I sometimes wonder ... How have the projects gone on to have lasting direct impacts in Afghanistan? Certainly, the training fostered leadership and administrative skills that the Fellows will have taken forward and I'm certain that their contributions to their country have been huge.

Final Thoughts
Afghanistan has been impacted by international forces for decades. It can seem that these are immutable and beyond the control of a smaller country like Afghanistan. The Fellowship was a wonderful demonstration that in the midst of the internal and external pressures the actions of individuals' matters. I was inspired by the leaders in Afghanistan, Japan, United States, and Canada who developed the Fellowship and nurtured it over many years. The Coaches, Resource Persons and Mentors in Afghanistan grew in number and abilities each year and in the final years of the Fellowship their pride in the program was wonderful to see. The Fellows had significant responsibilities in their jobs and to their families, but their dedication and commitment ensured the Fellowship flourished.

I am honored to have been able to play a small role in the UNITAR Fellowship for Afghanistan.

A Mosaic of Projects for Transformational Change
Steven Polunsky[22]

It's all David Eaton's fault. Somewhere in 2009 Dr. Eaton, the Bess Harris Jones Centennial Professor of Natural Resource Policy Studies at the Lyndon B. Johnson School of Public Affairs at the University of Texas at Austin (UT/A), and UNITAR Senior Special Fellow, distributed to LBJ School alumni a notice about the Fellowship and an invitation for mentors. In 2009, I was a Texas Senate committee director with state agency oversight responsibility, which made this a terrific opportunity to extend what I was already doing and make a difference beyond Texas. It was also persuasive that Jennifer Fox was involved, as I knew her through her legislative agency work and had the highest regard for her. I offered my resume and soon was accepted into the project.

It was only when I started to research Afghanistan that I learned how ignorant I truly was about the country and its people. I knew nothing about the terrain, the history, the culture, the Independent Directorate of Local Government (IDLG), NRAP, MRRD, the complexity of project delivery under difficult circumstances, including sporadic electricity, internet availability, and unwieldy pre-Zoom conference software. Even the unusual time difference took some adjusting to – two o'clock in the afternoon my time is eleven thirty at night in Afghanistan; we had meetings at 6:30 a.m. my time and

---

[22] Steven Polunsky worked as the Director of the Texas Senate Committee on Business and Commerce, more recently he joined the Texas A&M Transportation Institute (TTI), where he helped develop infrastructure finance options for transportation policy. He served as Mentor from 2009 -2018

midnight. I may have missed a coordination meeting or two due to my misreading a time calculation. I read as much about the country as I could get my hands on, talked to people who had spent time in Afghanistan, and prepared for my first program cycle.

For the first group I was teamed with coach Jamal Nasir Pashton and mentors Anjum Khurshid, Elango "Raj" Rajagopal, David Scott, and Meredith Melecki of the Texas Legislative Budget Board. I think we worked well together. In particular, Meredith's addition was a true stroke of genius, as she had a knack for finding the key areas needing improvement and communicating that in a resourceful, constructive way. Her deep knowledge of governmental functions and processes was a great asset, and I learned a lot from her during this process as well. We focused on sharing the state-of-the-art practices in leadership, management, planning, budgeting, ethics, and project development in the public sphere.

Our first Afghan group was full of leaders and highly accomplished people – Abdul Bari Balakarzai, Mohammad Bashir Dawar, Nasir Ahmad Ebrahimkhel, Sameer Ahmad Raz, and Javed Sidiqi – which gave us a running start in developing the project and approach. The project selected was "Development and Implementation of Electronic Human Resources Management Information System (HRMIS) to the IDLG" which required me to augment what I knew about the subject by calling on my friends implementing information technology in the public sector for tips and things to look for. They helped me with suggestions such as: keep the program simple to accommodate different levels of computer literacy, create unique IDs, have a drop-down menu for frequently used phrases, don't underestimate training needs or costs, and be as specific as possible in defining the system's purpose (payroll is one thing, personnel development is another), list reasons why the program should be implemented including short and long-term benefits such as consistency and fairness. The Fellows were up to the task, citing speeding up HR processing, providing accurate information, and improving decision making through better information. In some ways their work was groundbreaking – today we call this data-driven decision-making, and it is a major goal of public policy.

We reviewed Fellows' survey forms, survey results, study proposals, project development, and related papers throughout the course of the cycle. We participated in multiple audio web conferences, team project working sessions, and all-day web seminars as well as progress conversations with Coaches, Afghan Resource Persons (ARPs), and Mentors. The consistently high quality and innovative thinking evidenced in these materials made these tasks enjoyable, and I looked forward to each revision or new generation.

In the 2010 cycle, Meredith and I teamed with Coach Nasser Nazari, ARP Zianalubadin Hamid, and Fellows Farkhanda Ghoossy, Sharifullah Hashim, Najeeb Ahmadzai, Elham Arash, Mohammad Nasir Figar, and Besmillah Maiwand Akbari to take on an issue at the heart of public agency and confidence, the tax system. In our conference calls, we had wonderful discussions about how to make tax collection more accurate, uniform, and fair, and make it easier for the public to fill out tax forms. I was able to apply what I had learned in Texas directly to this issue, as the public's concerns about taxation are universal. In particular, the public's perception of how taxes are collected and used is extremely important. The Fellows developed a thoroughly researched and well-thought-out approach that we were all proud of.

We introduced the Fellows to the six-step problem solving, conducting an environmental analysis, organizational needs assessments, project planning, results based management, and methods of dealing with difficult team members (which was not an issue during our time in the UNITAR program, of course). This cycle also demonstrated an early and meaningful commitment to include women in the program.

For 2011, Maiwand Akbari was promoted to become Coach, a true treasure for his patience and sense of humor. Our ARP was

Dr. Gul Afghan Saleh, whose professional approach kept us on track along with the Fellows Mohammad Yunus Rahyab, Amir Javed, Mariam Rahmati, Matiullah Omaid Fazli, and Abdul Nasery. We discovered that the work we were currently conducting in Texas to update and implement uniform and useful performance measures was directly transferable to government and nonprofit operations in Afghanistan, so we developed and delivered mini courses on inputs, outputs, and outcomes using the latest materials that were already found on our desks.

In 2012, we were joined by Mohammad Sediq Sahibzai, a highly qualified Coach; our excellent ARP Nasir Ebrahimkhil, and Fellows Feriba Quraishi, Ahmad Zia Saidkhily, Hayatullah Ahmadzai, Nasir Ahmad Ahmadi, Aminullah Amini, Mohammad Reza Fayq, and Fardin Sediqi. As the group sizes increased, Fellows showed themselves highly capable of adjusting to the different group dynamics, developing, and competing for projects, then successfully combining talents to focus on the selected project.

Each subsequent cycle we saw creative and productive approaches to important project proposals. These included travel fraud reduction, internal operational improvements for provincial officers, and addressing mortality and morbidity rates. We were privileged to work with outstanding leaders like Ahmad Shah Naqshbandi, Mohammad Sohail Kaakar, Abdullah Fahim, Abdul Malik Farah, Friba Quraishi, and many others.

Over time, I think I learned as much from the Fellows as they may have from me. I certainly found plenty of inspiration in the dedication, ingenuity, and perseverance seen over the course of the program. As we worked together, I from relative comfort in Austin and they are enduring constant threats, danger, and uncertainty, the minor discomfort for me of late night or early morning conference calls fell away as together we looked at the world's hardest problems and explored how we each, in our own way and as a team, could take them on.

This synergy, the sum of our work being greater than its parts, and this feeling of having expanded what our minds are capable of is what leads me to believe that the UNITAR Afghanistan Fellowship Program was successful in its goal of transformational change – not just incremental change but leaps in advancement. With the benefit of time, I have seen Fellows become teachers and leaders, change-makers who themselves become mentors with impacts felt around the globe. AF alumni are now found in non-profit organizations, universities, and businesses the world over, as well as in almost all of the ministries of the Afghan government, the Afghan Parliament, and the highest offices. We are truly now in a time and place of a new level of innovation, collaboration, and inspiration.

My one regret, and it is a great one, is that I was unable to travel to the work sessions. We built so many friendships from a distance that I know would have been greatly enhanced, and so many new relationships created to last a lifetime. I am very glad that the Fellows were able to have multiple in-person group workshops and form life-long bonds that are so important as we progress in our careers and lives. The true test of any society is how its people relate to each other, and it's easier to relate to a friend than a stranger. It's putting into practice the words of Ahmad Shah Naqshbandi, whom I am proud to call my friend, who says, "You cannot be fully human, fully civilized, unless you recognize humanity in everyone."

I am most grateful to UNITAR and the government and people of Hiroshima Prefecture and the City of Hiroshima, with special appreciation to Sharapiya Kakimova, Berin McKenzie, Nigel Gan, Annelise Giseburt, Johanna Diwa, Sokout Sabahuddin, and of course Humaira Kamal for their friendship, guidance, and hard work to bring this program to success. All of the Coaches, Resource Persons, and Fellows, far too many to list here, are integral to the success of each cycle and always will be a part of my memories. Every day I think about the people of Afghanistan and how well-served their future is by these amazing public servants and leaders. I wish nothing but future success to all.

From Fellow to Donor

Musa Kamawi [23]

My engagement with UNITAR started from 2008 when I was Assistant Human Resource Manager at the Afghanistan Investment Support Agency (AISA), and came to know the excellence and substantial impact of this important program. I was keen and enthusiastic to join the Fellowship myself though I had to wait for six months for the upcoming cycle.

Eventually, in the 2008 cycle, the application was open, and the nominations started. I asked my immediate boss to introduce me to the program to enter the first round of application. There were only two slots for AISA in the Fellowship that year, and around 10-14 candidates were competing for the two slots. It was a lengthy examination and selection process. Fortunately, I along with one of our regional directors were selected for the 2008 cycle as Fellows.

The Fellowship was a unique program of its kind as I learned a lot and gained so much experience that has brought my life substantial change, both personally and professionally. Especially it equipped me with team building skills in the workplace, coordination, effective communication skills, change management within departments and organizations, and many other skills that really changed my professional life. It helped me become a successful manager in a public sector organization.

---

[23] UNITAR AF 2007 – 2018 – Fellow, Coach, ARP, Mentor, Faculty Member, Afghanistan MOF Donor Representative

After completing AF, I started working as HR Manager at AISA and subsequently was promoted as Director of Human Resources at the Ministry of Finance in 2009. Hence, the importance and impact of AF in changing my career is clearly visible.

Luckily, I was also selected as a Coach in 2009 to serve the Fellowship in a different role. In 2010, I became an Afghan Resource Person, and in 2011 I was selected as the first honorary Faculty Member for AF which I have the privilege of holding till now.

This brief message does not encompass all my thoughts, however. I would say without a doubt that as a Fellow and a professional in this program, I found AF unique and effective with superb and more tangible results among all the other training programs conducted for Afghanistan. This statement would be highly supported by the majority of public institutions and private organizations benefiting from it either directly or indirectly.

Lessons learned as a Fellow
UNITAR was an outstanding platform in building workforce capacity, and it has always been a privilege being part of the UNITAR family. It substantially helped Fellows build on their existing capacities of their professional and personal skills, while offering high-level support and inviting active engagement from the Fellows. AF also focused on developing expertise in social capital development, the impact of teamwork and development, organizational behaviors, professional discipline, organizational need assessment, and project planning and implementation in both public and private sectors.

At the same time, apart from the professional objectives, Fellows were acquainted with the culture in Japan and specifically, with the history of Hiroshima. From individual and personal points of view, in the context of our country, it was important to learn how to develop consensus in post-war or conflict countries.

Reflections as a Coach, Resource Person, Honorary Faculty Member, and then Partner

As an AF Coach, I helped the Fellows better analyze and digest the knowledge disseminated during the Fellowship, explained the program's orientation and role expectations, and helped to determine the teams' action plans. More critically, I provided quick and positive feedback to encourage more participation from each Fellow, while acting as a bridge between Fellows and Mentors.

The following lists the things that I believe I could have done better as a Coach:

1. Lacked knowledge and utilization of Fellowship norms and experiences
2. Being overly dominant and subjective
3. Overly influenced the individual and team projects
4. Provided overly negative and subjective feedback
5. Insufficiently prepared teams for the assignments
6. Insufficiently motivated or encouraged team members

After the successful completion of two important roles in the program, as Coach in 2009 and Afghan Resource Person in 2010, I was much honored to become the first UNITAR honorary Faculty Member. This tenure was filled with many significant experiences, one of which was to deliver presentations for AF in Kabul and Hiroshima. I also had the privilege to present the first case studies on successful and failed projects in Afghanistan within public and private sectors. It helped the Fellows to better understand Dr. Michael Fors' session on project planning and implementation, providing a practical examination of why public sector projects succeeded or failed.

In 2009, I was honored to become Mentor for AF to ensure on-time and better responsiveness of each team and the Fellowship as a whole, maintain smooth communication, strengthen coordination among teams, and facilitate equal treatment such that all group members were provided with equal opportunity during the program. I supported the determination of roles, identification of assignments, and expectation setting. I was responsible for engaging closely with the Fellows and preparing them for difficult situations such as professional or interpersonal challenges arising during the programs. At this stage and especially at the end of the Fellowship, Mentors needed to be more available and involved to help Fellows complete their assignments and projects more efficiently.

The Ministry of Finance of the Islamic Republic of Afghanistan maintained and extended its strong engagement as a core partner with UNITAR not only for AF but also initiated other professional programs and Executive Master Programs, Customized Technical Programs in 2011, 2012, 2013, 2014 and 2015 respectively. The partnership and cooperation, that was initiated with the Fellowship program, gradually was promoted in a joint Executive Master Program for the Ministry's core senior staff and other key ministries and organizations.

The first technical training program for 25 senior provincial staff of the Ministry of Finance was conducted in Hiroshima focusing on finance, budget, and revenue learning from the best practices in Japanese organizations in these areas. The one-week training was conducted in November 2012 followed by other two public finance training programs for our staff in Hiroshima in 2015 and 2017.

Executive Master Program in Public Policy
In 2013, on the sidelines of the World Bank/IMF spring meeting in Tokyo, the former Minister of Finance Dr. Omar Zakhilwal met with the former Head of the UNITAR Hiroshima Office and discussed extending the cooperation to promote the existing Fellowship

to an Executive Master Program for the Ministry of Finance staff. Both sides agreed to start the Executive Master Program with the Graduate Institute of Geneva. The first batch of 20 senior officials at Director General and Director level were enrolled in the 7-month Executive Master Program partnering with UNITAR in 2014. With the first cycle, the second and third cycle in 2015 and 2016 totaled 55 participants hailed from the Ministry of Finance and other organizations.

Tangible Impact of AF and Customized Training Programs
The Fellowship had a substantial impact on the professional careers of those who participated from the Ministry of Finance and other government entities and were later promoted to higher positions in government and international organizations. It is worth mentioning some of these Fellows from the Ministry of Finance:

1. Mujeeb ur Rehaman Shirzad: Fellow in 2008 with UNITAR Executive Master in 2014 became the DG Revenue and Tax Authority in the Ministry of Finance and was later promoted in 2017 as Deputy Vice CEO of Afghan Audit Department.

2. Said Mubin Shah: Fellow in 2008 became Deputy Minister of Customs and Revenue in 2013.

3. Dr. Najeeb Wardak: UNITAR Executive Master in 2015 was DG Customs and then promoted as Deputy Minister for Customs and Revenue in 2017.

4. Syed Amin Habib: DG Policy and UNITAR Executive Master Graduate in 2014 promoted as Acting DM Policy in the Ministry of Finance in 2016.

5. Khatera Sadat: UNITAR Executive Master graduate in 2014 was sector Manager in Budget Directorate, later promoted as Deputy Minister of Administration at the Ministry of Urban Development and Housing in 2018.

6. Ahmad Naweed: UNITAR Executive Master graduate in 2016 working as mid-level official in Nangarhar Mustofiate and became Head of Revenue in Nanagarha Mustofiate, later promoted to Director of Nangarhar Customs and currently serving as Head of Mustofiate Nanagarhar.

7. Ahmad Masoud Tokhi: UNITAR Executive Master graduate working as Director General Civil Service, IARCSC Afghanistan.

8. Musa Kamawi: UNITAR Fellow in 2008 as HR Manager in AISA and then promoted as Director of HR at the Ministry of Finance in 2009, later in 2017 promoted to DG Insurance Affair.

These are some of the few examples of Fellows, who benefited from either the UNITAR Fellowship programs or other Customized programs.

Critical Analysis of AF
When I was a Fellow in 2008, AF's quality and standards were up to the mark and acceptable to all Fellows and partners. However, in the subsequent years, it was downgraded due to numerous challenges highlighted below.

1. Sufficient Budget from Donors. In 2008 and 2009, the donor agencies trusted and assisted the whole program and Fellows bearing good capabilities were selected by both counterpart organizations and UNITAR.

2. High Quantity and Low Quality. When donors started to downsize the funding for AF considering it not a priority for Afghanistan, the UNITAR management was obliged to find alternative sources to finance AF and reconsider self-financing in 2010. However, line Ministries also demanded more participation in AF, and some ministries had allocated budgets for the program. The UNITAR management

positively responded to the ministries' request to increase the size of the program.

3. Coordination Problem with IARCSC[24]. At first AF had smooth coordination with the Civil Service Training Institute. This coordination and harmony lasted for two years with IARCSC and after this period, the relationship between UNITAR and the Civil Service Training Institute was problematic as IARCSC did not own the process within AF when the self-financing scheme by the Ministries was introduced to the program. Thus, during the whole process from the planning, launching and conducting the program to graduation, the coordination between IARCSC and UNITAR was not strong enough while other stakeholders wanted to see a smooth implementation of projects. The Civil Service Training Institute did not want to share the authority over incoming scholarships, and the process of nomination of civil servants to AF with line ministries. They argued that UNITAR should financially sponsor the Fellowship 100% and channel funds and management through IARCSC Institute, but UNITAR did not have the funding to do so, and the AF alumni community was too invested in the opportunity that AF presented, to let the lack of resources or the administrative red tape prevent them from sponsoring their colleagues and team members to the program.

Recommendations

My recommendations for making program administration smoother with local government partners in the future are below:

1. AF successfully concluded after 15 cycles, so this is the right time to revisit and re-think about the program.

---

[24] Independent Administrative Reform and Civil Service Commission (IARCSC), Afghanistan

2. Secure future funding. Future programs should have both external and internal sufficient funding sources to ensure quality control.

3. Social capital and alumni community. The UNITAR alumni community should utilize the social capacities built and accumulated.

4. Fellowships should be promoted to Advanced Fellowship or the Executive Program. There is a high demand for programs like the Fellowship to offer advance or executive training certification or even executive master's degrees in relevant fields.

5. The UNITAR curriculum should continue to be adapted to changing needs. The current curriculum and syllabus need to be revised and matched with the needs and core demands of the line ministries as needs are different from time to time.

A Personal Journey

Hangama Hamid[25]

(Original in Dari, a rough translation in English follows)

بنام خداوند بزرگ و توانا

به نظر کمی عجیب هم میاید، که تقریبا بعد از یک ده یا اندکی بیشتر برنامه آموزشی "یونیتار" یا بهتر بگویم، سفر آموزشی "یونیتار(1) " را مرور میکنم.

سفری که برای من با اشتراک در این برنامه آموزشی منحیث یک اشتراک کننده در سال ۲۰۰۹ آغاز گردید و در ظاهر با تقبل مسئولیت مربی یک گروپ کوچک چهار عضوی در سال ۲۰۱۰ ادامه یافت و فکر میکنم، که این سفر به طریق دیگر هنوز هم ادامه خواهد داشت. چون با اشتراک در این برنامه ایجاد یک شبکه را با افراد مسلکلی و مستعد برایم فراهم ساخت و دستآورد های فراوان را برایم به ارمغان آورد. شاید این برنامه نه فقط برای من، بلکه برای اکثریت اشتراک کننده گان رهنمود خوب برای راه یافتن به قلعه های دانش، کسب مهارت ها و جاگزین شدن به مقامات بلندتر در ادارات دولتی، خصوصی و اعم از کاریابی در نهاد های معتبر و غیر انتفاعی بین اللملی بود. اکثر دوستان که از این طریق با آنها آشنا شدم، به وسیله تلاش های خسته گی ناپذیرشان و با استفاده از مزایای همچنین برنامه های آموزنده چون برنامه یونیتار اکثرا امروز در مقام های عالی مرتبه در داخل و خارج کشور مصروف اجرا وظیفه استند و اکثرا انسان های موفق و با تعهد در امورکاری خویش اند.

---

[25] AF Fellow 2009, Coach 2010. Currently serving with Culturally and Linguistically Diverse (CALD) in Australia

در حقیقت برنامه "یونیتار" برای اشتراک کننده گان خویش زمینه آنرا فراهم ساخت، تا به اندوخته های خویش دقیق تر بنگرند و مهارت های خویش را شناسایی کرده و از آنها به شیوه های بهتر بهره مند گردند. به طور مثال رهبری و مدیریت یکی از آموزنده ترین بخش این برنامه بود، که به ما اشتراک کننده گان آموخت، تا چگونه در یک جامعه پر چالش افغانستان اعم از مسایل ناامنی های سیاسی و منطقه وی و نا به سامانات اجتماعی و فرهنگی مخصوصا با موانع فراوان اجتماعی برای زنان توانایی های خود را بهتر شناخت و آنها را به طور ارزنده مورد استفاده قرار داد. برنامه رهبری و مدیریت این برنامه آموزشی مخصوصا نیاز مبرم برای جامعه افغانی ما در آن زمان بود، چون ما آموختیم، که با حوصله مندی و استقامت بیشتر به تلاش های خود ادامه دهیم و با چالش های و سد های فرا راه پیشرفت و ترقی خود بهتر کنار آیم و خدمات با کیفیت را به جامعه خویش عرضه کنیم.

از جمله دستآورد های بزرگ که به تعقیب اشتراک در این برنامه برای من فراهم شد، اشتراک در برنامه ماستری در بخش صحت عامه در استرالیا در سال ۲۰۱۱ بود. با اتمام این درجه تحصیلی زمینه کار و فعالیت در نهاد های مختلف در کشور استرالیا مانند "ایمز استرالیا" (2) ، " کو هیلت" (3) و "برادر هود" (4) برای من فراهم شد. امروز از اینکه دانش و تجارب بدست آورده به وسیله این پروگرام را برای عرضه خدمات به جوامع با فرهنگ و زبان های مختلف مقیم استرالیا به اشتراک میگذارم، احساس افتخار میکنم. تقریبا شاید در هیچ مصاحبه کاری نبوده، که تجارب بدست آمده از طریق این برنامه را به اشتراک نگذاشته باشم و از آموخته های آن مستفید نشده باشم.

به هر حال سفر "یونیتار" نه تنها فرصت خوب برای بدست آوردن معلومات، تجارب ، آگاهی های جدید و مطابق به روز بود، بلکه همچنان زمینه بازدید، مرور تجارب و چالش های کشور های دیگر مانند جاپان و سنگاپور را در عرصه ها و سکتور های مختلف مانند صحت عامه ، تعلیم و تربیه، اقتصاد، انجنیری و سایر بخش ها در قبال داشت.

از جمله خاطرات فراموش ناشدنی این سفر که برای همیشه در خاطرم باقی خواهد ماند، بازدید از یارک صلح هیورشیما (5) و بنای تاریخی و تخریب شده در اثر پرتاب بم اتومی در سال 1947 (6) بود، که همیشه مرا به یاد مشکلات سد راه مردم افغانستان و آن مملکت که سالیان متمادی دستخوش تحولات، نا هنجار ها و نا به سامانی های سیاسی داخلی و خارجی گردیده است، می اندازد. امیدوارم ما مردم افغانستان با حسن نیت و اتحاد ملی مانند مردم جاپان روزی را تجربه کنیم، که از مخروبه ها به عنوان میراث های تاریخی گذشته یاد آور شویم و شاهد شگوفای مملکت خویش باشیم و بیت زیبای از حافظ شیرازی مصداق تلاش های خسته گی ناپذیر مردم ما باشد، آنجا که بیان میکند:

فلک را سقف بشکافیم و طرح نو در اندازیم

بیا تا گل بر افشانیم و می در ساغر اندازیم

سخنم را با ابراز تشکر و امتنان از دست اندرکاران این برنامه آموزشی،
مخصوصا خانم حمیرا کمال، آقای صباودین سکوت و خانم نجلا صبری و اعم از
تمامی مربی های مجرب که با حوصله مندی کامل اشتراک کننده گان را راهنمایی
کردند و اندوخته های خود را با ما شریک کردند، به پایان میرسانم.

با سپاس فراوان

هنگامه حامد

اگست ۲۰۲۰

لست واژه ها:

UNITAR .1

AMES Australia .2

Cohealth .3

Brotherhood of St Laurence .4

Peace Park in Hiroshima .5

The Hiroshima Peace Memorial .6

English translation

In the name of God, the Great and the Mighty

It seems a little strange, to review the UNITAR Hiroshima Afghan Fellowship or rather the UNITAR journey, so many years after the program.

The journey started for me as a Fellow in 2009 and continued when I got responsibility as a Coach for a four-Fellow group in 2010, and

I think it will continue in other ways. Participating in the program offered me the gift of working with a marvelous network of professionals and talented people.

The Fellowship was a good guide not only for me, but probably also for the majority of the participants, who could attain summits of knowledge by gaining new skills, thus helping them to acquire higher positions in governmental and international organizations, as well as national and international non-profit institutions. Most of the professionals I have met through the Fellowship are now working as high-ranking officials both inside and outside the country; it might be because of their tireless efforts and the benefits from informative programs such as AF in their real lives and workplaces.

In fact, AF provided its Fellows with a platform to identify their skills more accurately and utilize these same skills in a better way. For instance, leadership and management sessions were among the most informative parts of AF, which taught us how to better recognize our own abilities and use them in the challenging Afghan society, including political and regional insecurity, social and cultural issues, and especially, the many social barriers for Afghan women.

The leadership and management sessions were particularly necessary for the Afghan community at the time because we learned to continue our efforts with more patience and endurance, to better address the challenges, and deal with them in order to provide quality services to the society.

Among the great opportunities that the Fellowship opened to me following the training program was participating in a master's degree program in Public Health at La Trobe University, Australia in 2011. I successfully completed the degree, fieldwork, and activities, which gave me access to a number of institutions in Australia such as AMES Australia - Education, Employment and Settlement Services, Cohealth, and Brother of St Laurence. Today I am proud to share my knowledge and experiences through AF to provide services to the Culturally and Linguistically Diverse (CALD) in Australia.

The UNITAR journey was not only a good opportunity to obtain information, experiences, and new and up-to-date awareness. We visited the sites and reviewed the experiences and challenges of some other countries such as Japan and Singapore in various sectors such as public health, education, economy, engineering, and other sectors, which were the most useful sessions.

The experiences and the memories so far from AF were the strong management of the Fellowship, which began from a needs assessment of the workplaces in Afghanistan, reviewing the policies and strategies of the Afghan sectors, and designing small projects to solve the challenges to bring positive change. Creating a network with professionals through the UNITAR alumni also promoted the continued learning and further development of these communications.

Among the unforgettable memories of this journey, which will remain with me forever, was the visit to the Hiroshima Peace Memorial Park and the A-Bomb Dome (Genbaku Dome). Hiroshima was destroyed by an atomic bomb in 1945, which always reminds me of Afghanistan's conflicts and its diverse impacts, as well as all the monumental challenges faced by the Afghan people and the country after decades of war and chaos, external and internal conflicts, underdevelopment, and injustice. I hope that we, the people of Afghanistan, will like the people of Japan, one day experience goodwill and national unity,, remember the distortions and legacies of past conflicts, and witness the birth of a peaceful and developed

Afghanistan. It can be achieved by the tireless efforts and commitment of our people to bring about positive change. It reminds me of the famous poem of Hafiz, as he says:

فلک را سقف بشکافیم و طرح نو در اندازیم

بیا تا گل برافشانیم و می در ساغر اندازیم

Come, let us scatter flowers and cast wine into goblets

Let us rip the ceiling of the heavens and throw in a new draft

Hafiz Shirazi

Once again, I appreciate the efforts of the Fellowship coordinators especially Ms. Humaira Kamal, Mr. Sabahuddin Sokout, and Ms. Najla Sabri, and all our experienced trainers and facilitators, who had been patiently guiding the Fellows and Coaches and sharing their valuable experiences with us.

UNITAR's Afghan Legacy: A Tribute
Dr. Vinod B Mathur[26]

I was delighted to recently receive communications from Nassrine Azimi and Humaira Kamal, the two architects of the UNITAR Hiroshima Fellowship for Afghanistan (AF) to contribute towards an initiative documenting the special lessons, bonds, and connectedness achieved through this exceptional 15-year program, which began in 2003 and trained almost 500 mid- to senior level Afghan professionals. My association with UNITAR and AF covers four different categories viz. Alumni, Mentor, Faculty Member, and Partner. While the first three categories have their own highlights, the one as a Partner of AF has a special significance, which I would like to share.

I had just returned to Dehradun from Hiroshima after providing inputs in the UNITAR training series on Management and Conservation on World Heritage Sites, when I received a call from Nassrine saying that AF was likely to run into difficulties as the UN had issued an advisory preventing overseas experts to travel to Afghanistan on account of "tensions," and thus AF could not be organized there. She asked, "Can AF be organized in Dehradun?" So impressed was I with Nassrine's commitment to plan and conduct super quality training programs at UNITAR Hiroshima, that without waiting for a second, I replied, "Yes, we can do that in Dehradun." Thus began the partnership of the Wildlife Institute

---

[26] Former Director, Wildlife Institute of India, Dehradun

of India (WII) (www.wii.gov.in) with AF. The course design and delivery were meticulously planned and stalwarts like David Eaton came to teach interactive sessions with young men and women professionals from Afghanistan.

Since WII had no on-campus guesthouse accommodation to house over 25 Afghan participants, we lodged them in a hotel in downtown Dehradun. The first week of the AF ran as scheduled, and the participants enjoyed the "learning" experience as well as the choicest of Indian cuisine. It was during the second week that we noticed a "fall" in attendance in the classes. In some sessions, " men" groups were missing, and, in some sessions, " women" groups were missing. As this absence in the classroom sessions became both frequent and noticeable, it became intriguing as both the quality of learning and catering had remained the same, and the hotel staff confirmed that the participants were not spending time in their rooms after bunking the classes.

I then decided to deploy a group of my staff to investigate the matter and "follow" these groups when they went out of the hotel. They came back with the information that the "men" groups were visiting the schools and colleges in Dehradun gathering information about educational courses and admissions of their wards, and the "women" groups were going to clinics and hospitals for consultations on their health-related matters. We could easily understand the reasons for their absence and also appreciate the additional opportunities that organizing AF in Dehradun was providing to these participants. We then talked to the participants and offered to facilitate these interactions outside the classroom sessions, to which they all readily agreed. I feel that this is an important lesson to be learnt while planning and conducting such programs for adults. Flexibility and facilitation have to be an integral part of all adult learning programs, irrespective of their location, as each site would have multiple things to offer beside the course contents.

I must also write about another interesting experience that relates to organizational style. All UNITAR courses were very meticulously planned and delivered with a great eye for detail and a zest for perfect execution. I had noticed in person all the above when I was attending UNITAR workshops to provide inputs in the heritage training programs. Every morning Nassrine and her team would go into a huddle and go through all the details and activities of the day, in addition to the hard copies that had all been distributed and gone over by the team members ahead of this meeting.

So once it was decided that the AFP would be organized in Dehradun, Nassrine sent Sharapiya Kakimova, a trusted and competent young UNITAR professional staff, in advance to assist me with the course planning. Sharapiya occupied a space in my office and observed the discussions and verbal instructions being passed on to different WII staff members and course material being delivered. After five days I asked Sharapiya about her impressions and if she thought anything was missing. She said, "Dr. Mathur, you are a magician – you utter something in Hindi or English to your staff, and the course material gets delivered in your office." Obviously, management styles are different at different places, but I feel that there is no match for the UNITAR and Japanese style, which is undoubtedly very reliable and effective.

As I look back, I realize what a powerful legacy the AFP has left in the minds of not only the almost 500 Afghan professionals who were fortunate to participate, but also their families and friends with whom the outcomes would have been shared in multiple ways. Afghanistan has tremendously benefitted from the UNITAR Fellowship, but the task of rebuilding still remains unfinished. How I wish that the world would continue with the capacity-building initiatives for young professionals in Afghanistan, in order to support and mainstream the Afghan society.

Transformational experience
Abdul Nasser Nazari[27]

When I chose to further pursue a career in the developmental sector, a colleague of mine in the field suggested I apply to a relevant fellowship program and/or possibly pursue a master's degree in the developmental studies. I had heard about the UNITAR executive training program, which was at that time closely coordinated with the Civil Service Commission of Afghanistan, where I was working as a World Bank contracted Project Manager. At that point I was not even aware of what the UNITAR acronym stood for or even what was the purpose of the UNITAR Hiroshima Fellowship for Afghanistan.

The road to selection for the Fellowship was not an easy one. I was awarded the Fellowship opportunity for the 2008-2009 cycle following an intensive selection procedure comprised of applications, placement tests, and interviews. I was informed that out of the 150 applicants or so, I had been selected as one of 25 participants for that year. Honestly, I was very excited and glad to get my first ever Fellowship opportunity. Along with the other Fellows, I spent around one year with the program, which I believe to be one of the most prestigious Fellowships for Afghanistan. My later experiences and promotion as Coach and subsequently Afghanistan Resource Person (ARP) were also excellent and productive learning experiences.

---

[27] Personal Recollections, Abdul Nasser Nazari, former Fellow, Coach and Afghan Resource Person (2008-2012)

The AF, which was implemented by the UNITAR Hiroshima Office and its Kabul-based dedicated local coordinator, Mr. Sokout, was an excellent experience for me, both for its academic as well as professional development aspects. I was able to improve my skills in leadership, management, and collaboration across multiple disciplines, as well as negotiation and teamwork. Moreover, I had the opportunity to experience new people and places, and to exchange thoughts, ideas, and perspectives with representatives of different cultures on multiple subject matters. I realized that the values of understanding, collaboration, and perspective-sharing, that the Fellowship fostered, were some of the most important tools to solve our local problems and to build a more peaceful and prosperous world.

After completing the Fellowship and during my later involvements with it, I came to appreciate how valuable such an experience was to my professional and personal development, and also how joyful it was, to share my experience and knowledge with my co-workers and colleagues. Some of my professional and personal development, to which the UNITAR program contributed, are as follows:

1. Leadership. Since my involvement in the Fellowship, I frequently utilized the skills I learned from the workshops, seminars, webinars, and group discussions in various leadership positions. I also contributed to many projects working with government institutions and local communities.

2. Management. The lessons I learned during AF have helped me improve my management skills and inspired me to further explore various topics in more detail. For instance, it motivated me to learn the Project Management Professional (PMP) concept at the Project Management Institute (PMI) and to pursue higher education studies in management of development overseas. I was granted an opportunity to use my knowledge in the field of project management gained

during my longworking tenure but also to move away from the classic project and leadership practices and toward more up-to-date and effective methodologies.

3. Volunteer work. Since the program was based on volunteer work principles, it not only inspired me to take part in volunteer activities but also motivated me to foster the culture of volunteerism among peers, co-workers, and fellows. I have participated in a number of social and academic activities and was able to share my experience with those in need.

4. Sharing experience and the transfer of knowledge. The Fellowship environment and working closely with expats in developmental projects encouraged me to share my experience and knowledge with my co-workers, peers, and subordinates, and to conduct training programs for project staff on paid or volunteer basis. It means that a large number of other individuals have benefited from my knowledge and experience ensuring sustainability of the transfer of knowledge.

5. Application of international best practices and lessons learned. One of the contributions of the Fellowship to my career was to advance my ability to collaborate across multiple disciplines. The multidisciplinary approach and best practices taught during the Fellowship program and other trainings I have obtained, have been accepted as the best viable approaches in today's situation of rapid changes and uncertainty, and in the volatile environment of Afghanistan. I also learned effective ways to communicate and to develop my presentation and negotiation skills.

As far as I know AF was a life-changing experience for every Fellow, especially for those, who had not had the opportunity to visit or engage with communities outside Afghanistan. The Fellowship allowed them to learn, understand, and share experiences, not just about the cultures, lifestyles, religions, and perceptions of each other, but it also helped them to understand how other countries have made economic, scientific, and social progress.

Our visits to the Peace Memorial Museum, Atomic Bomb Dome, Japan International Cooperation Agency (JICA) Headquarters, and academic institutions in Japan, and exposure to the botanical gardens in India through study trips were very productive for the program participants. Particularly, knowing the story behind the atomic bombing of Hiroshima and listening to the atomic bomb survivors were among the most unforgettable memories. The people of Japan really worked hard to overcome the effects of war and have successfully rebuilt their country. A dream of peace that I have always nurtured could also come true for my war-torn country Afghanistan.

From the various trips I have participated in during my involvement with the Fellowship, I came to the realization that the world is full of people who want to live with each other and extend love, compassion, and assistance. The study trips to India, UAE, and Japan made me realize that whether someone is from Afghanistan or another country, most of us want to respect, love, and assist each other.

AF was an empowering experience that my participating Fellows and I will never forget. The program was unmatched in terms of professional development in a relatively short and intensive period of time and opened incredible doors for Fellows to learn from some very impactful and experienced lecturers and mentors. The relationships cultivated through video conferences, webinars, e-mail correspondence, and traveling to attend workshops and seminars have truly enriched my work life. I was beyond grateful for the opportunity to see Japan through a new lens of economic and social development, which demonstrated how it improved its people's living standards.

All in all, I gained a lot from the Fellowship, was empowered to contribute as a Fellow and later as a Coach and ARP. I formed relationships that continue to nurture my growth in various ways. I have made a number of professional friends in various levels of the program and being in touch with them is joyful for me. I believe the UNITAR Fellowship was the type of opportunity that I would wish most of the working Afghan professionals at various levels of responsibility could have. We have been among the lucky ones to have become part of the program, but I sincerely look forward to seeing similar models of training being offered for other interested young Afghan professionals.

The Fellowship has changed the path of my life in so many positive ways – I have become more confident, and I feel more equipped to push harder to meet my obligations. It forced me and gave me the opportunity to learn more, and to intellectually wrestle with the developmental challenges and issues that are and will be affecting Afghan society in its recovery from the prolonged conflict in the country.

As rightly said by Gordon B. Hinckley, "Without hard work, nothing grows but weeds;" without comprehensive planning, execution, and quality control, the Fellowship would have not been such a tangible success.

The knowledge, intellectual, and professional strengths of those who took part in the Fellowship will be transferred to new generations, thus ensuring the sustainability of the Fellowship and ongoing benefits after its successful completion.

The Fellowship for Afghanistan – A Case for Systems Thinking[28]

Ernest Lee[29]

My mother used to be a schoolteacher and taught the Chinese Language in primary school. So you can probably imagine that apart from the strict upbringing during my childhood days, she taught my late sister and I that we should grow up to be people who would be "useful" to the society.

Back in 2008, I had spent about 12 years with the Inland Revenue Authority of Singapore (IRAS). IRAS is a public service organization handling Singapore's tax administration and advising the Ministry of Finance on tax-related matters. My career experience then included business development, corporate services, human resources, training, knowledge management, running an academy, organization development, and organization excellence. I was grateful for the career opportunities and experience gained in IRAS. Being one of the key public service organization's that was leading organizational transformation, we were often invited to share our best practices with others. Doing so brought great satisfaction to me personally because the impact of the work that I was involved in went beyond just my own organization, to other public organizations and Singapore as a whole.

---

[28] Systems thinking is a way of making sense of the complexity of the world by looking at it in terms of wholes and relationships rather than splitting it down into its parts

[29] Ernest Lee was Director of Organization Excellence with the Inland Revenue Authority of Singapore. He served as Mentor and Resource Person in the Fellowship for Afghanistan from 2008 to 2018.

Having completed some major projects and having a little "extra" capacity (which my wife would disagree because my youngest of four children was less than five years old then), I began to look for opportunities to use my experience to contribute at the national or transnational levels. I sought out the Singapore International Foundation (SIF) and ended up as a Mentor with the UNITAR Hiroshima Fellowship for Afghanistan. The Program attracted my interest because we were venturing into a new model of web and online mentorship and my experience would be suitable for the Fellows, many of whom were in the civil service. The Program would also give me the rare opportunity of interacting with Afghans, other Mentors and Resource Persons from whom I could learn as well.

Looking back, we might have been one of the earliest groups trying web and online meetings. The most common phrase used during our online meetings then (when we used Skype) was "can you hear me?", and we are still using that phrase now when people use Zoom, Teams, Slack, Webex, etc. because of the Covid-19 pandemic.

My eyes were opened
It was not difficult getting to know the Fellows. After all, there were just a handful of them for each group of Mentors. There were another two Mentors in the team from Singapore in the first batch – Patsian Low and Hooi Yen Chin. Between the three of us, we reviewed the proposals and reports submitted by the Fellows and had Skype sessions periodically.

Having spent all my life in a cosmopolitan and relatively stable country, I have taken many things for granted, have been schooled to have a certain perspective of things, and conditioned to a different culture. Through the AF, I also learnt some aspects of the Afghan culture and how those who have studied abroad might see things differently from those who have not had the opportunity to do so.

Thanks to the comments and questions raised by the Fellows, we saw the needs of the Afghans and the passion they have for their country. My heart goes out to them, both then and now, whenever I read about the challenges they face there. I am sure things have been improving and we continue to have hope for the future.

Together with the Mentors from Singapore, I had the privilege of conducting a few online workshops for the Fellows and recall a particular session when one of the Fellows shared that there was an explosion that morning near where they were gathering. As people of courage and determination, they continued with the work-shop where they were. Such disruptions, however hard, were not uncommon to them.

Our Fellows often addressed us as "Respected Mentor." I recall feeling uneasy and had asked that they just address us by name. However, I think it is their culture to show respect and courtesy. I have not told any of the Fellows before, so let me take the opportunity to tell them that they have my respect, especially when I heard one of them saying that they have decided "never to leave Afghanistan again," that [Afghanistan] is their "homeland" and they will "work very hard to bring peace back." So in a way, I felt I was able to con-tribute indirectly to the betterment of their country. The Fellows were always an intelligent bunch and most of the time it was not as though they did not know their stuff. What I felt they needed was more of affirmation, support, and friendship.

Workshops in India and Japan
Apart from the online coaching sessions and workshops, the Fellowship included two face-to-face workshops conducted by the Resource Persons and Mentors. With my boss' support, I was able to participate in these overseas workshops in 2008. The first workshop was held in Dehradun, India while the second one was in Hiroshima, Japan. These physical meetings were very helpful

to break the ice between the support team and the Fellows. There were team-building activities and small group discussions. I must say the Afghans I met were a very friendly, outspoken, and jovial group. They come from a rich culture. Seeing them interact, and dance their traditional dance warmed my heart. One cannot tell that they were in the process of rebuilding their country. I have never seen one of them appearing lost or dejected because of their country's situation then.

Apart from the interaction with the Fellows and the team at the workshops, I will remember both trips fondly as it was my first visit to both countries. I remember the five-hour bumpy car ride from Delhi to Dehradun, the wailing in the middle of the night at the Dehradun hotel where a wedding was held, the visit to the Hiroshima Peace Memorial Museum and the Children's Peace Monument. May the late Ms. Sadako Sasaki's wish come true.

Playing host

When I was at the workshop in Hiroshima, it crossed my mind that the Fellows could actually stop by Singapore on the way to Japan or on their way back. What started as a wild idea came to fruition when SIF and UNITAR managed to set it up.

Needless to say, the suggestion to include IRAS as one of the site visits was mooted and I was glad my boss supported the idea. I was among pioneers to introduce the Learning Organization (LO) Tools and Concepts in IRAS and opened the way for organizational transformation to take place. Having seen its success in IRAS and shared with fellow public organizations it was quite natural for me to share about the "LO" journey which I thought could also be helpful for the Fellows.

More than sharing knowledge, I wanted to give my team's Fellows a glimpse into life in Singapore, so I invited them to visit my home.

I could not accommodate more as I was living in a four-room Housing and Development Board (HDB – public housing) flat which is about 100 square meters. Of course, I have to thank my wife for her support and her help to tidy up the house before the visit. While on the way to my house, I took time to explain some of the HDB policies to them, for example, how we promote interaction among various races, promote neighborliness at the void deck and community areas. If I remember correctly, I brought them to Satay Club for dinner that night. I also had a drink with one of the Coaches at Equinox. Some of my friends wondered why I would open up my house for people to visit. To me, these were not just any ordinary "people" – these were my friends.

A Community of Friends

Indeed, it was not easy keeping in touch via long distance. But thanks to Facebook, some of them are my Facebook friends and I am always so happy to see updates from them every now and then on their work and family.

I have benefited as much, if not more than the Fellows, from the Fellowship. It is a great privilege to be able to contribute towards another country's success. If you understand systems thinking, you will see that we are connected with one another. The world will have a higher chance of enjoying peace if we see ourselves as a community of friends.

Beyond Covid and What Not

Every country has her own challenges and needs to take care of her citizens' interests. Similarly, every head of the household would have to take care of their family's interests. The Chinese have a saying that goes something like "nation before family, family before self." It is often easier said than done especially when you have a spouse and children – because your decision affects your family.

Some of the Fellows told me that they have dual citizenship. I suppose a decision may have to be made at some point whether to remain or to move. Often times, decisions are made because of the children's welfare. I would not suggest that there is right or wrong to such decisions. We are not in the other person's shoes and even if we are, we have not walked the same journey in those pair of shoes.

While Covid-19 is a pandemic affecting the economy and everyone's lives, it provided opportunities for family members (who are in the same country or state) to be around one another more often, for us to be more reflective and for us to get used to online meetings. Even my elderly mother can now use WhatsApp video call (but she needs more practice!) The distance between people seems to have been shortened, although face-to-face meetups are always preferred.

The World as a Better Place
Strangely enough, Covid-19 also revealed that some family members get into more conflicts when they spend extended time together. During this time, more people sought help for their mental stress due to the financial challenges and strain in relationships. I know because I have since joined the Samaritans of Singapore (SOS, a social service agency in suicide prevention) in May 2019 after 25 years in the public sector. I think my mother should be quite pleased that I am still (I hope) contributing positively to society.

We have heard that it takes a village to raise a child. Would it then not take a community of nations to make friends and help one another so that the world as a whole will become a better place? I will always remember what Nassrine Azimi said at one of the workshops, "May the pull of the future be greater than the push of the past."

Afterthoughts Post-August 2021
December 18, 2021

Ernest Lee

My first reaction when I learnt about the events in August 2021 was whether our friends and their families were safe. The next thought was whether the efforts and dreams of the Fellowship were dashed.

Have you tried building a tower with cards or built a domino structure? It may not be difficult if it was a tower of 52 cards or a domino structure with 520 pieces. It would be rather strenuous and could even be frustrating if more pieces were targeted to be used. It would require a great amount of patience, resilience and inner peace. Was all the time and effort wasted when the structure falls apart during construction? Some perhaps, but not all.

I am sure many have heard about the saying, that there is a time for everything, and a season for every activity under the heavens. As I have shared earlier in my article, I have found the Fellows to be of courage and determination. They are passionate for their homeland and desire peace. Parts of the structure has fallen, but the knowledge and experience gained through the Fellowship would not be made naught, the impact made by the Fellows must have benefited many and the friendships established live on. I wish all our Fellows and friends well and may I echo these words – may the pull of the future be greater than the pull of the past. May peace prevail.

Dreams of Leadership in Public Health
Mohammad Saber Perdes[30]

I am a physician by training, though I am not practicing medicine right now. I studied through primary school, high school, and most of my faculty of medicine in Pakistan as a refugee.

We went to Pakistan because of the war. First, we were displaced from Kabul to another province in 1985. Then in 1988, we moved to Pakistan. We lived in a refugee camp where there were no facilities, where life was hard and most of the people were living in poverty. I can recall the days when I went to English language classes at a private tutoring center in Peshawar, Pakistan. I took four classes of English language obtaining ranking first or second in every class, but I could not continue due to financial problems. My father was keeping a farm of honeybees, and we had a lot of honey at home, but we could not sell it. So, it was a hard life. I did not give up, and my family supported me.

In fact, at that time, the situation got even more difficult in Afghanistan because there was the civil war in the early 1990s and then later on the Taliban, and we did not have any future to look forward to. The only two professions that were bringing in money were engineering and medicine as everyone needed those, even the Taliban needed a doctor. Since my elder brother was a doctor and I had worked with him at a clinic as an assistant for some time, I

[30] Mohammad Saber Perdes, M.D., MPH; UNITAR AF 2008 Fellow; Technical Specialist – Health; Afghanistan Holding Group (AHG)

was motivated to study medicine. In Afghanistan, when you obtain the highest marks in the university entry test (Kankor), then you go to the school of medicine, so mostly it was the cream of the crop. Until 2001, I only understood basic English, but I could not talk for more than a minute. Then, when I was in the final class of my medical courses, I decided to continue studying the English language. I went to a very famous center in Peshawar; it was called the English Language Program (ELP) established by the International Rescue Committee. Before that, I had procrastinated for a long time saying that I will do it this year, next year...

At that time, English was not important since all of our classes were in local languages, and the professors tried to prepare notes for us. We had very few reference books, but the professors were not considering them during exams. They would give us a reference like, "If you want to study more, you can read this book." It was not a required reading; it was just recommended reading. But I thought that if I studied English, it would make me stand out among my classmates. And when I completed my classes in July 2002, not only did I rank the first, but I also made a record score for that center. It motivated me a lot.

Taliban's government collapsed in 2001, and I came to Afghanistan in 2002. I started teaching English, and I did my residency at different hospitals in Kabul. Still, the financial situation of the family was not good. I was receiving some money from my brother while I was teaching English and doing small jobs in translation services. So, I started to translate his articles for a children's magazine called Parwaz , which means flight. And when I translated an article, I think they paid me ten dollars. They were translating one article every two months, so ten dollars for every two months. It was only pocket money for me. I was traveling mostly on my bike to different areas of Kabul. Kabul was not crowded like now. There were very few cars, and I could ride my bike even in front of the US Embassy as the roads were open. Now, they are all closed to the public.

By teaching English and doing some translations, I improved my English language capacity. In 2003, I got my first job in the private sector, and I worked there for the next three years.

I joined the Health Promotion Department of the Ministry of Public Health (MoPH) in the capacity of Technical Manager/Trainer in late 2006, although I did not have any previous experience working in the government. I was working closely with numerous donors and implementing partners on coordinating and launching communication campaigns, producing Information, Education and Communication (IEC) materials, and developing project documents such as proposals and reports. Expectations were high, and it was not easy to handle all my tasks.

In 2007, I heard about the UNITAR Hiroshima Fellowship for Afghanistan. I was curious to know the details of the program. Two of my colleagues told me about the Fellowship contents and process. Then, I applied and luckily, I was selected for the 2008 cohort. It was an eye-opening and life-changing experience. The program was designed as a seven-month on-the-job training program for mid-level managers. Participants were divided into several groups, and I was part of the health group. Every group had a Coach, and we had individual and group assignments.

Now that I know more about the team building process, and I recall our group assignments, sometimes I laugh aloud because the transition from Storming to Norming took us a long time. We had a lot of heated arguments, and I thought it was not going to work. However, things changed as the team members started to connect with each other. I made a strong commitment that I would get the most out of the Fellowship, and I confess that I learned from every activity, whether it was a lecture or a site visit. Some activities were supposed to be completed or attended through the internet, but we did not have good internet connection in Afghanistan. I had to go to the Independent Administrative Reform and Civil Service Commission

(IARCSC) to attend audio conferences. Once, I was caught up in a traffic jam and I could not reach IARCSC on time, so I tried my phone's 2G internet, and I was able to inform my group and professors that I was following their discussions.

The bonding among participants got stronger as we travelled together and had more in-depth conversations. Most of us had one thing in common, and that was a strong belief in the future of Afghanistan and commitment to take an active part in the rebuilding of our beloved country. Since the program was very condensed, I had to give it enough time every week and make sure that all assignments were completed on time. I believe the Fellowship program had academic, social, and transformational goals. There were lectures, site visits, group exercises, and recreational activities. I learned proposal writing, report writing, presentation skills and time management throughout the program. Since then, my life is more organized and more productive. I have more control over my self-regulation, and the soft skills I gained during the Fellowship are my strength.

Visiting Hiroshima was like a dream come true because I had heard about its destruction at the end of World War II, but I had never expected to go there in person. When I went to the Atomic Bomb Dome, the T-bridge, and the Peace Memorial Museum, I felt as if I was part of the people who had suffered the tragedy. Later, I listened to an A-Bomb witness and how he survived. His story and the Peace Museum were strong motivations for everyone. While I was shedding tears, I was thinking about how I could make a difference in the life of our people when I got back home.

In short, I see that my soft skills have helped me a lot during my career. In 2009, I got a Fulbright Scholarship and studied for a Master of Public Health at St. Louis University in Missouri. My area of expertise was health policy. I finished with a Grade Point Average (GPA) of 3.9 and distinction at comprehensive exams.

I spent just under 400 days in the US in total. It was a great time, I learned a lot from my professors, classmates, and friends. It was not only learning about public health, but I also tried to serve as a cultural ambassador of Afghanistan. I attended different social events and gatherings and delivered speeches at events where I was requested to do so. I talked to them about the differences and similarities in our cultures. Some of them had never seen an Afghan in person before. I remember that at one social event, I talked to a group of Americans and answered their questions. One of them said, "You are just like us!" I made a lot of great friends. I had host families with whom I am still in contact. What I want to say is that there are good and bad people everywhere. Most of the people I met in US were very kind, honest, and friendly.

After coming back to Afghanistan, I have worked in different capacities in the government and non-governmental organizations. In a voluntary capacity, I am currently serving as vice president and board member of the Afghanistan Cancer Foundation (ACF) and International Relations Coordinator at the Afghanistan National Public Health Association (ANPHA). I am a founding member of ANPHA and the Afghanistan Fulbright Association (AFA), and I served as executive board member of ANPHA from 2012 till 2015.

To conclude, I believe the UNITAR Hiroshima Fellowship for Afghanistan was a great opportunity for learning, networking, belonging, and looking at the purpose of my life from a different angle. I have stayed connected with many of the Fellows, who are in key positions in the government and the private sector, and I think we need to work together and strive for a better future for our beloved country. As a next step, I suggest that we hold a reunion for the whole community and revisit our goals and promises. Alone, we are strong — together, we are stronger!

Learning to Manage Change and Take Ownership
Zainulabuddin Hamid[31]

I was introduced to the UNITAR Hiroshima Fellowship for Afghanistan by my organization, the United Nations Office for Project Services (UNOPS), where I worked as Deputy Project Manager for the Kabul area.

The management and leadership skills required for the reconstruction of Afghanistan posed a serious challenge. Although a critical requirement for a better future and prosperous Afghanistan, the skills and capacities were limited, and reconstruction was an unknown territory in the new Afghanistan. The UNITAR Fellowship offered me an opportunity, as a young engineer, to tap into resources on modern management and leadership. I was able to use this opportunity to learn new skills in:

1. Needs assessment
2. Team development
3. Change management
4. Conflict resolution
5. Communication
6. Coordination and facilitation

---

[31] UNITAR AF 2008 Fellow, 2009 Coach, 2010 ARP

My journey started with UNITAR as a young Fellow in 2008. It advanced in 2009 as a Coach and blossomed in 2010 as an Afghan Resource Person (ARP).

The first year was, of course, a steep learning curve, where I tried to learn as much as I could. The skills I learned during my Fellowship year were further advanced during the coaching year. I had the unique opportunity to provide coaching for a group of Afghan Fellows from different ethnic groups. This tested my skills and knowledge to the maximum. Being an ARP was more fun as it was interesting for me to participate in the preparation of case studies, review of reports from Fellows, providing feedback etc.

I want to take this opportunity to shed some light on my four-year collaboration with the UNITAR Fellowship for Afghanistan and its impact on my life and performance.

The Fellowship
The Fellowship provided me an opportunity to take my management skills to a higher level. It convinced me of the urgency and importance of the learning offered by the Fellowship for professionals in Afghanistan. It also broadened my perspective, allowing me to look deeper into my own country's failures and what needed to be fixed.

The Fellowship program gave me skills in resolving conflicts, team development, needs assessment, and communication skills --all skills that had either been lacking in Afghanistan or were neglected for years.

Change management is a major issue in Afghanistan, and any new initiative faces opposition and obstacles in various ministries and even in universities. Change, and resistance to change, has been a major topic at the Engineering Faculty, Kabul University, where something as simple as a new generator needed to work

Autocad for Drawings, SAP for Design works, etc. was resisted for a long time. Instead, the professors preferred to stick to their old handwritten notes and techniques, which were good, but outdated for today's generation. It took at least five years with numerous meetings and discussions to adopt the new curriculum in the university.

There are many more examples where the lack of the skills mentioned above can be highlighted, but we would need a book to include them all!

Coaching

Coaching provided me with a unique and immediate opportunity to implement the skills from the Fellowship Cycle. Being an Afghan myself, I knew all the frustration of Afghans with their government and system.

I wanted to coach the Fellows on the need for team development, an essential shortage in the Afghan institutions. Lack of effective team development and teamwork prevents the ministries from achieving their goals, and in some cases even leads to donors cancelling the projects.

The absence of the use of tools such as needs assessment by the ministries was, and still is, a huge obstacle for donors and funding parties. Most development initiatives are carried out without understanding the exact needs of the community. A failed program by the Ministry of Urban Development, where they were procuring generators for electricity dramatically failed, because the villages could not pay for the fuel and maintenance. This failure could have easily been avoided if an assessment of available resources had been done prior to implementing the project, and the traditional fuel sources had been replaced by Solar Power, making the generator fuel sources relatively free and easy to maintain.

When coaching, I made sure the team understood the above issues. I learned interesting techniques on how to facilitate the team towards its goal, within the specified timeline, and focused on specified concepts already identified. I facilitated the team's work while keeping myself neutral, not imposing my own ideas on the team, and letting them make their own decisions, while all the time ensuring that the team stayed on track. I carefully involved all the group members to work together and facilitated managing conflict.

My goal was to ensure all members of my team would go back to their respective ministries, become change leaders, push the skills they had learned, and work for a prosperous Afghanistan.

As Afghan Resource Person
In my role as ARP (also my third year with the Fellowship), I had the opportunity to work closely with the Fellowship Mentors and UNITAR facilitators to prepare and present case studies specific to the Afghan organizations and context. Meanwhile, I also reviewed the Fellows' assignments, provided feedback, especially based on my coaching skills, finally evaluated the group presentation, and shared constructive comments for improvement.

We had real case studies within the ministries, which were developed and shared with the Fellows. We wanted the Fellows to identify the shortfalls and find ways to overcome them.

Special emphasis was given from my part to communication skills. Being involved in construction projects and infrastructure in Afghanistan, I knew that the communication lines were not always open, and sometimes, even simple access to the main stakeholder within the government could be blocked by the secretaries and other staff, which added real impediments to achieving goals.

Coordination and Facilitation (Logistical support) – Taking Ownership

During the Fellowship Cycles from 2009 to 2012, beside the given roles, due to my enthusiasm and the good feeling I had for the program, I wanted to be involved in coordinating activities and facilitation with Mr. Sokout, UNITAR Representative in Afghanistan. I was involved in logistical activities supporting Mr. Sokout to smoothly handle training events in Kabul. One such instance was when there was a need to provide buses for the Fellows to be transported from the ACCI to CIDA office. My commitment to the continued success of the program resulted from believing in the vital impact it was having on my country's professional development goals. To support the UNITAR representative, I volunteered to work with the vendors to negotiate for transportation vehicles sponsored by local businesses. It was an honor for me to support the program as I believed this was something everyone needed to join and learn. This was a unique dynamic for an international training program. Participant and alumni involvement in the logistical and practical activities of an international program, especially on a voluntary basis, almost never happens. It happens even less long after the training program is over. But the UNITAR Fellowship proved its uniqueness in the way it inspired and engaged its community.

As Director of My Own Company

I established my own construction company in 2007. With a young company at its early stages, I wanted my partner to have the same authorities I had as Director. This was a bad strategy setting us up for failure, because having two heads never works although the company had kick-started with relative success.

My partner left the company in 2010, and at that point I understood very well, how to lead the company. The skills I applied were taken from the UNITAR Fellowship Program, and I wanted to implement the methodologies and systems learned in my own company without any further delays.

First, I did a needs assessment to see what went wrong during our partnership and why we did not last long. I realized that the first mistake was having both Director and Deputy Director working at almost the same position and having similar authority. Second, we were lacking team development, and of course inter-staff conflict was another major issue.

I identified and prepared a list of changes that needed to be made, brought a major overhaul to the company, and found a new partner. Within the new partnership, we ensured that duties and responsibilities were clearly formulated to avoid conflict. Finally, decision-making at higher levels became my responsibility, with my deputy supporting in various aspects of the company.

Changes have been brought, where the system is centralized to Director as Top Authorized Person, Deputy Director as second-in-command while providing a helping hand to the Director. The projects are run by an authorized project manager who manages his or her own scope of work and staff. A team of young engineers has been selected in various positions within the company. They are advised by managers and the head of the company.

I managed to develop clearly designated teams such as the Design Team, Implementation Team, and Finance Team within my company. Furthermore, multi-tasking has been developed as part of the company's long-term visions. Multi-tasking training is to make sure that the teams are able to perform various tasks and be productive at all times. This reduces the risk of laying staff off because we have a team which can be busy all year long, and the company can offer employment security, even if there is no project for a while.

Lines of communication have been open to all staff. The communications with clients and donors are established on the basis of honesty and integrity. There has never been any miscommunication since 2011, because now the communication is managed from the top level. Conflict has been at a minimum and where it has arisen, it was usually resolved amicably within the staff. No conflict has been raised with clients and donors.

My company's project portfolio has dramatically increased, and I credit this success to what I have learned from my continued involvement with the UNITAR Fellowship Program.

سوله

باني

ملح

مانی

和

صلح

平和

Afterthoughts Post-August 2021
Anonymous submission, AF alumnus
December 23, 2021

Before the Taliban government, the Afghan youth were passionate about only one thing: building the country and their homeland in the hope of having a good future, regardless of security, economic and social problems, such as discrimination against minorities across the country. Everyone was trying to facilitate the work of international friends of Afghanistan to do the same, by providing voluntary support. I don't want to be negative or say that all the achievements of the past two decades have been merely a waste of time and resources, but after the collapse of the republican system by a group which advocated terrorism and suicide bombing, and whose aim seems to be to distance non-Pashtun ethnic groups from the government, there is a sense of frustration among Afghan youth and intellectuals as they foresee a dark future. Based on the past experiences from the previous Taliban government and the current situation in Afghanistan, the frustration has spread among different segments of society, especially young people, who were born into a relatively free society and grew up with democratic values. Many have left Afghanistan to achieve their aspirations and to taste life again in a free and democratic society, and a significant number are trying to find a way to escape from the Taliban, particularly scholars and youths. The Taliban are seeking to establish a single-ethnic Pashtun government in Afghanistan, which leads to internal wars and causes ethnic conflicts across the country. As long as the Taliban is in power, there will be no hope for social development, economic development, or any other sustainable development in Afghanistan.

"A prosperous and sustainable future can only be secured through greater equality and collaboration."

Joseph Rain

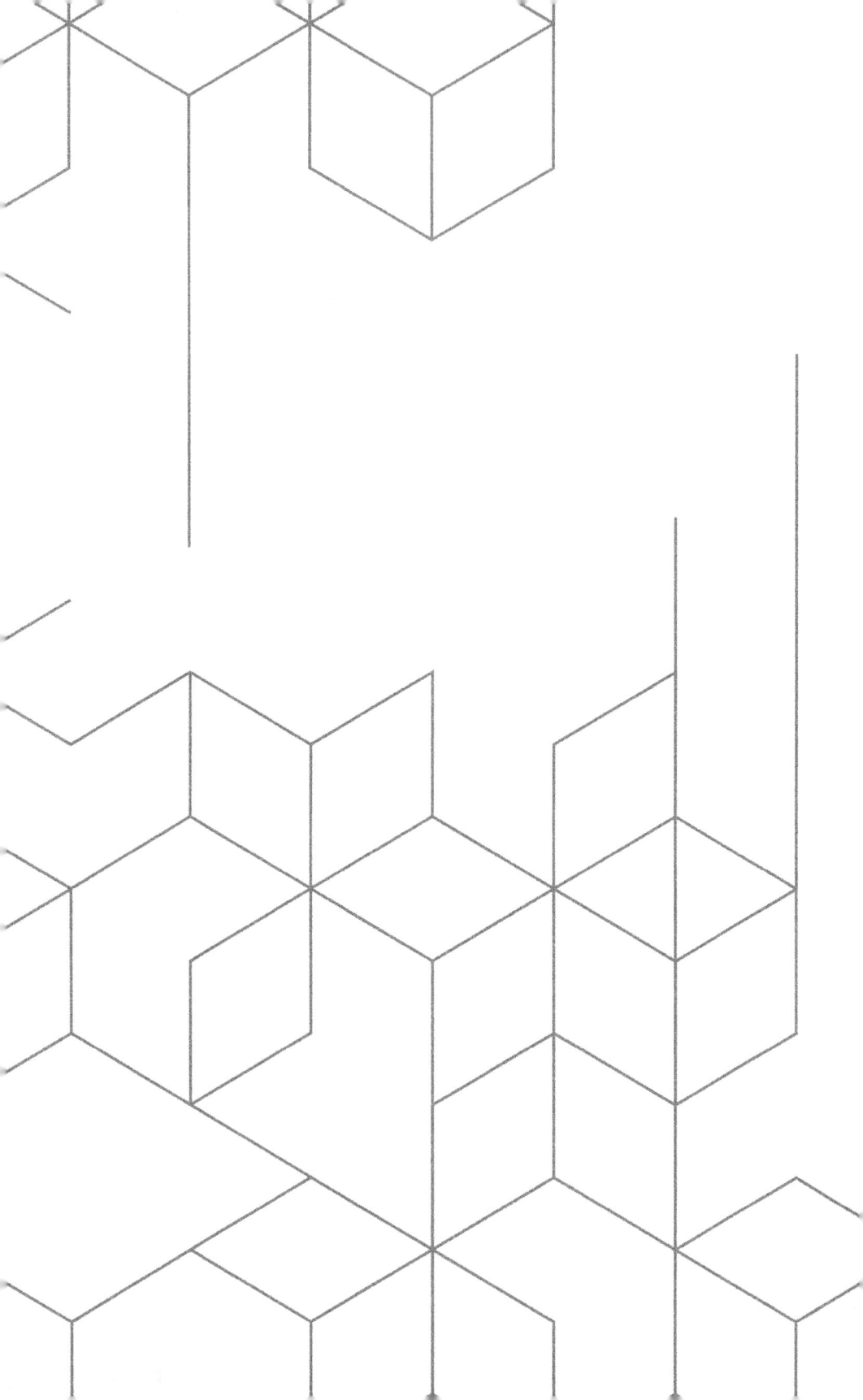

PART IIIA

THE WOMEN OF THE
FELLOWSHIP

UNITAR: The Full Package, from Learning to Professional Networking
Najla Sabri[32]

In 2007, not long after the collapse of the Taliban, things were slowly and gradually getting better in Afghanistan, and there was still a severe need for capacity-building and networking opportunities for young professionals in the country. I heard about the UNITAR Hiroshima Fellowship for Afghanistan from one of my friends. The Fellowship sounded very interesting to me. To be honest, the traveling part of it and having the opportunity to visit Japan were very attractive too because I, like all other Afghan youth at the time, had seen nothing in life but war and the experience of being refugees in neighboring countries, where life was not so different and, in some cases, even worse than what we had experienced in Afghanistan before fleeing to other countries from the civil war.

After learning more about the Fellowship, I soon became even more interested as I learned that I would have the opportunity to meet other youth and young professionals, something I really needed after living 10 years in Pakistan and only being in Afghanistan for five years after repatriating. My network of friends was very limited. And, of course, I wanted to learn and develop new skills for my professional growth. At that time, I was working with the Office of the European Union Special Representative, as Personal Assistant to the EU Envoy for Afghanistan. It was a job which I was enjoying

---

[32] UNITAR AF 2007 Fellow, 2008 Coach, 2009 ARP

but, at the same time, I was ready to explore other fields of work, less political (the EUSR office was a political organization) and more interesting. Looking back, I think I made a wise decision to apply for the UNITAR Fellowship even as a self-financed applicant as at that time the program was not financing those, who were working with international organizations. The program contributed a lot to broadening my professional choices and changing my career path. Through AF, I got introduced to topics, which were new to me: project design, project implementation, team building, needs assessments, etc. all related to development work which, unlike political work, could bring tangible results in a shorter time frame. I became very interested in development work, and in my second year with UNITAR when I had become a Coach, I got a job with the World Bank in Afghanistan. Since then, I have worked with this major development organization in the country in different capacities, contributing to the development agenda in my country. The focus of my work is on gender and social inclusion.

My UNITAR journey has been one of the most beautiful experiences in my life so far. I found it as a full package from learning to networking. The Fellowship helped me learn so many new things in the most effective way. The very design of the program as such helped me learn complicated concepts by doing and experiencing. The group work on which the program put much emphasis was indeed the best way for adult learning - being supported by a local Coach, who knew the program intricately, and who had gone through the same process, and an international Mentor, who provided technical support to our work, helping the group on course material and course assignments.

The most interesting and challenging part of AF was the group work! As per the design of the program, each cohort (around 60-70 Fellows) was divided into smaller groups of four to six members, who had to stick to the group they had been assigned to. Interestingly, our group was the only one in which all members were female. I was very happy about this, but, at the same time, I and perhaps my other team members were worried and somehow felt extra pressure. In Asia including Afghanistan, as a female professional, you have to work two or three times as hard compared to men to prove yourself. We must be so accurate in our work, and whatever we do should be flawless; otherwise, our professionalism would be linked to our gender. The very common social perception applied would be, "Women don't make good professionals," or "Women's professional capacity is lower than men's." I was lucky enough to have two other team members, who were great professionals and capable women. The three of us came from different backgrounds and different age groups, and, of course, had different personalities. One was very talkative and extroverted (yes you are right, that is me!), the other was somewhat introverted but always tried to keep us on track, and the third one, somewhere in between, always looked very serious. But once you got to know her, she would be the most lively and fun person. With all these differences, at the beginning and until we got to know each other well and realized each other's skills and strengths, we had a difficult time in our group. However, slowly and gradually our team was built, and we became – I would dare to say – one of the strongest teams in our cohort. We complemented each other, we became each other's support and strength, and most importantly we became lifelong great friends. In the whole process, one cannot ignore the role of our Coach and Mentors – their guidance, support, and the many ways they helped us to become a successful team - were instrumental. In the final workshop in Hiroshima, each team presented their joint project in front of all the Fellows, Coaches, Mentors, and external audience. I would say, it was an opportunity to actually present months of hard work and professional development, demonstrate leadership skills, and how we had come along as one team. It was the toughest part, at least for me, especially when I came to know that our team was the first to present. Again we, as the all-female team, were so nervous. We had our unconscious biases which were socially constructed in us making us think that men would do better than us. With all these feelings and doubts but yet having confidence in our hard work and ourselves, we presented our team project, a research paper on "Women's Leadership Role in Afghanistan." I will never forget all the great comments we received from the jury and from the audience. Indeed, being different from other teams gave us a great opportunity for being at the center of focus of our audience, who thought our team was unique not only in its composition, but also in our work and project.

After the successful completion of the Fellowship, I couldn't detach myself from UNITAR. I was fortunate enough to have the opportunity to become a Coach and Resource Person and stay with AF for three consecutive years. Even after that, UNITAR has always been with me in one way or another. I loved the Fellowship for what it had offered to me. Besides learning and enhancing my skills, it gave me the opportunity to make new friends and expand my network, which is really important in both my personal and professional life. As a World Bank employee, I work with many projects and ministries and for a successful and effective partnership, trust-building with counterparts is critical. I feel so privileged when I see that in most of these projects and ministries, I know someone from our UNITAR family from mid-level to the most senior level positions. I immediately think that half of the work is done especially on trust-building as we know each other. Having such networks is so important, especially when there is so much hierarchy in the government system and so much politics in everything. In normal circumstances in Afghanistan, one cannot easily get access to a Minister or even to a Deputy Minister to pass an important work-related message or get any urgent work done, but I have been very lucky in many instances. For example, once I heard that in one of the projects, they had eliminated the gender officer positions, both at the central and provincial levels as they thought that these were not important positions. I, as the gender specialist for that project from the World Bank side, came to know about this, and knowing the importance of these positions for that project, I immediately reached out to the acting Minister, who was one of the UNITAR AF alumni, and brought it to his attention. Thankfully, he immediately resolved the issue on the spot. I have many such work-related examples in which my UNITAR network has played a very strong role, And it is the same with my personal life. Some of the AF alumni and staff are now my best friends on whom I can really count, and there have been many occasions when we have supported one other.

I will always cherish the great memories from the UNITAR Fellowship, value what I gained from it personally and professionally, and remain grateful to all the supporters and staff of UNITAR.

Ernest LEE KIAN MENG

A Journey Gladly Taken — My Thirteen Years
of Volunteerism
Chin Hooi-Yen[33]

At 09:52 on June 11, 2007, I received an email with the subject heading, "Seeking volunteers for UNITAR Hiroshima Fellowship for Afghanistan." It was written by Margaret Theravakom, an intelligent and warm lady, who is now, 13 years later, someone I am proud and happy to call a friend.

Margaret was from the Singapore International Foundation, and they were calling for volunteers to serve as Mentors for the UNITAR Hiroshima Fellowship for Afghanistan. I applied out of a desire to make a "positive impact on the world" (I suppose I was much younger, and perhaps equally, idealistic).

Margaret interviewed me – she told me the UNITAR team was interested to know about my experience with the legal aspects of contracts and grants administration and management, an area I had consulted in for several years with a Singapore statutory body.

The Beginning of the Journey
Soon, I was in. I found myself being called a "Mentor" (a title I was more than a little nervous about), and I met Patsian Low and Henry Kwok, my fellow Mentors from Singapore for that cycle.

---

[33] Chin Hooi Yen is a lawyer and currently serves as Adjunct Associate at Republic Polytechnic, where she lectures and facilitates classes for B101 Entrepreneurship. She served as an AF Mentor from 2007-2013.

Soon, I found myself at the World Bank office in Singapore, using their video conference facility and being introduced to Sabahuddin Sokout, who was the Coach of Group III, and the members of Group III, Sayed Mobin Shah, M. Ayaz Azizi, Fazil Malik Qasim, and Ab. Samad Yadgari.

The Challenges
Thus, began my journey with the Fellowship. Those early days were a whirlwind. There was all the material provided by the UNITAR Hiroshima Office to review (as I write this, I am looking at the "Guideline for Mentors" and the "Fellowship Requirements for Graduation"). I read through the profiles of the Fellows and the biographies of Resource Persons, Coaches, and Mentors. I went through all the background readings meant for the Fellows on topics such as needs analyses and environmental analyses. I reviewed all the work produced by the Fellows (often several times) and tried to be as helpful as possible.

During each cycle, I set aside lunchtimes for calls with the Group I was mentoring, which would be early mornings in Kabul, after lunch in Hiroshima, and who knows what time in Phoenix. The Singapore-based Mentors would meet or have calls to discuss any difficulty or web seminar we had undertaken to conduct. I recall several lunches and coffees with Ernest Lee and Patsian to prepare for a workshop we were conducting.

There was the travel to attend workshops in Hiroshima, Dubai, Abu Dhabi, or Dehradun, where we would get to meet the Fellows and the UNITAR team in person, but which would themselves be a tornado of workshops, team building activities, assignments, speeches, and dinners, all conducted whilst I spent nights and early mornings responding to work email and holding calls with clients and bosses.

There were other challenges. The first one was cultural. I found it difficult to read the Fellows. Did they agree or disagree? Did they grasp my point? Was my choice of words and expressions appropriate? These questions often swirled through my mind when interacting with the Fellows, who seemed very formal and respectful, and almost never pushed back on any of our suggestions or comments, especially as the medium of our communications was remote and added to the sense of distance and formality. In Singapore, we tend to be informal and direct when expressing ourselves as compared to the Fellows, and I wondered how this came across to the Fellows.

The second set of concerns I had involved my gender. Would this present any issues? I also wondered if the formality I was treated with had something to do with my gender. In any case, I soldiered on as thoughtfully as I could. On one of my trips to Hiroshima, my hotel room phone rang in the middle of the night. I was not sure if the caller said anything, but I do remember, after having spent the night replying to my work email, I picked up the phone, immediately said, "Go to sleep!" and put it down. The next day, the UNITAR team announced that some female Fellows had received unwanted phone calls the night before and asked if anyone else had experienced the same. The UNITAR staff then raised the matter with the Fellows.

The People
Beginning with the 2007 cycle, I volunteered with the 2008, 2009, 2010, 2012, and 2013 cycles. My desire to contribute got me to apply, but the people I met brought me back again and again.

The stories, backgrounds, selflessness, and determination of the Afghan Fellows blew me over. So many had left Afghanistan with nothing, and returned as doctors, engineers, finance professionals, and administrators to rebuild their country, one project at a time, one day at a time. They taught me about their culture, their diversity, their languages, their history, and the beauty of Afghanistan (I promised myself to visit Bamiyan one day, thanks to a video from Amir Foladi).

While workshops were generally full-on serious affairs, there were light moments, such as an impromptu song and dance session led by the Fellows after dinner one night in a restaurant in Hiroshima. During team building and other activities, we got to know the Fellows better and hear their personal stories. Their stories were so powerful and gave intense human dimensions to the headlines and news reports I had previously only read or watched, but now also feel. For me, these opportunities to interact with the Fellows made workshops the bedrock of the Fellowship.

Some of the people I will never forget include the atomic bomb survivors, whom the city of Hiroshima arranged for us to meet on several occasions, and who told us their stories. Despite their pain in recalling the events of that day in August 1945, they wanted to tell their stories so that we would never forget the horror of that day.

The Program
Throughout the years that I was involved, the Fellowship evolved and expanded. Afghan Resource Persons were introduced, adding greater depth to the program. The role of the Coaches

expanded. ACTRA (an alumni association for the Fellowship) was established. Team projects were implemented, reviewed, and reported on. Feedback and reviews at the end of each cycle were analyzed in-depth and acted on. It seemed the UNITAR team was ambitious and tireless in their efforts to provide more opportunities for the Fellows to learn new skills and expand their roles within the Fellowship, as well as opportunities to keep in touch and network after the conclusion of their cycle. To me, this was another aspect of the Fellowship that made it so special. The program learned, grew, morphed, and developed every single cycle. The Fellowship gained depth, alumni, and supporters, and its reach expanded.

At workshops, web-seminars, video web conferences, and audio web conferences, the Fellowship seemed to have the support of a galaxy of experts, development professionals, management consultants, scholars, and business executives from countries as diverse as Afghanistan, Japan, Canada, the United States of America, and Singapore. This was testimony not only to the importance of the objectives of the Fellowship, but also to the ability of the UNITAR team to inspire and lead a diverse international group of professionals.

In July 2009, the Fellowship held Workshop I for that year's cycle in Singapore, during which the Singapore International Foundation facilitated the Fellows' visits to various ministries and statutory bodies. One of the Fellows mentioned to me that he was inspired by the racial harmony in Singapore, where the national language is Malay, and the parliamentary proceedings are conducted in the official languages of Malay, Tamil, Mandarin, and English. I recall my reply: I in turn was inspired by the drive, spirit, and warmth of the Afghans we met, and that we in Singapore and Southeast Asia, were not too different from the people of Afghanistan in terms of our racial, language, and religious diversity.

Thanks to the dedicated UNITAR team, the Fellowship seemed to come together each cycle and move forward seamlessly as one. They made the forming, storming, norming, and performing seem painless. The orchestra was conducted by UNITAR, the musicians played their hearts out, and the music was being written for Afghanistan.

Reflections

During each cycle, the Fellowship immersed itself in the world of needs assessments, key performance indicators, monitoring and evaluation, conflict management and organizational development. Every activity was followed by an after-action review, with Fellows penning their reflections in their journals.

My reflections start with the many fond memories of the people I have met, and gratitude for the many chances the Fellowship has given me to meet and learn from experts and professionals from all over the world. I am humbled by the city of Hiroshima for generously supporting the post-conflict reconstruction efforts of another society. My thanks go too to the Singapore International Foundation for enabling our participation and extending their support for so many years.

Above all, I take heart that there were many dedicated professionals from around the world, who selflessly contributed in so many different ways to the Fellowship, perhaps inspired by the stories of the courageous people of Afghanistan and the dedication of the Fellows. And when such individuals put their hearts and minds and hands together, they can create a unique collaborative effort, which is both international in scope and human at heart.

I am not sure how much I have changed the world, but the people I have met through the Fellowship have certainly changed me.

The Impact of the Fellowship on
Women's Leadership and Development I
Jennifer Fox[34]

I knew the first time I heard Dr. David Eaton speak about the UNITAR Fellowship for Afghanistan that I wanted to be a part of it; I do not think that I had ever been so certain of anything in my life. I knew that I wanted to play a role, even a small one, to help improve the lives of Afghan people. And there was also something powerful about the idea of civil servants in my country, like myself, supporting Afghan civil servants to rebuild their country. I had first become interested in Afghanistan after reading several books that chronicled people's journeys across the land. I knew there had to be more to the country than what I saw on the nightly news, and I saw the Fellowship as an amazing opportunity to learn more about this place, people, and culture.

I was, however, still a little apprehensive about serving as a mentor. I was not sure what my team members, all men, would think about me, a woman and an American. At that time, I had already faced my share of challenges as a young professional woman and emerging leader. I had worked with men whom I believe did not treat me as an equal because of my age and gender. Even though they were polite, I did not feel that they always took me seriously. I also

---

[34] Jennifer Fox has over 10 years of experience providing technical assistance to governments across the globe and serves as an advisor with the U.S. Treasury Department's Office of Technical Assistance (OTA). She served on and off as a mentor in UNITAR's Fellowship for Afghanistan since 2009 till 2018

believed that I had to prove myself more than my male colleagues which often meant that I worked late hours and even weekends to have as perfect a deliverable as possible with few, if any, mistakes. I started my journey with the UNITAR Fellowship in this mindset and with this life experience.

My apprehensions quickly dissipated, however, when I first walked into a Fellowship workshop. Everyone I encountered seemed warm, friendly, and funny. I bonded with my team very quickly. My first workshop was an incredible experience; I loved working one-on-one with my team to discuss their needs assessments and proposed projects, helping them choose a project, and develop a draft proposal. I was inspired by the team's project ideas and strong determination to improve their departments, ministries, and country. In our free time, we chatted about everything under the sun from religion to Texas politics to Bollywood movies. I even spent an evening with my team listening to Afghan music and watching Afghan music videos. When I was not hanging out with my team, I enjoyed getting to know the other Fellows, mentors, and the wonderful members of the UNITAR family.

At the time, I did not realize that it was another part of my life experience that had made it so easy to socialize and even bond with my team members. For many years, I had not only worked with male colleagues but had spent hours socializing with these same colleagues getting to know them and my other female coworkers on a personal basis. Whether I knew it or not, that socialization helped to level the playing field in my professional world. Although on the flip side I had encountered disrespect and lack of support from some male colleagues, I had many colleagues who very much respected me and my ideas. I believe some of that respect was due to the relationships and community that had been created and the ideas that had been shared outside of the work setting. I felt this same ease and connectedness with my UNITAR teammates – especially my male colleagues. I think in some ways I experienced the concept of western women being classified as a "third gender," where my colleagues did not quite see me as another guy but also did not quite see me as equivalent to an Afghan woman; I was essentially somewhere in between.

Early on in my time in the Fellowship, I did not connect very well with the women in the program. Of course, quite frankly, there were very few women to connect with and most of them were in other teams like health and education. That all changed, however, one evening when I was invited to one of the ladies' rooms after class. The minute I walked into that room and saw the women taking off their head scarfs and shoes, I felt a whole other energy. Everyone was so much more relaxed. That evening I got to know these amazing, dynamic women a little better, to hear their stories and learn a little more about what life was really like for educated, urban Afghan women. I realized after that time that the best way to get to know the women in the program was one-on-one or in small groups (like this), and that at least, in general, these women had not had the same experiences I had had of socializing as commonly with male colleagues. It just was not as much part of the Afghan culture.

During my years as Mentor in the UNITAR Fellowship, I got to see some of these dynamic women really come out of their shells and some of the unconscious gender biases start to fade. In addition to the Fellowship teaching invaluable, core project management and leadership skills it also created a relaxed environment that allowed male and female Fellows more opportunities to socialize and to come together to solve problems and support each other in meaningful ways as teammates. The result of this was a community that started to break down some of the walls that had previously existed between Afghan men and women, and between people of different ethnic backgrounds and from different regions. As the years went on, I started to see amazing friendships form between men and women and between people of different ethnic backgrounds. I realize today that this was the real power of the Fellowship. It was not just the skills learned but it was the opportunities for people of different backgrounds to work together and to get to know each other; this is what helped open minds.

During my time in the Fellowship, I met amazing people and made some good friends. Two of the people I became the closest to were Mariam Ghaznavi and Mina Naikmal. I met them in 2016 when Mariam was Coach on my team and Mina a Fellow. I liked them both right away. I was impressed by Mariam's intelligence and her ability to motivate and lead her team members, and I found Mina to be a quick learner and very approachable. We became good friends, hanging out together at workshops, and having wonderful in-depth discussions about family, relationships, professional life, etc. Our relationship evolved from Mentor/Fellow to genuine friendship, and we became each other's confidants and sources of support on various occasions. They also helped me understand on a personal level some of the daily challenges they faced as women in Afghanistan and helped me understand why women, particularly, needed opportunities like the Fellowship to advance professionally but also to grow personally. I believe what powerfully sets the UNITAR Fellowship apart from many other capacity building programs is the peer-to-peer learning element – Afghan colleagues mentoring and learning from Afghan colleagues through work as Coaches and Afghan Resource Persons. I learned this best from watching Mina and Mariam. I watched Mina beautifully put into practice coaching skills she learned first-hand from Mariam to both manage and motivate her team when she became a coach herself. I also got to watch how Mina mentored a young woman named Sahar; she befriended her and took her under her wing to become an effective member of her team. I believe this kind of peer-to-peer learning was particularly powerful for women in the Fellowship and the growth opportunities of serving as coaches and Afghan Resource Persons were invaluable.

On a professional level, the Fellowship ignited my passion to do reform and development work for a living. It helped me see this work in a different light. Before the Fellowship, most of the development projects I was involved in were top down, often driven by outsiders. I learned from the Fellowship how important it is for local people to be the ones identifying and developing solutions to their problems. In 2012, several years before I met Mariam and Mina, I left my job working with the Texas Legislature to take a job with the U.S. Department of the Treasury's Office of Technical Assistance (OTA) to serve as a budget advisor to the Ministry of Finance (MoF) in the Dominican Republic. In this position and in subsequent assignments in other countries, I used many of the hard and soft skills learned from the Fellowship to help MoF colleagues better manage and oversee their budget reform projects. My work with OTA ultimately led me to become an intermittent advisor to the Afghan MoF to help the government improve their budget processes. In this position, I had a unique opportunity to work with Afghan women outside of the UNITAR Fellowship.

During my time working with the MoF, I saw two contrasting themes. On the one hand, I got to see amazing young female leaders like Mariam, Mina, and other women I met through the Fellowship in action in their various positions in the MoF. I saw how they were able to incorporate some of the valuable lessons they learned from the Fellowship into their leadership style. I heard from their bosses about the good work they had done and saw firsthand some of the impressive reform initiatives they were involved in, although I did not work directly with their directorates. I was also so pleased when I heard about these women's promotions to even higher-level management positions. My female colleagues expressed, however, that they were not always provided genuine support in these new positions which often involved difficult decision-making. This led me to believe that perhaps some of these promotions were motivated by external forces such as a need for international approval as much as a desire to promote these well deserving women to higher-level positions.

On the other hand, although I only worked with a few MoF teams directly, the teams I worked most closely with had few women on them, and these women were often in entry- and mid-level positions. Very few women spoke up in meetings and were less likely to engage in discussions. I also observed during training breaks that the women who attended the trainings rarely chatted with their male colleagues, it seemed like they were often the odd ones out. Looking back, I realize that I was so focused on my training that I did not do enough to try to engage these women who all seemed smart and very capable; I regret that now. On average, though, these women seemed so different from the women I had met and worked with in the UNITAR Fellowship who had so much more confidence and who had taken leadership roles in their departments' activities. It is important to note that the Afghan MoF was one of the major supporters of the UNITAR Fellowship in the later years and many of the Fellows, both male and female, were MoF employees.

My experience working in the MoF shined a light on the impact the Fellowship had had on former female Fellows and Coaches working in the MoF. It was also clear, however, that there was a need within the MoF greater than what could be met through the Fellowship. To meet this need, I talked to Mariam and Mina about developing a mentoring program in the Afghan MoF, modeled in part on the UNITAR Fellowship and in part on a mentoring program I helped developed at the Texas Legislative Budget Board (Texas' equivalent of a ministry of finance) when I worked there. I believe that the Legislative Budget Board (LBB) mentoring program was one of the best initiatives I was involved in at the LBB. Over the years, more than a hundred people participated in the program which continues until today. The overall premise was for mid- and senior-level employees to mentor entry- and mid-level employees, respectively. Like the Fellowship, there was great value in peers learning from other peers as opposed to outsiders. Part of the mentoring program also included specialized skills building sessions. Also, much like the Fellowship, I believe as a mentor in the program I got as much out of it as any mentee. It was an excellent opportunity for me and other mentors to hone our management and leadership skills.

I talked to Mariam and Mina about developing a similar mentoring program in the MoF but incorporating more of the UNITAR Fellowship elements like team building, DISC tests, change management elements, etc. into the program. I helped Mina and Mariam develop a basic program concept and Mina was able to push the proposed program further forward but, regrettably, the program was never fully implemented in the ministry; it apparently was not the right time. It is unfortunate, though, that this women's mentoring program never took hold in the MoF. I think it could have been game-changing to help bring women like the young women I met out of their shells and empower them to play key roles in reform efforts in their country. If the program had been successful, it could have been implemented in other ministries in Afghanistan and perhaps in ministries and agencies in other countries as well. From my personal experience, in general, most government bodies do not often do enough to support women, particularly emerging women leaders, and a mentoring and leadership program like this could be as useful in Austin, Texas as it could be in Kabul, Afghanistan. Although the timing was not right in 2019 when we tried to implement the mentoring program, perhaps in the future a program like this incorporating key UNITAR Fellowship elements could be implemented in the MoF; it could be an important legacy project of the Fellowship.

It is not, however, just women who are at the beginning of their careers who need support in Afghanistan. I often heard from my friends like Mariam and Mina and others that what was also lacking was a good support structure and training for women who are in leadership and top management positions. There has never been a formalized program to help support these women who often find themselves in difficult, sometimes politically sensitive, situations in the ministry. In addition to a mentoring program for entry- and mid-level employees, it would also be very beneficial for the MoF and other ministries to implement an executive leadership program for women to provide them with key training needed to navigate difficult situations and build other hard and soft skills to give them the confidence they need to effectively lead and manage large ministry teams.

The simple reality, though, is across the globe, professional women face many challenges, particularly those in leadership positions and those with leadership ambitions. Sometimes, women are lucky enough to have the support of a program like the proposed executive leadership program or some other kind of mentoring program, but many do not have this kind of support and programs like this take time to implement. Also, for various reasons, women often lack the full support of their families and spouses to pursue leadership opportunities and to take on greater responsibilities. In these situations, women must look for support from others and who better to support them than their peers – other professional women and women in leadership positions. Women all over the world have been providing support and mentoring other women to achieve both personal and professional goals, mostly as part of informal networks. Sometimes, these networks are among office co-workers although at times that can be difficult given competition for positions and promotions. Other times, these informal networks are simply among friends with similar career and personal goals. For example, Mariam, Mina, and I have essentially formed our own support network to help each other move forward on professional and personal objectives such as pursuing master's degrees and new management opportunities. We also support each other and are there to listen when we are dealing with personal problems. We have basically created our own little mentoring network – supporting and learning from each other.

It occurred to Mariam and I last year that perhaps we could expand our small network into something larger by creating a UNITAR Fellowship Women's Alumni Network if there was enough interest from women who have participated in the Fellowship program. Given the challenges that many Afghan women face in both their professional and personal lives, we thought that it would be useful to have an informal mentoring network of colleagues and friends from the Fellowship to discuss shared interests and hardships, to be sounding boards for each other, and perhaps to come together collaboratively to discuss innovative solutions to shared problems that are faced. The alumni network could also be a way to share information on job opportunities and create connections for future job search needs. We also thought it would be a great way for old friends to re-establish contact with each other and for others to make new friends and create a new UNITAR community. We envision that if there is enough interest and support for something like this that the UNITAR Fellowship Women's Alumni Network could include a database of women alumni, the organization of virtual and, perhaps, later in-person events organized by alumni, speakers, and informal chats through breakout groups that could be modeled on the organization Lean In. We also envision international mentors and UNITAR resource people playing a role in this network if there is interest. At the end of the day, though, this network is about what the alumni see as needed most and the program would be designed around their needs and could certainly evolve over time to meet additional requirements. It should, if possible, though, be primarily self-run by the alumni themselves. If there is enough support for such a network, the first step will be to reach out to female alumni and access their level of interest in implementing such a program and do a sort of needs assessment to determine their priority interests. I think it would be wonderful to be part of such an initiative however this network develops. I cannot think of a better way to continue my UNITAR journey and to honor the Fellowship legacy.

The Impact of the Fellowship on
Women's Leadership and Development II
Mariam Ghaznavi[35]
To Be the Change I Want to See – A Quest to Transform
Myself and My Surroundings

I once read in a book the following lines, "I set out to change the world but failed. Then I set out again to change my country, but to no avail. I then decided to change my city and village but failed yet again. Finally, I decided I could change only myself. And then, suddenly, I changed the whole world."

This lesson has always been the philosophy grounding my behavior in almost any context. It has helped me overcome the external forces that could have pressed me to keep narrowing my vision of the world and myself.

After cherishing four years of academic, professional, and social activities related projects in 2014, I graduated from university. Due to the altering political environment because of the reduction of U.S. forces in Afghanistan, many social and academic projects were completed and closed, including my NGO's programs. Most of my friends and many of the people I knew within my network left the country. Left with overwhelmingly emotional, empty and lost feelings, I was curious about my next steps for capacity development programs and professional growth in my job and career.

---

[35] UNITAR AF 2015 Fellow, 2016 Coach; Mentor and Resource Person South Sudan Fellowship

I was a junior employee working in one of the U.S. Government Projects, with little knowledge about the higher-level issues, but highly motivated and excited about working with the senior staff, who had extensive business experience. Fortunately, my employer, who had had prior affiliations with UNITAR's professional development programs, provided me the opportunity to join the UNITAR Hiroshima Fellowship for Afghanistan in 2015. Since then, my association with the UNITAR programs for Afghanistan, South Sudan, and Iraq grew. I had the privilege to work with various programs in different capacities as a Fellow, Coach, International Mentor, and Resource Person, with distinction as a medalist for Afghanistan Sustainable Development Champion.

I started the program with the objective of developing my technical skills; however, to my surprise, the Fellowship experience turned out to be a combination of both technical and social development. At the end of the Fellowship, I knew how to design and run a project and make sure I had sponsors to get everyone's buy-in. We practiced team building with informed decision-making and awareness about different personalities, leading to reform and changes that were not significantly different from adaptive leadership. Not only that, we developed a sense of connection; I completed the Fellowship with the feeling that I was not alone in my journey, but had a robust support system, including the Mentors, Coaches, and other Fellows. They all joined the Fellowship from all walks of life with diverse backgrounds, experiences, and personalities.

I remember when one of the sessions started with an activity on DISC Personality Assessment, followed by a presentation on change management with emphasis on self-monitoring, ego states, and reaction versus response concepts of conflict management. It was not merely a routine lecture, but truly a transforming experience that affected my concept of self and surroundings to a large extent.

It broadened my knowledge of intra- and interpersonal dimensions of human behavior and developed tolerance and patience in me toward different personalities and ideologies.

Further, with this learning and my involvement in various other activities, I have come to acknowledge two things about myself and others. First, the ethnic make-up of my country is like a mosaic, each piece different in size, shape, and color from another, which readily makes it hard to be synergized. Second, despite these very strong ethnic and cultural differences, I still observed unbelievable behavioral and preferential similarities among people from different ethnicities, genders, and cultures. During the Fellowship, when the teaming and grouping of Fellows and Coaches were announced, given the volatile and unpopular background of my countrymen concerning ethnic tolerance, team diversity seemed like a weakness in the beginning. It did not give me any much-needed motivation. However, to my surprise, the teams' rapport and performance were phenomenal. I was overwhelmed by the harmony created by the teammates from different ages and gender groups, nationalities, and ethnic backgrounds creating such a beautiful and mesmerizing whole. The credit goes to the inspiring leadership, applaudable management of teammates, and collaborative teamwork as part of the team building exercises. Later on, I heavily capitalized on my learning in the next year's program when I was selected as a Coach in 2016. The feelings of a shared goal, teamwork, direction, and needed motivation to go on regardless of the hardships were beyond words.

It was amazing to see at the end how all the pieces came together so perfectly. The international Mentors and Resources volunteered their time and resources with dedication for years to support the Afghan Fellows. Likewise, to be part of a meaningful contribution, the Afghan Coaches made sure to keep everyone motivated and focused while also learning and practicing the art of coaching.

In 2015, when I traveled to Japan for the last phase of the Fellowship, I visited the Hiroshima Memorial Park, Peace Museum, and the Atomic Bomb Dome. What astonished me was that the people of Hiroshima had kept the remnants of war as a sign for peace. They believed that the Hiroshima and Nagasaki incidents must be lessons for their people to maintain peace. Another important aspect was that, soon after the destruction of Hiroshima and Nagasaki, people started building their country, out of love to rebuild their country. This is where I truly understood for the first time the human urge not only to manage change but to lead it. The main difference between what happened in Japan and what was happening in Afghanistan is that we didn't have a lot of our human capital and lost whatever was there to war. Therefore, there was a critical need for professional development programs like the Fellowship.

As part of the empowerment agendas, I was asked as a Coach to deliver a presentation on "Gender Biases." It amazed me how much I learned from the mentors throughout the process before delivering it to the Fellows. We all come with hidden biases, especially regarding gender and sex differences and the leadership attributes of the different genders. However, what fascinated me was that despite our diverse backgrounds, we still had a common interest – we all wanted to bring about positive changes in ourselves and in our societies. The training, though different and indirect in approach, was not limited only to the Fellows but to everyone, including Coaches and Mentors. Understanding the concepts about human behavior, different personalities, openness to different ideologies, and dealing with gender biases inspired me so much that I decided to be a future influencer and bring significant improvements in others' lives the way this experience had brought improvement in us. Now the question, which needed to be answered, was whether the realities and practices on the ground would be the same as the ones we had faced in the classrooms. To answer this, we required more experience and commitment.

The realization of self in a constantly changing and unstable society has been a challenging but beneficial process. This realization was further amplified when I was promoted as the first female Director in the Afghan Customs Department. I grew as a technical person and gained confidence in my abilities as a woman while learning that human effort is useless without a purpose and direction for the whole.

Initially, except for the immediate team with whom I worked, others did not have much confidence in my ability to lead an essential directorate. Despite my increasing enthusiasm for improvements, I was also overwhelmed with some significant challenges. I received much attention from everyone. Colleagues that I worked with closely gave advice and showed their willingness to assist. Despite their good intentions to help, there was a subconscious bias against women to take over challenging work. Some officers believed that my good manners and soft behavior made me incapable of dealing with the system's harsh realities. Some even referred to my promotion as a government measure to merely promote gender equality, overlooking my competence. However, with a little time, I was able to gain the trust and support of most.

To adjust to the male-dominated working culture, I wondered if it was necessary and proper to adopt some of the existing male-dominated working traits, i.e., authoritarianism and strictness in dealing with my employees. The advice I received from colleagues was to adopt a strict task-oriented authoritative position and keep my circle small to a group of heads of departments, who should deliver to the rest of the employees. Initially, it sounded appealing given my priorities and obligations and as a way to be able to fit into the working culture and professional protocols. However, as I reflected on my work, I realized that my long-term motive was beyond occupying a senior official position in the government. I realized that fitting overly into the system would only lead to holding authoritative positions and reinforcing the initial stereotype of women officials. That was never my aspiration, and maintaining a position was never the end. The job was a means to greater responsibilities.

I believed my work must never end with a few quick wins. Therefore, I started meeting everyone in my team and listened to their problems, which helped me support them and take over essential projects from there. In addition, I also met with clients and provincial officials as they walked into my office without prior confirmation for their pending issue. I took the first two months to learn about my surroundings and assess the existing problems. This was because when I joined the UNITAR Fellowship, the very first session started with organizational assessment, understanding that it is not realistic to think of a change without having insight into the problem, which requires an environmental assessment. Vision without practical tools will only remain an idea, and tools without vision leads to no direction. Two years have passed since my work with the Customs Department, but even now, not a month passes without a message from my former employees with good wishes or quick chats.

Working in more prominent organizations requires enormous teamwork, political support, and diverse leadership and working styles. As much as compassionate and empathetic leadership is needed to listen to individuals and move beyond general labeling as corrupt or incapable, employees also benefit from a stronger leadership, a revolutionary style, strict and dominating personalities that could push through good changes. Likewise, steadiness to assist with the change process and analysis and conscientiousness to ensure legal and technical breakthroughs, when everyone moves out of their comfort zones to implement their agendas, are also part of teamwork. Conscious and informed appointment of capable individuals in various positions would have been enough to pursue technical and procedural reforms or enhancement; however, structural and systemic reforms require political will and support at the country level. For women to pursue their careers and thrive in the government and in an insecure and unstable society, is it enough to be transparent and technical officials? Is it sufficient to bring youth into the government without providing systemic support and protection to them? Discussion of this subject is beyond the scope of this piece. My own experiences and reflections on my work are all that I can discuss here.

My countrywomen are resilient, passionate, committed to working, building their country, making a career, and carving their own destiny. What I see as a challenge is a lack of equal opportunity for women, from the grassroots level to the top leadership level. Second to that is a lack of proper mentorship and guidance. We are now provided the chance to work; of course, not all of us have this fundamental right and opportunity, but even those who have it need the right skills and support system to make our way up the ladder.

Direct employees and co-workers may or may not receive women well, regardless of their leadership and management styles; however, unfortunately, their merits have not significantly affected their status and promotion in the government. It does not add any value to the sustainability of their jobs, which could be replaced anytime. As much as a technical perspective is important for women to be able to stand by their counterparts' sides and professionally counter the stereotype that women are promoted as part of the government and international benchmarks for gender equality, while emphasizing their capability and the different perspectives that they can bring to the workplace, it is equally important to provide them the necessary support as they move up in their career ladders and encounter issues politically at the higher levels.

Despite the support from Afghanistan's Former First Lady for women's empowerment, there was never a systematic and strategic move or program to support them after their appointment in senior positions, support needed when there are hundreds of factors that pave the foundation for women officials' failure. As much as technical and professional development programs are necessary to enhance women's opportunities to grow in their working environment, there is also need for an executive leadership program that builds their political and strategic stamina.

Gender inequality and human rights as a whole and women's rights precisely, is a global issue, and Afghanistan is not an exception. I believe we still have a long way to go. As it is not very unusual for women to put in extra effort to be accepted, it is equally optimistic and evident that women can deal with heated issues. I don't recall the exact reason for the protest, but I remember a mob coming out on the streets in 2019 in the same area where my office was located. Everyone told us that it was unsafe to travel to work as there could be a potential attack on the government vehicles. I traveled to the office, where almost over 80 percent of the employees did not report to work as the roads were blocked, and it took them hours to get there through other routes. Women, who reported to work for a few hours a day, had issues with their families due to increased worry and frustration, and at the same time, they had to handle the work in the office. Balancing personal and work life at times of crisis and danger was not easy for anyone. However, they made it shoulder to shoulder with their male colleagues. We do not want sympathy and compliments for our work just because we are women. Women can deliver and should be treated as equals. In this walk, I want to make sure that I hold as many hands as I can.

Overall, this was not my first time experiencing all this. It is an unfortunate situation that women are not only looked down upon, but certain areas of normal work are considered impenetrable for us too. Within less than two years of working in my position, it was pleasantly joyous to hear colleagues in the leadership meetings say, "It would be great to bring in more women into Customs' in junior and senior positions."

Through my years of work, these are the type of statements I want more women to hear when they are in meeting rooms. This is the mindset I want to create and the legacy I want to leave behind for my country's women through what I do, to make sure that no work area is considered impenetrable for us or to say that women "cannot do." I know my work is a droplet in the ocean, but I genuinely believe that droplets make the mighty ocean.

Many structural, technical, policy, and value-based issues directly or indirectly lead to women's challenges to thrive. There was a point when I was thinking about where all those efforts went. As officials are replaced, visions and directions change too. Wheels are reinvented again and again rather than institutionalizing the reforms. These come from a culture of quick wins to receive incentives and legitimize one's positions, or to maintain status in politically complex environment.

Every time I have taken a job in the public or private sector, I put more effort into delivering on my responsibilities for two important reasons: to reshape mindsets and leave a legacy behind. However, one thing that I regret is I could have done more work in gender empowerment. I did not do enough to provide support to other women while I was working at the Customs. My work and policy formulation for capacity-building was more about merit-based systems and procedures. Given my own experiences and struggles, I always believed women should earn the position, respect, and seniority. I still believe in that; however, to ensure women are ready to compete as part of the merit-based programs, they should be provided the environment and support to be prepared to compete. It is always easy to complain or criticize but equally challenging to look into ones' shortcomings and admit them. We may blame the state, but we should not forget that each and every one of us has a role in shaping that state. An honest realization is never too late to direct us into a meaningful path. I could have helped provide equal opportunities to them to further their knowledge and skills. As much as I regret that, I know that I cannot go back and fix it, however, I do not lose hope on doing better going onwards.

Reckoning about my experience in the government and realization of my shortcomings reminds me of the adaptive leadership lesson, "Balcony Analogy." When you are in the dance field, you play and dance along with everyone and feel the heat; however, sometimes you have to sit back on the balcony and see others dancing. When many are dancing, some may sit back and check out others silently. Not only do you not feel the heat, you are also able to see how everyone else dances or quits. Likewise, every sit- or set-back in life is not a failure. Sometimes it is about getting ready for doing something more meaningful, if not more significant.

In 2019, when I moved to the Ministry of Industries and Commerce (MoIC) as Development and Consumer Protection Director, there was only one other female Director besides me. Unlike the usual perception of women – competitiveness, we were highly and genuinely supportive of each other. In the minimal time, in addition to having a seat at the leadership table, we became the vocal voices. We had never felt that powerful and supported before, with due respect to all our male colleagues, who were also genuinely respectful.

Whereas women in leadership struggle with political complexities and fight for their rights, women at the mid- and operational levels face classically similar problems but in different forms. In MoIC, I developed a close professional relationship with the women in my team who worked as officials and supporting staff. I used to dedicate one hour twice a week to each of them individually, to learn about their background, hardships, concerns, and ambitions. Based on my learning from my experience with Jennifer and my UNITAR mentors, I needed to build trust before developing the same relationship with my employees and eventually work with them based on their availability, preparedness, and involvement level. I did not want to move ahead with my own views and standards of how professional women should perform at work. When I asked them why none of them chose to meet me before I asked for a meeting, their response was they no longer relied on or trusted the system as Directors were replaced quite frequently in the government. Every Director, in the beginning, came in with promises, but they could not even secure their own jobs. I did not have any answer for them. Deep inside, I knew that they all were affected by the overall governance. However, I tried to tell them how relationships evolved in the digital world, regardless of our positions. But unfortunately, they were the working class who earned 100 to 200 USD a month and could not afford the internet expenses when they had other priorities. They needed support within the system that could help them learn and be promoted.

At the same time, they shared their happiness about seeing a woman leading the Directorate. They had higher expectations from a woman leader in understanding their psychological and social issues. Each one of them had a different story — a widow whose priority was to provide better educational opportunities for her children, a woman close to her retirement, who worked as a cleaner and lived alone with her husband, a divorced woman with a background of torture and abuse, who did not earn enough to raise her son with a better life but did not lose hope and was pursuing her higher education, a woman in her 50s who sacrificed her life to serve her mother who passed away and a paralyzed older brother, who was unable to establish his own family either, and two newly married mothers with young children, trying to balance work and personal life balance. Given all the issues, they still wanted to be promoted, learn, and be valued. They all complained about being invisible. No one saw them, listened to them, or helped them. I still think about them. They are the real faces of resilience.

As much as I am happy to see how we all always find meaning in our ways of living, it also scares me when I think of the internalization of the unjust norms, that may become a new normal for the might through the reinforcement of the conservative image of women socially, when no one will dare to raise their voices. I hope as the new peace deal is in progress, the marginalized and vulnerable groups should not be seen merely as a number, but living individuals with fundamental rights. I hope we will not go backward when it comes to human ' and specifically, women's rights, but we should also be wary of not allowing the internalization of sexism socially, which is silent but more powerful. It is not only about women having jobs, but actual presence both intellectually and practically – a real empowerment, not symbolic representations.

Through all this, Jennifer Fox, my Mentor in the UNITAR Fellowship, provided me selfless support throughout my journey. I have known Jennifer since 2017, and since then she has been always there to provide support during the good and bad times. We make many connections, but only with a few of them, do we maintain a long-term positive relationship. Jennifer is a walking-talking inspiration, who always led through concrete action when we needed her the most. Even though Jennifer served the Ministry of Finance through U.S. Government Funded Projects, we never heard about each other until we met in the UNITAR Fellowship. After I was promoted, Jennifer was no longer working for our Ministry; however, she still introduced me to her colleagues at the U.S. Treasury, who were willing to voluntarily provide support in different areas given their expertise. She lives in the U.S. and traveled to Africa for work, yet despite the time difference, she always made time to talk to me whenever I got overwhelmed, lost, or frustrated with the challenges. She still hopes for the establishment of fundamental projects, that can have meaningful contribution in the capacity-building and systems development for her Afghan Fellows. Looking at her never-ending motivation and enthusiasm for giving back keeps me motivated too. She is a brilliant mentor, good friend and beautiful human being. Jennifer and I hope to extend this into a bigger women's support system network where we women, should feel supported by and connected to each other and be able to give back better to everyone.

At the end, I would like to extend my gratitude to UNITAR for supporting the program in Afghanistan and paving the foundation for us to make lifetime connections and friends – a safe network that we still feel happy when we think of having each other in addition to the capacity- building programs. Sabahuddin Sokout, who leads the UNITAR programs in Afghanistan, was a great support in keeping everything going so perfectly. Sokout is such a positive influence on all of us. Besides, I am happy to utilize this opportunity to thank my Mentors Michael Fors, Shona Welsh, Tham Chien Ping, Rama Kannan, Kelly Dugan, Humaira Kamal, and Rahul Gopalkrishnan, who were always there to help. Especially Rama and Rahul, when I was lost in my own world of fights and issues, never forgot to check on me. I am always so grateful for making good friends – Mina, Qane, Didar, and Azmat. And finally, Nigel Gan, a perfectly nice, open, and understanding face in the UNITAR office, who made the programs possible without us facing any issues. With UNITAR, we not only have a professional connection, but also an emotional one that will continue.

The Women Building Afghanistan – A Multilayered Affair?

Rama Kannan[36]

November 2010, Hiroshima: It was Zakia Nouri's[37] turn to present, and I was sitting at the edge of my seat – she took the microphone and started speaking, words rolling off her mouth confidently and persuasively. It was clear she knew her part and the entire audience, that included her fellow Afghan civil servants and the UNITAR folks, were mesmerized by her quiet authority. She finished her part, handed over to the next person in her group and then it was time for Tamana[38], the other project leader and young professional woman in the group to wrap up the presentation. Tamana presented just as confidently, asking for approval of the project and it was clear from the reactions, that they had won the hearts and minds of the audience! The project that they were presenting was on Fixed Asset Management Training for Da Afghanistan Bank Finance Unit Staff.

---

[36] Rama Kannan is a Master Coach, Mentor and Advisor in both corporate and social sectors to formulate and achieve goals for their holistic success. She served as AF Mentor from 2009 to 2018.

[37] Zakia Nouri was Administrator at the Director General Office of CSMD at the Independent Administrative Reform and Civil Service Commission (IARCSC) of Afghanistan. From 2006 to 2009, she was Administrative Manager and Senior Translator in the HR Policy and Legislative Department.

[38] Tamana Naderi in 2010 was working as an Accountant in the CFO Department of Da Afghanistan Bank in 2010, having previously been employed as an Administration Assistant at Bakhtar University.

Project Goals and Objectives were:

True valuation of assets in the Da Afghanistan Bank and greater efficiency and effectiveness in use of the organization's resources (fixed asset). Following were the objectives of the project.

1. *Production of clear, comprehensive, and on-time information on fixed asset*

2. *Availability of a comprehensive database categorized to calculate asset's depreciation rates*

3. *50% decrease in expenses through maximizing the lifetime of the fixed assets*

4. *Ability of line manager to make on-time decisions on auctions, disposal, and other activities in regard to asset management*

5. *The Bank to have a proper fixed asset management database containing data/information of organization assets*

6. *The bureaucratic manual system to be replaced by a standard up-to-date computerized software system*

There were a few questions asked, which the group, with the two ladies pitching in, answered to the satisfaction of the audience. Their group got the loudest applause and everyone in the Jury gave them a green signal! I had goose bumps and clapped till my hands hurt, mistily watching them, and feeling utterly thrilled! When I look back, I can say with some certainty that my future career as a Coach was inspired and born at that moment, in that sense of fulfillment I experienced then.

I thought back to the start of my association with the Fellowship almost a year back – I was based in Singapore, and someone from the Singapore International Foundation (SIF) had connected, asking if I would be interested to be a Mentor for the UNITAR Hiroshima Fellowship Program for Afghanistan – it sounded so unique, I said yes without knowing anything about it. I met Margaret, the head of the SIF program for the Fellowship, got even more convinced and joined it with pleasant anticipation. I met the group I was assigned to – Group 9 – in a video conference call, where I saw the two girls for the first time, along with the other group members. They didn't speak much then, and not much either when I finally got to meet them in Abu Dhabi for the first workshop. There were not many women in the program, around 10%, and most of the women wore Hijab and spoke little.

We had many group meetings and the two girls (they were in their early twenties, so I could only think of them as girls) stayed quiet and didn't contribute much, but they appeared smart, visibly understood the issues well, and the little they said without raising their eyes made a lot of sense. I thought to myself, "I want to know more about these girls, and I wish they would speak more assert-ively," and wondered what I could do. Over the next few days that we were in Abu Dhabi, I spent a lot of time with them informally and got to really enjoy their company. I was impressed with their knowledge and understanding. I was convinced then that the girls had to be part of the final presentation, and I was going to try and have them show their extensive potential to the whole. I realized over the course of the next many months that Afghan women were not naturally the quiet withdrawing types; they had immense strength and confidence, and didn't shy away from expressing their opinions! It was just that the Taliban over the many years of oppression had tried to suppress the public demonstration of these strengths. However, it seemed that these young women were ready to own these strengths in public and participate in rebuilding their country.

I realized later that something that we started in Abu Dhabi that year helped in that journey! And it became a tradition. At each workshop the groups would present a cultural program, and during one such evening as part of the Afghan presentation, the performance ended with the Afghan men dancing the fabulous Atan! The women were dressed in rich traditional clothes and looked stunning but did not dance – I asked them if they did not dance at all, and Tamana said of course we do but only among the women. On an impulse, I asked if I could see them do so, and she immediately agreed and got all the ladies in the group to consent as well. Within a short time, she had organized the whole event and invited me to one of the girl's rooms later that night. What a memorable experience! The girls were a different species from what I had seen of them so far!! They laughed happily, spoke loudly and animatedly, and moved and spoke with so much confidence and assurance. They blasted me with questions about my life and work, and how I came to be doing what I was doing. They shared what their life at work and home was like, how they were expected to behave. They danced, they sang – Bollywood songs mostly – and dragged me in to join them. I had mentioned this meeting to Humaira, the UNITAR Program Leader, and asked her to join too. She did and the two South Asian women – the Pakistani Humaira and the Indian me – kindred spirits and South Asian "Music Aficionados" sang along with the Afghans, laughed at their pronunciations of the Bollywood lyrics, and transcended boundaries through mutually shared passions and experiences.

We did this every year – Humaira and I were constant, we had other women Mentors join in too. New woman participants shared their stories, we shared ours, we laughed and bonded, and in the next days, the women were more relaxed in the meetings, smiled at us and each other, and became more confident! One of my fondest memories is how in one of the years, late one night after the singing and swapping stories, some of the women asked if they could go out in the streets in Hiroshima – it was past midnight – and we all happily went out. We walked by the river, some started singing and all started dancing, forgetting everything and just being happy. For the girls and myself, that memory is etched as the highlight of the program!

There are so many other ways that the Fellowship has enriched my life, and the amazing perspectives and learnings include many stories that are etched in my mind and heart:

1. The video calls with our groups in the initial years were held at the UN office. One time in the first year when I had gone to the UN office, the group was late to join the call from Kabul, and I waited with impatience for the group to join in, planning in my head that I would tell them why discipline and commitment were important. The Afghan Resource Person finally joined after 25 minutes and with apologies said they had had a bomb go off in the heart of the city, there was chaos, and the Fellows were not able to reach the office for the call, and he had reached there with great difficulty because we were waiting. My heart stopped, and I felt ashamed. I had harbored harsh thoughts about them, cocooned in the privileged position I was in. Never again did I question their ethics or wait in impatience for any call. It also taught me not to pre-judge anything.

2. Every year in Hiroshima we had a survivor give a talk and share their experience of the nuclear bombing. I was in tears the first time I heard an 85-year-old survivor talk and share about her entire family being wiped away. When one of the young Afghans asked me about it, I mentioned I didn't know what it was like for them. They have had their share of the tragedies – he told me calmly, "Yes, my father died of a bombing 6 months ago." Another shared, "Our tears have dried up, we've all had many losses." I truly did not know

what to say or how to console them, and just looked at them through tear-filled eyes.

3. After the talk by the Hiroshima survivors, everyone would gather in a room and be asked to write what they thought and share if they wanted to. I thought I was going to hear sad stories, people saying they were depressed, seeing and hearing the survivor. I was in for a huge surprise – some had written poetry, some a note to themselves, some their ideas. ALL of them positive, all in essence saying, that if after the unspeakable tragedy of the bombing, Hiroshima could be rebuilt and achieve huge success, they had belief that Afghanistan could be as well. The positivity they showed imbued me with confidence and gave me a path to look for the pluses in everything.

There are many such stories that I experienced, learned, and wondered about. It was always the people, the wonderful people that I met who I remember with much fondness. Nassrine, the architect of the program, is a true visionary, wise and warm! Michael, who taught many of the courses and who used his holidays from Microsoft to come and teach for the two weeks. Berin, who was in charge from the Hiroshima Office and who took it upon himself to show us around. Sokout, a Fellow of the first cohort himself but later the UNITAR representative of the Fellowship in Afghanistan, who worked hard behind the scenes and personified servant leadership. And most important of all, Humaira, who ran the program for most of the years and was so invested in the Fellowship and with such passion – she ended up with tears at the close of the Fellowship every single year. There were many others too, instructors, other wonderful co-Mentors from around the world, and the people from the Hiroshima Office. Humaira, Michael, and I resonated the most and spent many evenings giggling and laughing over some innocuous thing, the special bond that we share will always endure.

10 years as a Mentor with the Fellowship has undoubtedly been one of the best things in my life. I have seen the Fellows grow enormously over the 10 years. Initially as Mentor, I used to be constantly in touch with the Fellows, looking at their projects, editing, asking questions; the Coaches and ARPs in Afghanistan would be a little hesitant and keep checking with the Mentors. By the last year of the Fellowship, the Fellows were far more assured, and they knew what was needed to be done for the projects. The Mentors did not have to chase them but only nudge them occasionally. The Fellows made great presentations. The local Coaches and Mentors (many of them had gone through the Fellowship as Fellows) guided them wonderfully; big changes were seen among the women as well – the women I had seen in my first cycle were mostly shy and quiet and would not talk in the groups and hesitated to present. By the last year, not only were the woman Fellows more confident and as ready to talk as the men, but there were also many woman Coaches, who did not hesitate to question and advise the men (Fellows) when needed! The Fellowship has produced many senior officials in the Afghan government. To our joy it includes a few women, like Ms. Lema Khurram and Ms. Mariam Ghaznavi, Directors in the Afghan government. With the progress, it felt only natural when the Fellowship ended, even though most of the people associated with it felt sad.

I have grown with the Fellowship: I have wider perspectives and more belief in people, have built great bonds, and have a better understanding about myself and what gives me joy and purpose. That has led to the successful coaching career that I now have! I feel very lucky to have had the opportunity to be connected to the Afghan Fellowship and to the wonderful people, who were a part of it.

There is indeed a long way to go for the country. I tear up every time when I hear of a bomb or any atrocity there, and yes, there is huge corruption. Yet I know there are capable people and am confident they will find their way some day.

Is it possible to feel deep connections with a country you have never even visited? Every time I hear from one of the Fellows or anyone associated with the program, I feel very happy. When Afghanistan does well in cricket (even when it beat India a year back), I am thrilled! I follow with keen interest the political and economic affairs of the country, and whenever I hear of a bomb attack in Afghanistan, my heart sinks. I contact people I know, and I send a silent prayer to keep people safe. Afghanistan is deep in my heart and will remain so always.

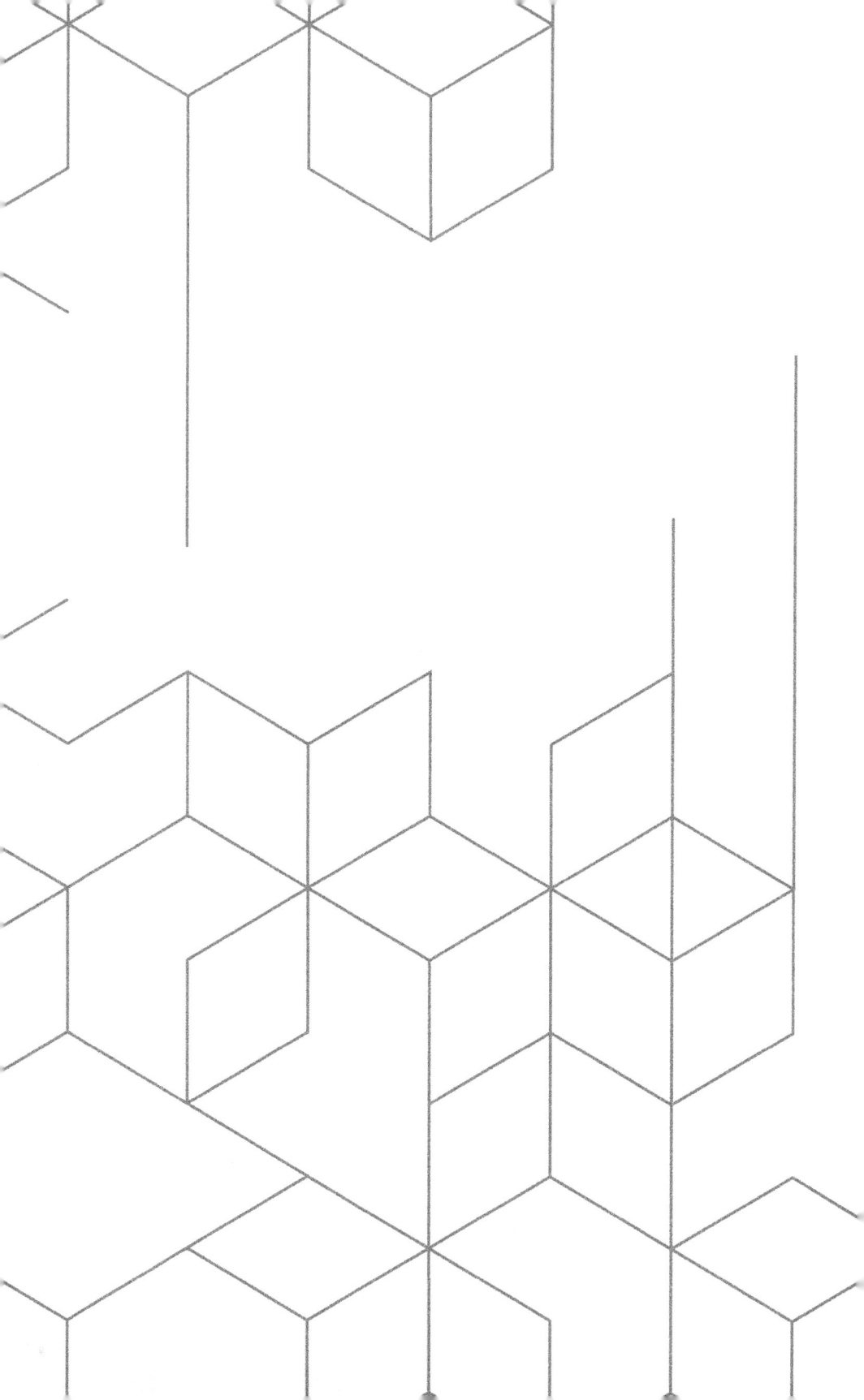

PART IIIB

IN MEMORIAM – EARLY
VOICES NO LONGER
WITH US

سوله

انی

صلح

ماني

صلح

平和

Editors' Note:

Over the years more people than we could ever thank, or even name, gave their all to the Fellowship. They gave of their time, their know-how and resources, their networks, their knowledge, wisdom, and life experiences. They influenced and were, in turn, influenced by the Afghan Fellows. Some have left us already, a few far too early, and their names will appear and reappear throughout the pages of this book.

Here we pay tribute to three — three pillars, in truth pioneers of the Fellowship, three individuals who articulated and formulated the core concepts that carried the program over a decade and a half. Their inputs have marked and transformed the Fellowship. But it has been their very presence — their moral authority, their intellectual rigor, and their human generosity — that have impressed and transformed so many of us.

Nassrine Azimi and Humaira Khan-Kamal

سوله

ملح

انی

مانی

صلح 平和

Jonathan Moore
By Nassrine Azimi

I first met Ambassador Jonathan Moore in 1998. At the time I was chief of the UNITAR New York Office. He was in the city to present the book he had just completed as editor on behalf of the International Committee of the Red Cross (ICRC), entitled *Hard Choices: Moral Dilemmas in Humanitarian Intervention*. I had a keen interest in the topic, having recently worked on two books about the genocides in Cambodia and Rwanda. I did not know Jonathan personally, but everything he said at the book event that day, the way he formulated his ideas, deeply impressed, and moved me. I recall at times he would be on the verge of tears, at times cantankerous and unrelenting. Throughout, his intellectual brilliance, but also his humanism, shone through. Not for Jonathan, any of the platitudes.

Very quickly we became friends, and quite naturally my team and I turned to him when a few years later the chance to design a training program for Afghan civilians on behalf of UNITAR's Hiroshima Office arose. Few in the United States could have brought us a richer, broader professional experience in the international development realm — throughout his intense and colorful career, Jonathan had served six US administrations, been an Associate Attorney General of the United States, acted as the State Department's Director of the Bureau of Refugee Programs, and later Ambassador to the UN Economic and Social Council. By the time we met, he was mostly involved in academia, nurturing younger scholars and practitioners. His main base was Harvard University, where he had established and directed for many years the Shorenstein Center at the Kennedy School of Government.

We made two trips together to Afghanistan, the first in 2002 as a fact-finding mission, the second in 2006, to assess the impact of the Fellowship. Everyone we visited — from officials at the fledgling new government to the UN and the EU, at NGOs and the diplomatic community — there were people who knew and admired him. I was nominally the head of the mission, but it was clearly Jonathan's reputation and his intellectual and moral authority that opened us doors. We conducted many interviews, and each time I was impressed by his diligence and focus, listening intently and asking questions with great precision and clarity. Following him around was like a masterclass in international humanitarian work. The Afghan Fellows just loved him, and he visibly returned the sentiments. His depth of feelings, and his ability to articulate the importance of the work we were all doing, fired up all of us in the team, young and old alike.

Of the many shared experiences two personal images, snapshots of the man of heart that he was, stand out for me.

The first was during our initial mission to Afghanistan in 2002: we had been visiting an elementary school in the outskirts of Kabul. After years of war, nothing was left of the original buildings, but the undeterred teachers had all the students spread out in one large circle outdoors, delineated groups by class and seated them on blue plastic sheets laid out on the dirt floor. For each "classroom" there was a blackboard of sorts, standing precariously by the rare trees that marked what seemed an otherwise desolate landscape. And yet what energy! It felt like a real school, with boisterous, giggling students — many diligently writing, despite half broken pencils and shabby notebooks, with utterly palpable *joie de vivre*. We could not resist sharing in their happiness. I turned to say something to Jonathan, and saw him standing spellbound in the middle of the school encampment watching a class of the youngest students, tears flowing down his cheeks.

Another image: it was 2006. By that time, the security situation in Afghanistan had deteriorated significantly. The initial wave of hope and enthusiasm had passed — and the realities of governance, the shortcomings of national capacities, and the distractions of international assistance were becoming more evident by the day. Many Afghans had become unhappy, and quite a few had again turned to arms. During our stay, an incident with the US military brought violence to the streets, and international staff on temporary missions were asked to leave or take precautions. I quickly started working on repatriating members of our mission, and ultimately only Jonathan, my colleague Sharapiya Kakimova, and I remained in Kabul, asked to remain at the World Bank compound until further notice. Jonathan was supremely calm throughout — he had seen far worse. But at one point I found him sitting alone, on a plastic chair in the garden. He looked uncharacteristically despondent. I asked him what was wrong. He looked at me with tearful eyes and said, simply, of his wife of 50 years: "When I left Boston this time, I forgot to tell Katie how much I love her."

Jonathan Moore passed away in March 2017, pained and worried like the rest of us by trends in Afghanistan, but never hopeless, never giving up.

> "*Looking to a future containing promise, hope, danger and uncertainty, the key resources of Afghanistan nation-building lie in the willingness of its people to be forbearing, persistent, unified, and resilient. This social psychology is essential, as in any prodigious human endeavor...continuing to do what can be done as well as possible, not being intimidated by the imposing difficulties, and respecting the need for time. Capacity-building, training at different levels and in a variety*

of formats and focuses, and where Afghans and internationals collaborate, is a critical component, helping to develop both the competence and confidence to be able to continue to move forward."

Jonathan Moore, former US Ambassador to the United Nations and Senior Special Fellow, UNITAR Hiroshima Office, in "Post-Conflict Reconstruction in Afghanistan," notes prepared in the context of the Hiroshima Fellowship assessment, October 2006.

Ambassador Jonathan Moore during the initial Fellowship fact-finding mission to Afghanistan (2002, above and center), and second evaluation mission (below, 2006)

سوله

صلح

مانی

平和

Iqbal M. Khan
By Nassrine Azimi

How to describe Professor Iqbal Khan? Those who met him would know immediately that they were in the presence of a very special person, and those who had only heard of him invariably wanted to meet him. His charisma, brilliance, and humanism were palpable. When he spoke, you knew it was from the heart, and from deep personal experience. And when you spoke, you knew that he would be listening, really listening.

Quite early on in the Fellowship, Humaira and I realized that modules on business management and entrepreneurship were key but lacking. The Fellows needed to better understand, and train themselves with an eye to the real world, not just focused on lofty but unpractical concepts. Yet we had no budget, and no experts we could turn to. I pleaded with Humaira, to ask her father — Professor Khan — if he would be willing to help the Fellowship. Despite a hectic schedule, he accepted right away.

Iqbal Khan's experiences were extraordinary — precisely what the Fellowship needed. He had studied, researched, and taught entrepreneurship in many universities and research centers in Pakistan and around the world, established and directed banks, worked for international organizations, and advised national governments and corporations on business strategies and entrepreneurship. He had also found the time to write and edit prolifically, including publications on women and enterprise, and social entrepreneurship

—works that encouraged not just the Afghans, but many women and men across the Islamic world and beyond.

He joined us as one of the lecturers in Kabul in November 2004, and then as workshop leader in August 2005, and it is difficult to describe the ease with which the Afghan Fellows took to him, the depth of their attachment, and the power of his teaching and also his empathy. The management examples he used in his training were not from textbooks but from his own direct experiences — applicable to the milieu he knew the Afghans could recognize and maybe one day emulate.

A small compact man, Pathan by birth, debonair in appearance and exuding a kind of benevolent intelligence and the refinement so typical of the residents of Lahore, Iqbal's sense of humor and wit often made me crack up. During one Kabul workshop, we all stayed in what had been a former residence of an Afghan family, a dark, gloomy house, which had seen happier days but now resembled the homes described in the novel The Kite Runner. Due to the security situation and the day's exhaustion, every night our group of lecturers would eat together at the house. These would have been rather somber gatherings were it not for Iqbal, who kept the fire and light at those dinners. I now recall those evenings with great nostalgia —thanks to him our conversations became lighter, richer, scintillating — in short so very deep and cultured, exactly in the image of the man himself.

Iqbal passed away in 2015.

> *"I would like to end by saying that there are lessons to be learnt from every culture, every society, and every thought that has been spelled out. We need to devote our scholars and researchers and thinkers to those areas of requirements that our societies need. We need to empower enlightened intellectuals to look for ways to come out of the mess that we have created for ourselves. We need a lot of research in*

almost every area and consequently in the area of economics and finance and banking. We must know what we possess and understand it. It's only after that are we able to develop new ideas. Otherwise, we have no claim on anything. And in the words of Goethe "What we do not understand, we do not possess."

Iqbal M. Khan, a paper Small Enterprises and Modes of Financing shared as part of project funding module in training

Iqbal, Kabul November 2004

Kabul August 2005

سوله
مانی
صلح
صلح
平和

Howard Lamb
By Humaira Khan-Kamal

On his first trip to Swat, Pakistan (near the Afghan border), Dr. Howard Lamb and his wife and partner Ms. Sue Lamb, were commissioned to conduct a workshop on leadership and organizations. Howard fit right in from day one. With his Afghanesque abrasive straight talk, his ability to laugh at himself, his generosity of knowledge, his faith in the power of storytelling, and above all his grumpiness and absolute amenability to being managed by his soft-spoken wife (like any red-blooded Pathan or Afghan!), it was obvious that he had found his "other people" in this region. The first time they started calling him Pagal Gorah (Crazy White Man) was when he tried on an Afghan turban and shawl in one of the bazaars in Swat and started twirling in circles. From the mountains of Swat, it was a natural progression for him and Sue to accept the invitation by Nassrine and I to become a part of the core team charged with developing and delivering the Fellowship for Afghanistan.

Howard Lamb specialized in organization development and management with special attention to organizational change in both the public and private sectors. This seemed to be exactly what the Afghans needed. He was passionate about interpersonal relations, group dynamics, consulting skills and training of trainers. All of this could of course be offered by any number of equally qualified experts, but what made him perfect for this very hands-on project was the ability to cut through the cacophony of voices on nation-building, global games, and politics – and understand that to make any impact, our project had to be focused on one Afghan and one small project at a time, and to stay with them for as long as we possibly could. This fortunate consensus among the Fellowship core team and the Afghans themselves came through in many of the program mechanisms that were introduced by Howard and Sue, and which became part of the signature design of the Fellowship.

All the Fellows who had the chance to learn from him or be his mentees felt the warmth and ownership of the relationship, so much so that any time that any of the alumni visited the US, they reached out to Howard and Sue, visited them in person if possible and always stayed in touch. Till the time that he passed away, Howard's connection to the Fellowship and deep commitment to the Afghans and their plans and projects was always an important theme of his and Sue's life. The mutual warmth between the Fellows and him came through equally during in-person workshops in Hiroshima, Kabul or Dehradun, or online early morning webinars from Washington DC. He clearly told me on a number of occasions though, that distance learning forums were no substitute for him being in the same room with the Fellows, and feeling their energy and passion for rebuilding their country. The Afghans, needless to say, had the same feelings.

Howard passed away in 2017.

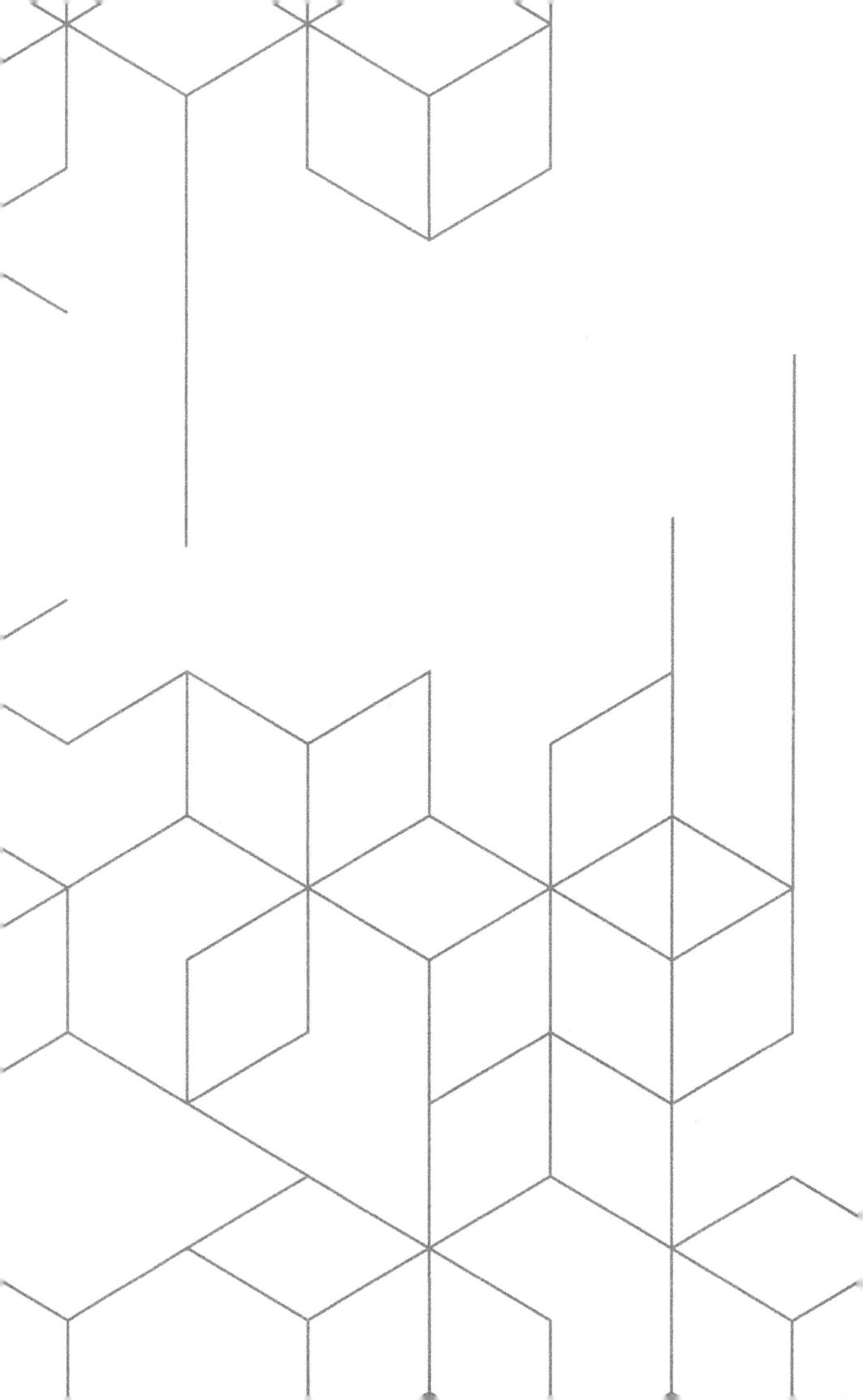

PART IV
THE FELLOWSHIP'S
MANY LEGACIES

The Fellowship's Legacy and Impact on
Other UNITAR programs
Interview with Mihoko Kumamoto[39]

In your assessment what is the impact and meaning of the Afghan
Fellowship, for Afghanistan and for Hiroshima?

UNITAR opened its third office, after Geneva and New
York, in Hiroshima in 2003. Hiroshima is historic and
unique: as a city that has experienced atomic bombing in
1945 and was reborn from its ashes into a beautiful, modern city, Hiroshima has witnessed first-hand the darkness as well as the brightness of humankind. Based in this
symbolic place, the UNITAR Hiroshima Office strives to
serve countries in difficult situations such as countries
affected by conflict and least developed countries.

The Hiroshima Office started the Afghanistan Fellowship
Program as one of its first projects in 2003. Many dedicated
professionals were involved in the design and launch of
the program including Mr. Jonathan Moore (Former US
Ambassador to the United Nations), Professor Akio Inoue
(Tenri University), Prof. David Eaton (Natural Resource
Policy Studies, University of Texas at Austin), Dr. Howard
and Mrs. Sue Lamb (Organizational Development and
Leadership, Lamb & Lamb Associates), Dr. Nassrine
Azimi (Former Director, and Senior Advisor UNITAR),

---

[39] Director, UNITAR Hiroshima Office 2014 to date

Ms. Humaira-Khan Kamal (UNITAR AF Team Leader), and Ms. Sharapiya Kakimova (UNITAR AF Team). With support from many people in Afghanistan, Japan, and other parts of the world, the Afghanistan Fellowship became the Hiroshima Office's flagship program. It now boasts almost 500 alumni. From the start, the program was designed and implemented to enhance local ownership – a critical element to make it impactful. It took a demand-driven approach, was built on close consultations with local stakeholders, and engaged local people in curriculum design and delivery. For the people of Hiroshima, supporting Afghanistan, a country that has suffered from conflict for so many years, makes moral sense and is a source of pride. And it helps Hiroshima establish itself as a world center for peace.

What was your goal and vision for the continued success of the program as it progressed under your leadership in its last five years? How did you need to change the Afghanistan Fellowship approach and strategies given the new Afghan environment and needs and the geo-political priorities and financial realities of this period?

I had two visions. The first one was to replicate and scale-up the success model of the Afghanistan Fellowship in other countries. With the generous support from the people of Hiroshima Prefecture and Japan, the Hiroshima Office has been able to expand our activities to other conflict and post-conflict countries such as South Sudan and Iraq over the past five years. Our programs in these countries have adopted key elements from the Afghanistan Fellowship, tailored to the local contexts.

My second vision was to transition the Afghanistan Fellowship to the next stage. When I joined the Hiroshima Office, more than ten years had already passed since the program was initially designed. Over these years, the situation in the country has changed significantly, and so has demand from the people of Afghanistan. While maintaining the Fellowship's success factors, it was important to match our services to the constantly evolving situation and demands of the country. After consultations with local partners, we launched the next phase of the Afghanistan Fellowship in late 2019, focusing more on leadership and innovation. Unfortunately, the Covid-19 pandemic has forced us to slow down the activities, but we hope to resume activities sometime in 2021.

Tell us about your experience during your visits to Kabul and how it informed your strategic vision for programs for Afghanistan.

I try to visit Afghanistan at least once a year so that I can meet with stakeholders including ministries, universities, bilateral and international organizations, and UNITAR alumni and hear from them directly their experience with the Hiroshima Office programs and any suggestions they may have. Everything we do – the overall strategy and programs – must be aligned with the priorities of our beneficiaries. This is the only way for us to contribute in a meaningful and sustainable way.

Each visit to Kabul has been memorable and eye opening. People were extremely hospitable. Almost everyone I met invited me to their home, and I needed to decline their offers because of my schedule. I also met many brilliant people who were articulate, had exposure to different countries, and had great ideas and visions for the future of Afghanistan. Many of them were young. I truly enjoyed having in-depth discussions with them on challenges and opportunities and how to shape a better future for Afghanistan.

On the other hand, I saw first-hand the extent and magnitude of the challenges people in the country face every day. I visited a hotel in central Kabul with beautiful, well-kept rose gardens, which was vibrant with many customers. A few days after my departure, the hotel was attacked by a militia group, causing high casualties. The capital was densely populated and suffered from severe pollution. Unemployment, corruption, inequality, and many other issues are hindering sustainable, equitable growth of the country. Covid-19 poses another serious risk in addition to many other risks that the country has already faced. Afghanistan is filled with opportunities and challenges, which drives home to me the importance of continued support from our office.

As development professionals, what can we learn overall from the program about conflict/post-conflict capacity-building interventions? What can we do better, or differently, when a similar intervention or partnership is needed?

I have had the privilege of working for many countries in different parts of the world through my 20-year career with the United Nations. One of the key lessons I learned from serving in conflict and post-conflict countries is that there are additional risks, and we need to stay flexible to respond swiftly to changing conditions. In a conflict situation, the situation can change suddenly. For example, the Hiroshima Office has been supporting South Sudan since 2015. In 2017, a few days before we planned to hold a workshop in Juba, the capital of South Sudan, major violence erupted that caused a high number of casualties. We immediately coordinated with local stakeholders, changed plans, and rescheduled our workshop for everyone's safety.

Another lesson is the importance of inclusiveness. Inequality based on gender, ethnicity, location, and other aspects tends to be more pronounced in conflict and post-conflict countries. It is therefore crucial to invite participants from various backgrounds, so that we are not contributing to inequality, and we give a safe space to learn from each other.

What lessons were learned when UNITAR applied the Afghanistan Fellowship model to other conflict or post-conflict countries such as Iraq and South Sudan? For example, lessons of applicability, cultural nuances, stage of conflict...

> As I mentioned previously, we have replicated the Afghanistan Fellowship model in Iraq and South Sudan. The keys to success remain the same: we need to be demand-driven, enhance local ownership, and promote local solutions. At the same time, there are many differences among countries, such as history, culture, politics, infrastructure, socioeconomics, and others. So, tailoring the program to the local context is critical. For instance, in Iraq, the Internet is relatively accessible, and many people use it as a main source of information. So online means are effective for communicating with our beneficiaries, delivering our services, and forming a network in Iraq. However, in South Sudan, access to the Internet is limited and digital literacy is low. We therefore use a hybrid style of communications involving computers, cell phones, and face-to-face discussions. We also make sure to include sessions to improve digital literacy. The key is to work closely with local partners and create a system where lessons learned are fed back into the activities in a continuous way.

You are committed to women's development and programs and have initiated a number of programs specifically for women professionals in Afghanistan and beyond. How did the Afghanistan Fellowship inform your strategy, and what do you envision for UNITAR's programs expanding in this area?

Discrimination based on gender is still rampant in many societies. Studies have also found that since the onset of the Covid-19 pandemic, cases of gender-based violence have increased in many parts of the world, and progress made towards gender equality is being reversed. Throughout my career, I have always sought to promote gender equality. I chair the UNITAR Gender Working Group and have had the pleasure of collaborating with many dedicated professionals inside and outside UNITAR to accelerate the achievement of gender equality.

The Hiroshima Office sets gender equality as a core value and has mainstreamed gender into all aspects of programming. For example, we aim for gender balance in the composition of beneficiaries, Coaches and Mentors, and Resource Persons. We have introduced a mandatory course on gender in all our training programs and use gender-neutral language. We also track how much of our budget and expenditures are targeted to promoting gender equality and addressing gender issues and provide gender-disaggregated data in our project reports. We will continue to incorporate a gender lens in all our activities, even the ones where gender equality is not the primary objective, and through them seek to create a wide network of gender champions – both men and women.

Given your continued commitment to Afghanistan, what are your expectations and hopes for the Afghanistan Legacy Project initiatives, and how do you think you can best help this unique campaign?

There is a significant need to enhance capacities in Afghanistan. I strongly believe that Japan, particularly Hiroshima, is uniquely positioned to provide much-needed support to the people of Afghanistan for multiple reasons. First, Japan has gone through several violent periods in its own history. During the Sengoku period (1467-1615), Japan consisted of many territories controlled by warlords. Civil war, conflict, and violence were common at the time. Japan was a main player in various modern wars including World War II, causing significant damage and casualties outside Japan and taking a heavy toll on its own people and territory. Japan has seen aggression and darkness of humankind. Second, Japan represents a success model of post-conflict recovery and reconstruction. Hiroshima was the first city destroyed

328 | The UNITAR Hiroshima Fellowship for Afghanistan, An Anthology

by an atomic bomb and burned into ashes. The city has been reborn into a beautiful, resilient, and modern city like the phoenix. Hiroshima is a pinnacle of post-conflict recovery and continues to give hope to people around the world. The Hiroshima Office aims to respond to needs of post-conflict recovery, peacebuilding, and sustainable development through training activities in diverse areas such as leadership, innovation, digital technologies, and entrepreneurship. The Afghan Fellowship Legacy Project is and will continue to be central to our work for Afghanistan, as it disseminates a universal and eternal message for humankind: treasure and protect nature and coexist with it. It will be a great honor for me to support the project and contribute to creating a harmonious and green future in Afghanistan and elsewhere.

Community Leaders Carrying the Legacy Forward I
Interview with Najib Sabory[40]

On the Afghan Fellowship (AF)
When and how did you get involved in AF? What was your background?

> I got selected for the UNITAR Fellowship in 2007. I was briefed by a university colleague who had already completed the Fellowship, and he highly encouraged me to apply. I was teaching at Kabul University, Engineering School, Electrical and Electronics department at the time.

What was your role in the AF? How did your role change over time? What about your performance, interests, and motivation?

> I started with being a Fellow in 2007. In 2008, I was given the role of Coach, and later, I remained with the UNITAR program as a Resource Person. After 2009, I continued my volunteer support and connection with the Fellowship program. The key motivation in being involved with the UNITAR Fellowship was learning. I was learning more than what I was contributing to the Fellowship. There were always windows of learning from the network.

---

[40] AF Fellow 2007, Coach 2008, ARP 2009

What was your project during the AF? Did you get to implement the project?

> Our project during the Fellowship was the establishment of an e-learning platform for engineering schools around the country. We were only able to initiate the concept. We were not able to implement it as we had planned and envisioned, but we were able to learn and benefit from thinking about the concept and implementing other similar projects.

Was there any professional and personal growth for you through the AF you had not expected in the beginning? Please share one or two memories of the AF.

> When I joined as Fellow, my expectation was to only learn about leadership and change management. However, it became much more than what I had expected. I learned not only from the lectures, but also from the network itself, resource-persons, site visits, group works were all other aspects of the program with educational value — I was not expecting to have such a broad exposure.
>
> I can recall visiting the Hiroshima Peace Memorial Park — that was a major experience and had a profound impact on us all. Visiting Singapore was another great experience. The exposure visits in Singapore were vastly productive and persuasive.

Given the AF goal of developing leaders for transformational change, how have you been able to apply the lessons from AF in your projects after the program?

> The concept of transformational change helped us move wisely towards bringing positive change in my

organization. After learning from the transformation and change topics, I learned to move slowly, but smartly. It also helped me identify potential risks and mitigation strategies during the change process.

On the AFLP Botanical Garden Network (BGNet) Initiative

What motivated you to get involved in the AFLP Botanical Garden Network (BGNet) initiative over and above your current job and commitments?

> I believed that by being in touch with AFLP friends, I could learn more. I accepted in the first call to volunteer in this initiative. I am super busy with my job and other activities, but I do enjoy working with AFLP colleagues.

What do you think the botanic garden can contribute to the Afghan society (i.e. food security, preservation of indigenous plants/biodiversity, local medicinal knowledge)? What does the BGNet partnership mean for your institution (Kabul University, Bamyan University, and Paktia University) and the role you would like it to play?

> Botanical Gardens are key components of the agriculture sector, so they are very important for the preservation of indigenous plants, local medicinal knowledge, and, of course, food security. Envisioning the AFLP project as a network of botanical gardens at the country level will furthermore help the initiative to grow faster, the BGs are also a place to learn from each other's experiences, and create a sound competition at the national level.

What are some possible challenges you might face with the construction of the botanical gardens, i.e. logistics, security, politics, etc.? What is your vision for your city's botanical garden for future generations?

There are very few people at the technical level, who understand fully all the various aspects of the BG, such as the economic and social benefits. They look at it only as a teaching supplement at the university level, while I think it should be discussed at a much higher level. I think the BG will support also related aspects of the higher education such as research for the students and faculty, and site exposure visits for the general public.

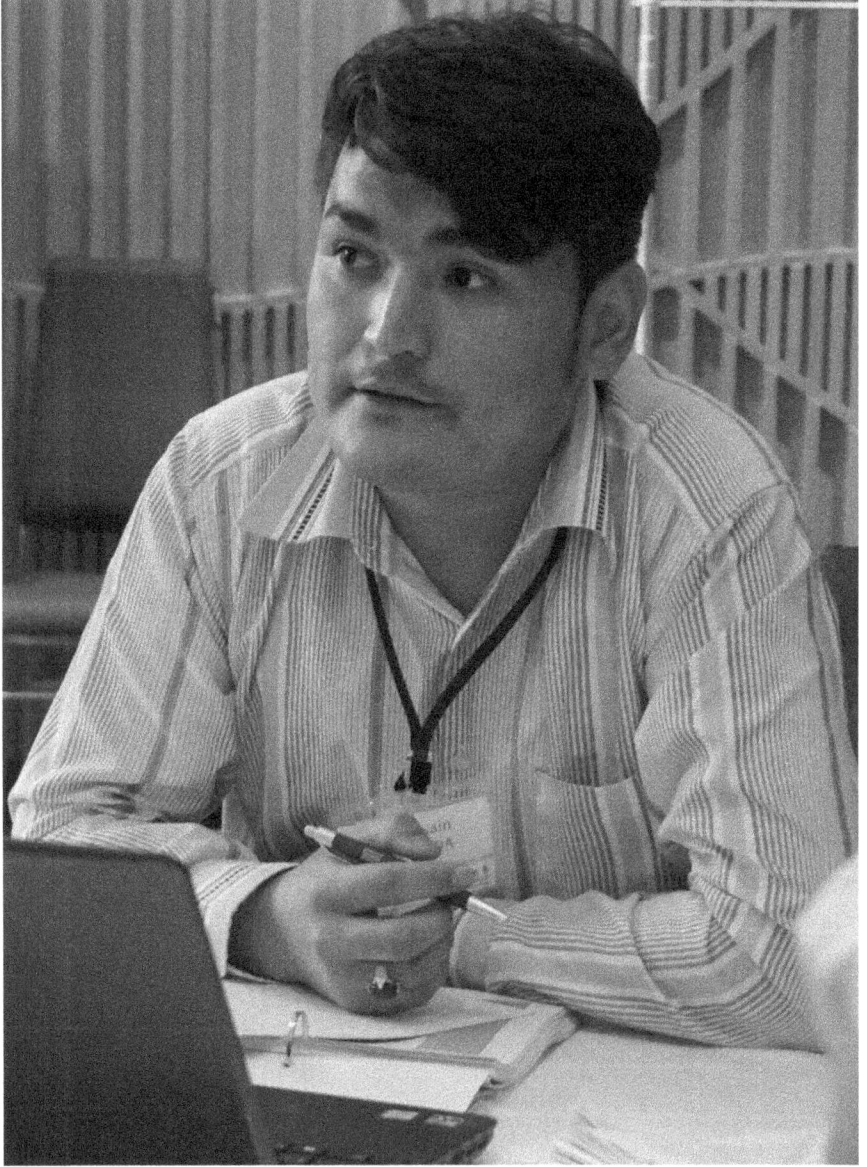

Community Leaders Carrying the Legacy Forward II

Zakir Hassazanda[41]

One Beautiful Journey

Back in late 2018, a simple conversation with my friend led me to the UNITAR Hiroshima Fellowship Program for Afghanistan. And I am glad it did.

My friend told me that when I participated in UNITAR Fellowship Program, I would forget other capacity- building programs for young leaders of Afghanistan. If I wanted to learn about the post-conflict reconstruction for the best and brightest Afghan public officials and civil society leaders, then UNITAR was the place.

The following week I was working on my application form to apply for the Fellowship 2018 cycle. Following the email address provided to all my colleagues through the Learning and Development Department, I called my supervisor Mr. Aimal Ahmadzai and told him I wanted to join the UNITAR program. He spoke to me in a kind and patient tone and told me he would do his best to provide all the necessary support. I sent my application to the UNITAR Team and was fortunately selected to participate in the training.

During that time, I was working as Regional Senior Monitoring, Evaluation, Research and Learning (MERL) Officer with the Bamyan Office of the Aga Khan Foundation. On my way to Kabul

---

[41] AF 2018 Fellow

to participate in the first week of the training, I was thinking about the Fellowship and how I was going to complete all the assignments successfully to pass for the next workshop. However, those thoughts and feelings were somewhat different to the ones I had earlier. They were hopeful but this time tinged with some doubt. I felt I had made a hasty decision, a decision that could be wrong. Maybe I could have pursued my higher education for a Master of Administration with a credible university instead of just participating in a six-month fellowship program. I did not know much about UNITAR, the environment etc. I was feeling doubtful, but little did I know that those doubts would only be around for a few days.

The following week, when I had my first workshop in Kabul, I was no longer in doubt. One by one, more participants from different government agencies and other international NGOs came, and almost all the seats were taken. Finally, Mr. Sabahuddin Sokout, coordinator at UNITAR, came and launched the training officially. I remember the first words I heard from him were, "Hello and good morning to all the Fellows." But it was not the words that made the impression. It was the way he said those words. He said those words with such joy that the training hall filled up with positive energy. It was quite obvious that he was happy to work as coordinator for the Fellowship and provide capacity-building support to all the participants. My first impressions of UNITAR were of high-profile participants and trainers who taught with joy and high motivation.

During the training, Mr. Sokout told us that every participant must join a group of five to six members in order to work on each and every assignment and identify a unique idea and project to be implemented after the Fellowship Program. On the first day, we were divided into groups. At first, I was not completely familiar with all the members of the group, but over time I realized that all my group fellows were talented, highly motivated, and hardworking, and I decided to learn as much as possible from these good people (when opportunity knocks, use it to the maximum). A little later, we met the group Coach, a talented, humble, and kind Mina Naikmal. At that moment, I told myself that I should have a good performance within the group to meet all the expectations of both my group members and professional career goals. I knew that UNITAR could help me achieve that. That was how my first day as a participant went at the Fellowship. It was enough to convince me that I had made the right decision by choosing UNITAR.

At the second workshop in Singapore, all group members decided and agreed to select the project Economic Development through Beekeeping, proposed by Mr. Ghulam Hussain Anees. We selected the project for the reasons below.

- The project could enable beneficiaries, particularly women, to have a sustainable income.
- It aimed to empower women economically.
- The women empowerment could continue to help women increase their confidence to take part in all the decision-making process at the household level.

We had a successful group among all the other groups because of the following reasons and considerations: mutual respect, consideration for the principle of teamwork, and individual efforts.

All the group members were responsible to participate in and promote the group's activities, and these principles helped our group to become the top group at the final presentation day (our group stood first). From all the assignments, group meetings and workshops, we learned about team development, conflict management, problem solving and effective communication that helped groups, communities as well as different teams to be successful in each and every project and program.

Despite relentless efforts to find resources to implement the beekeeping project, unfortunately, we were not able to implement our project. But we carried out our ideas and plans indirectly through the Aga Khan Foundation's rural development projects in remote areas of Bamyan Province. However, the Fellowship became an inspiration for me to become a changemaker, who could make a small but effective change in Afghanistan. I was an experienced professional in monitoring, evaluation, research, and learning, and had had over ten years of experience with the Aga Khan Foundation. I planned to meet my career objectives — hopefully a decision-making leadership position at top-level management of government agencies, donor agencies, or an international organization in the areas of monitoring, evaluation, research, learning and overall project management. The UNITAR Fellowship helped me a lot to fulfill my career objectives, and now I am working as country manager for Action – Aid Afghanistan and involved in top-level management decision-making and will be able to bring changes in development projects, programs for a better tomorrow in Afghanistan.

We had many unforgettable memories during the Fellowship. One of my best memories was from the second workshop in Singapore, we had been asked to do the LAVA game, the scenario was that a rescue team of four to five people should carry out rescue operations in a regular and coordinated manner to transfer people injured in a fire and smoke to a safe place as soon as possible. During the game, the injured person, whose eyes were closed with a piece of tape, could not go hand in hand with us, and I as the head of the team decided to take him on my shoulder and transfer him to a safe place. **Everyone was laughing but we did it!**

For many, the AF was only the place to learn about project management topics, but for me it was full of memories, and I learned a lot more than just project management. I feel incredibly happy when I think about the trainers, Coaches, Fellows that I have had and the lessons I have learned from them. UNITAR has been one of the main factors that has shaped me into the person I am today. I was a Fellow for the last two years, and I can proudly call myself a UNITAR alumnus. During these two years, UNITAR has become so close to me that I think I could even call it my second home and workplace.

I have already mentioned that Fellowship became an inspiration for me to become a changemaker. The AFLP BG-Net is the place where we can share our ideas with highly professional, dedicated, and motivated international friends to initiate a botanical garden. I would like to thank Sokout and all the AFLP team members for their trust in me and inviting me to be a member of such great team.

For me and for the Bamyan University Team, the botanical garden is not just a project to implement and leave after two to three years but the <u>botanical garden will be the seed of hope for further development across Afghanistan.</u> The only challenge we may face with the construction of the botanical garden is the unstable political situation of Afghanistan. We hope that the Afghan peace talks will end successfully, and all the challenges towards the development of Afghanistan will be eliminated.

The overall vision for the botanical garden here is to have a high-quality institution in the country and at the regional level, to improve scientific and research capacities. The botanical garden will play a vital role as a bridge between the provinces and other countries in terms of experience sharing, exporting the capacities, new ideas, potentials, scientific and research achievements of the universities in the long term.

In my opinion, for the growth and enrichment of the botanical garden team, it is necessary to have more Fellowship alumni on board, so that we will be able to mobilize more resources and establish partnerships with the government and universities in other countries. Furthermore, assistance, augmentation, and the use of collective capacities will be effective in accelerating the establishment and development of the botanical gardens.

Community Leaders Carrying the Legacy Forward III:
Three Parts

Najeeb Ahmadzai[42]

Part I: UNITAR Fellowship Program:
An Unforgettable Experience that Made Us Excel

Organizations, whether private or public, set goals and objectives for the purpose of achieving their mission – the reason for their existence – and for that they need skilled employees. Skills are always subjected to change as per the requirements of organizations and with changes in the environment in which a particular organization or individual is operating. There are various ways to improve the skills of an individual or an employee, and arranging various trainings for this purpose is an effective method, particularly when the training involves both theory and practice like the UNITAR Hiroshima Fellowship for Afghanistan.

Theory and practice are quite different, and there is no way that what one studies in a classroom setting can be 100% applicable in practice or on the job. Theory only gives an individual the capacity to think out of the box and make calculated decisions for the purpose of achieving organizational goals. The UNITAR Fellowship program helped me improve my skills to make calculated decisions during my tenure at various positions at the Afghanistan Revenue Department of the Ministry of Finance.

---

[42] AF 2011 Fellow, 2012 Coach

I remember one day when I was at the Foundation for Advancement for Science and Technology University in Peshawar, Pakistan, during my MBA studies, the professor was giving a lecture on profit and loss, explaining that there is always a risk-return tradeoff, which means that the more risk, the more return you have, and vice versa. So, I asked him a question that if it is the case in seeking a return that one is always faced with risk — then what was the logic in studying for an MBA, and what was the difference between me and an illiterate person on the street? The reply was that education and an MBA will enable you to have maximum return with minimum risk involved, but that's only possible once you get practical experience. The point was that the UNITAR Fellowship enabled me to gain theory along with practical educational techniques; we can't forget Michael Fors's lectures along with his various practical leadership techniques, especially that related to the elevator pitch.

I was a Fellow in 2011, and then in the 2011 cycle I became a Coach, which is an important part of my life. I give many examples when talking with my friends or colleagues. The reason is that it was not just a training program for me, but rather a process that has affected my educational qualifications, my experience, my social connections, my professional attitude, my professional development in my organization, the Afghanistan Revenue Department, and in my life even after I left ARD at the Ministry of Finance.

Professional Development
I joined the Ministry of Finance in 2009 soon after completing my MBA, and my first job was manager of the appeals and review unit of the Afghanistan Revenue Department, grade five, then followed by head of the special projects' unit of ARD, which was directly reporting to the ARD Director General. In 2010 when I was first introduced to the UNITAR Fellowship, I can't forget the oral and written entry exams, first in our ministry and then at the civil service institute. The speech by Farhad Osmani, Director General of

the Civil Service Institute, was great. When I was enrolled as a Fellow in 2010, at the same time, I was dealing by then with the HARAKAT investment support agency for funding the small taxpayer's reform project. I would say that my individual assignment, a taxpayer education program, which afterwards was selected as a group project and assignment, helped me learn in a practical sense how to do budgeting, make a logical project model, work plans, and proposals. This experience helped me gain actual funding of about 1.7 million USD, and I was promoted by top management as head of the Kabul Revenue Department also called STO. So. At STO our team became a pioneer in having a first ever client service unit for which I still feel proud. The stakeholders' analysis of our AF group project helped me make an effective client service unit. Since most of the taxpayers were illiterate, we distributed our client service unit into three sections, depending on various taxpayers and gave colors of the national flag to each section to help find taxpayers' areas easily, which at the end of the year helped me achieve organizational goals. In that year, we managed to achieve our revenue target while at the same time increasing the tax base.

Organizational Promotion

As previously mentioned, I was head of the special projects' unit when I started the Fellowship. The group project at that time helped me properly and professionally deal with the HARAKAT investment support agency that resulted in securing funds for STO. It impressed the top management, who promoted me as head of STO, where I worked for a year and a half. Then, I was promoted to director of the revenue services and systems directorate. That post was then followed by promotion to director of a large taxpayer office and ultimately, as acting Director General of Afghanistan Revenue Department, where I was responsible for supervising more than 3,000 employees at the national level in Kabul and in the rest of the 33 provinces. I had the privilege to represent ARD in 2014 in negotiations with the International Monetary Fund using skills I had learned. It helped me present the imposition of ten top-up fees (although not implemented as we proposed afterwards) over the telecom sector, which has generated more than 20 billion AFS so far.

AF Project Outcome

Our Afghanistan Fellowship group project was about a taxpayer education program later implemented at ARD through the Department of Foreign and International Development UK (DFID) funded tax reform project, implemented by Adam Smith International. Although the actual project implemented was of a broader scope, the essence was exactly that of the project we had designed at the Fellowship group project. I feel proud that ten years after that experience, and five years after I left ARD, ARD has managed to arrive at the same outcome designed initially in our taxpayer education project.

National Revenue has increased tremendously, although I have some reservations about that. The national budget, particularly the operating budget, is mostly funded by national revenue, and taxpayers' satisfaction rate has increased tremendously. There are other factors too that have contributed.

I am glad to say that now employees of the revenue services and system directorate (I was the first director of this directorate) of ARD are training taxpayers about e-filing of income tax returns, which was once considered as impossible, taking into consideration the capacity of employees and taxpayers.

Social Connections

In the 2010 AF cycle, we were a group of six people (Mr. Bismellah Maiwand Akbari from the Ministry of Finance, Nasir Figar from IDLG, Ilham from the Ministry of Foreign Affairs, Ms. Farkunda, Mr. Sharif Hashim from ARG, and I) coached by Hamidi Sahib and mentored by two brilliant Mentors, Ms. Meredith Melecki and

Mr. Steven Polunsky. I am in contact with many of them and have developed a strong relationship with the 2010 and 2011 cycles participants. In the Afghan context, making such relationships is of core importance because we give due importance to reaching one another in times of sorrow and joy. Thus we greatly appreciate Mr. Sokout for his continuous emails regarding funerals and prayers for the relatives of Fellows. The point is that AF has succeeded in creating strong and lasting bonds among most of us which would have otherwise been impossible. It is due to AF that we used to discuss various issues with our 2011 cycle Mentor, Ms. Jennifer Fox, and she has openheartedly given her sincere advice, and we are in contact with her till now. These are all the moral assets that AF has gifted us.

International Experience
The market value of an individual depends upon one's experience, especially international experience. Our trip to Japan during the 2010 Cycle was a great experience because it has helped me shape my values of life. I can't forget when we visited one of Japan's civil service institutes, and we took off our shoes because Japanese people respect their institutions like we do our holy places. Moreover, I learned the word "resource curse" during Iraq's ambassador's speech in Dubai and its implications for Afghanistan.

The Hiroshima Peace Memorial Park and Green Legacy Hiroshima associated with the city of Hiroshima were astonishing. Now I can say that after 2015 when I left the Ministry of Finance and got involved with civic activities, I made a strong team of dedicated people in my province, Paktia, and during the past few years, we managed to contribute thousands of plants to Paktia University, basically because of our values of giving to our institutions, which I learned in Japan. I would say that AF has greatly affected the unconscious part of my brain and has given me inspiration. We used to arrange university entry exam courses, and in a single year we managed to educate 1090 students on how to take the university entry exam. In short, AF has helped me shape my way of life to become a responsible citizen of the Afghan Nation.

Kabul, Afghanistan, March 2020

Part II: The Interview

On the Afghanistan Fellowship (AF)
Given AF's goal of developing leaders for transformational change, how have you been able to apply the lessons from AF in your projects after the program?

> AF shaped my entire career. It gave me the capacity to think out of the box. The international exposure I now have was not there before the Fellowship.

> AF has had a huge impact over my entire career. I had studied elevator pitch in university, but I had not used it practically until Dr. Michael Fors made us learn it. Previously, I did not have the capacity to work in a group — it was the able mentorship of Ms. Meredith Melecki, Mr. Steven Polunsky, Mr. Nasir Ebrahimkhail, and Mr. Akbar Hamidi who helped me achieve it. Through AF I learned how to lead a team, and I can say that I was fortunate enough to successfully lead ARD when I was Director General of the Afghanistan Revenue Department.

> Recently I ran for Member of Parliament in Paktia Province. It was a great experience of my life, and the various lessons and concepts that we learned at AF helped me a lot during the process. Although I was not able to get elected, the social exposure was tremendous.

On BGNet
What motivated you to get involved in the AFLP BGNet initiative over and above your current job and commitments?

Gardening has been my hobby for the last many years. I love to gift flowers and plants to others and get more energy when they grow over time. Moreover, as a social activist I have been involved with Paktia University for the last several years and have raised funds for various small projects and greenery of PU. Since AFLP BGNet has both aspects, i.e., involvement with universities and with greenery, that's why it motivated me to get involved with the project.

What do you think botanic gardens can contribute to Afghan society (i.e., food security, preservation of indigenous plants/biodiversity, local medicinal knowledge)? What does the BGNet partnership mean for your institution (Paktia University) and the role you would like it to play?

I think BG can contribute to all said aspects in one way or the other, but plant preservation and supporting research activities could be the most significant. BGNet is more than a project for Paktia University, it is considered as a possible outlet for expanding cooperation with international institutions in various fields. As an honorary technical advisor here, I want to be the core contributor in doing that.

What are some possible challenges you might face during the construction of the botanical gardens (i.e., logistics, security, politics, etc.)?

Every change is resisted in one way or another and with varying degrees. With respect to the Nakamura Botanical Garden at Paktia University, I think PU leadership changes and maintaining the current momentum could be some core challenges in the future.

What is your vision for your city's botanical garden for future generations? What kind of activities and partnerships can you cultivate surrounding the botanical garden? Do you foresee reaching out to other members in the alumni community to mobilize support or resources?

> Frankly speaking, at the start, I considered the botanical garden simply as a place with a collection of plant species, but with the passage of time I came to realize that it's not just collections of plant species but rather an opportunity to save our present and develop our future. I consider the project as a source of preserving our values, and that's why we have named the garden Nakamura Botanical Garden because Dr. Nakamura is considered as a symbol of dedication and hard work in Afghanistan. He was the one who devoted himself to Afghanistan, and the one who brought Japan into the hearts and minds of Afghans. My vision for the Nakamura Botanical Garden is to have a botanical garden, where we can preserve our plant species together with our values, where everyone can make a contribution in whatever form possible, either material or moral. I am of the firm opinion that not only our AF alumni community members, but rather every member of civil society in Paktia will be motivated to contribute towards the Nakamura Botanical Garden at Paktia University.

Part III

Afterthoughts Post-August 2021
January 5, 2022

Regarding the events of the past few months, I would like to share some thoughts. First, one should always be optimistic as I always believe that we should hope for the best and prepare for the worst. Every change, even a threat, brings new opportunities. We can try to consider the current situation in Afghanistan as an opportunity for our future. We have faced a setback, but, frankly speaking, the positive changes we have now were not possible before, irrespective of what's going on in the media and what they are portraying — in most cases, it is not the reality. Now we have top management, who rarely have masters or Ph.Ds., but they have the courage and capacity to listen and if convinced, to act. This was what we often lacked before, and I think that lack was one of the major reasons behind the fall of the regime.

Currently, I am working as an advisor to the Minister of Finance, and what I said above is based on what I have experienced. The leadership is cooperative to an extent that one could not have imagined before, and there are no vested personal interests involved, which ultimately results into success. You will, inshallah, see a major improvement with respect to Afghanistan in terms of the corruption index as no one at any government level can think of corruption. We have a daily average revenue of about 350 million Afghanis, yet with such a miserable financial situation we are managing; it was about 600 million before with the huge influx of resources and projects going on at that time. I am just saying this to elaborate my concept that we have a huge opportunity now to work and cooperate. It's time now when every penny invested can have an impressive cost-benefit ratio. It is a time when Afghans need the international community. The current situation is working like a sieve to filter out each one of us and to show who we actually are.

Personally, I feel more optimistic than before.

One thing that I, along with my Director General Revenue, am working on is an initiative named Public Welfare Initiative which will, without any outside aid, bring local capital (usher and zakat) into mobilization to improve the lives of people. Once again, things are not always as they look.

A "Chance" that Became the Beginning of a Journey
Fawad Akbari[43]

I once read an American humorist who wrote, "If you want to be successful, you must either have a chance or take one." This may sound like a joke, but it relates to my life in a significant way. My own experiences show that in addition to personal enthusiasm and dedication, environmental factors, including a chance (opportunity) to unlock one's potential, are critical to individual success. The UNITAR Hiroshima Fellowship Program for Afghanistan was "the chance" I had, to unlock my potential and take more chances in my personal and professional life journey.

This is how this journey began for me ....

It was mid-2008 and I worked at Cure International Hospital in Kabul, Afghanistan as Patient Services Manager. As part of my daily responsibilities, I was making my afternoon rounds of the hospital and as I entered the private patients' waiting area, a face I knew caught my attention. This was Sabahuddin Sokout, whom I was acquainted with from the time we lived in the same neighborhood in the Wazir Akbari Khan area of Kabul, but we hadn't seen one another for many years. As is typical in the Afghan culture, I warmly greeted him and asked him why he was at the hospital. Sokout and his wife happened to be at the hospital for a routine check-up of their expected baby. We updated each other about our lives and work,

[43] Senior Program Manager, Health and Humanitarian Response Portfolio, the Aga Khan Foundation Canada, UNITAR AF 2009 Fellow, Coach, ARP, Mentor

and Sokout passionately described his work being the local repre-sentative of a UN agency that managed a great Fellowship Program for Afghan professionals – that was the first time I heard about AF. Sokout's passion for his work and my eagerness to learn more made me ask him in detail about AF, unaware at the time that this was "the chance" in my life presenting itself. Sokout and I exchanged contact information, and I noted the UNITAR website, where he said the Fellowship call for applications would be announced.

The call for applications of AF's 2009 cycle was announced on 21 February 2009. At this point, I had already moved to the Aga Khan Foundation Afghanistan in the capacity of Health Program Support Officer. After securing commitment of partial financial support from the Aga Khan Foundation Afghanistan, I submitted my application on 18 March 2009 and was accepted to the UNITAR Hiroshima Fellowship for Afghanistan in May 2009.

At this stage in my career, I was a pediatrician with a year of clin-ical experience and about four years of public health experience as well as some basic project management, program development and management, leadership and team building knowledge and experi-ence. Because of the silo mentality of most national sectors, my pro-fessional network was limited to the health sector with little to no connection with other sectors. The only overseas trip I had taken was to Pakistan, so, in retrospect, it is safe to say I had little first-hand exposure to the world and to global issues. Even my post-secondary learning experience was limited to old-fashioned medical school studies and a few short courses on public health issues and monitor-ing and evaluation. The Fellowship has had a revolutionary impact on my career by touching all these aspects of my professional life.

Now in 2019, ten years after my initial engagement with AF as a Fellow, and subsequently as Coach, Resource Person and the first Afghan Mentor in the program, I work with the Aga Khan Foundation Canada as a Senior Program Manager leading a global health and humanitarian response program of over $250 million (about 50% in Afghanistan), serving close to four million women, men, girls and boys in 13 countries in Africa and Asia, including Afghanistan. While other opportunities and personal and environmental factors contributed to my success, I believe the UNITAR Fellowship was the key to unlocking my potential through the following aspects.

International Exposure – International workshops in Singapore, Dubai, Abu Dhabi, and Hiroshima, Japan, were a critical element of the learning program for a number of reasons. First, the mere better quality of life in these places inspired me as a future leader to desire better living conditions for my family, my community, and the communities I serve through my work. Second, in addition to in-class workshops, the AFP also included structured exposure to public policies and private ventures that benefited populations socially and economically. What I learned, for example, was how countries like Singapore and Japan that lack natural resources capitalized on their human resources in education and manufacturing sectors as main drivers of their GDPs. "There is something there for Afghanistan to learn," is what I noted!

International Faculty and Mentors – UNITAR brought together a group of diverse faculty members of global experts with a common goal and passion to contribute to rebuilding Afghanistan. I not only learned from them, but also practiced with them in international settings. This aspect of AFP has had a lasting impact on my professional maturity and later on promotions in my work.

Contemporary and practical content – AF offered a wide range of learning and development contents throughout the program. While program participants, including Fellows, Coaches, and Resource Persons, benefited from all sessions and topics, contents about leadership, team building and management, and coaching marked a turning point in my leadership and teamwork approach. Even now in my work in Canada, I still use the performance assessment tool and the Tuckman stages of team building introduced to us by Dr. Michael Fors. When I joined AF, I already had a few years of experience managing and leading, but AF was the first time I attended a leadership training. Contemporary leadership concepts introduced by Dr. Fors, coupled with his wonderful delivery methodology, helped me to set my on-the-job experience within a theoretical framework. This, in turn, inspired me to do further studies in leadership, hone my skills, and adopt my own leadership style. I proudly practice Servant Leadership, allowing me to be one of the best team leaders in my organization and to train and mentor others in the servant leadership approach.

Effective methodology – The blended learning, hands-on and interactive methodology used in AF as well as individual and group assignments grounded in the reality of our day-to-day jobs, was another strong trait of AF. For example, my individual assignment was a water, sanitation, and hygiene (WASH) knowledge, attitude and practice survey in Ishkashim district of Badakhshan, which was my first experience of independent primary data collection, which later on inspired a larger WASH project in the same province. My group assignment was a community-based monitoring of health services model that is still being implemented in Badakhshan province, funded by Global Affairs Canada and the French Development Agency and implemented by the Aga Khan Foundation Afghanistan. More importantly, the experience of coaching and mentoring Fellows was incredible. Through this experience, I had the opportunity to "learn by sharing," which I found an even more rewarding and powerful way of honing my leadership and facilitation skills.

Broad community – Fellows and alumni, some of whom served as Coaches, Resource Persons, and Mentors too, as well as the international Faculty Members and Mentors, developed a community that in my opinion was second to none in Afghanistan. This community defied organizational, sectoral, or managerial hierarchical boundaries, and brought people from different levels of management, and various sectors and geographies into one group working on one common goal. Over the past ten years of my engagement with AF, I was humbled to interact with a wide range of professionals, who have given me the confidence during the program and a network of professional and personal contacts after the program. This wide network ranges from parliamentarians to deputy ministers, heads of non-profit agencies, CEOs of private companies, diplomats, and so on. In a typical post-graduate program or in a conventional short training course, this network would be limited to a sector like health and education or organizations like NGOs and the government, but in AF the network went far beyond these boundaries, an asset unique to this program.

On a personal level, AF has had a huge impact. The same principles of leadership, team building, conflict resolution, coaching and facilitation, and organization and planning that I learned through AF and the subsequent opportunities, are perfectly applicable at home. I am the proud father of five empowered girls, and my daughters are stronger, more independent, inspired, and empowered because I motivate them as servant leaders, I coach them to be independent, I challenge them to be a stronger family (team) and better members of their community to pay back to their first home, Afghanistan, as well as their new home, Canada. All of this is possible, thanks to the skills, tools, and principles I learned from AF or was motivated by the program to learn later on.

In conclusion, the UNITAR Fellowship Program for Afghanistan was more than a capacity-building program for me. It was a foundation, on which I have continued to build a successful career, a new window for me to the world, and a chance presented to me to take many other chances by unlocking my potential to think better, do better, and achieve better.

November 2019
Ottawa, Canada

Under a Flying Tricolor Flag
Interview with Sohail Kaakar[44]
by Jenny Xin Luan

Sohail Kaakar at the time of this interview was based in Kabul, Afghanistan[45] working with the Ministry of Finance as the Director General for Coordination, Monitoring, and Reporting. He was part of the Reform Leadership Committee of the Ministry of Finance responsible for establishing innovative initiatives to reform the Public Financial Management system.

Which Cycle of the Afghan Fellowship (AF) were you in, and how did you get involved in the Fellowship? What was your background before that?

Before the Fellowship, I had attended several short and long-term trainings besides my academic education (I have a bachelor's in the social sciences). I had attended several capacity-building trainings, particularly in the field of management and leadership. I not only attended, but have even conducted some of the trainings myself for government civil servants, the private sector and civil society during my career. I joined the UNITAR AF program from the Ministry of Public Works (MoPW) in 2014, and was a graduate of the 2014-15 cycle. At that

---

[44] UNITAR AF 2014 - 18 Fellow, Coach and Afghan Resource Person, Mentor South Sudan Fellowship

[45] The interview was conducted in July and August 2021

time, I was working with MoPW and I was wearing two hats: I was Program Director for the Afghanistan Peace and Reintegration Program, and I had volunteered myself to be the Spokesperson of the Ministry as well. It was an awesome experience for me joining the UNITAR Fellowship. And then it started from there, I became Coach in the next cycle, and then Mentor for South Sudan, and Resource Person and Mentor for AF in the following years.

You have taken on many roles through the UNITAR Fellowship – Fellow, Coach, Mentor, and Resource Person for Afghanistan. What about your performance, interests, and motivation throughout the Fellowship? How did these experiences change you personally and professionally?

The Fellowship — the design, architecture and content, the way it was conducted — was extremely impressive for me. The mixture of the teams within the Fellowship, not only from Afghanistan, the Fellows, but also the Coaches and Resource Persons, the mentors from different parts of the world, and the curriculum, the Fellowship – everything was so impressive. My journey with UNITAR has been wonderful. It was a transformative experience for me because I learned a lot of things and built on my skills from different aspects and perspectives. I particularly developed leadership and team building skills, besides the technical subjects that we learned during the Fellowship. It's the collaborative and blended learning mechanism used by UNITAR and the practicality of the training that are really fundamental to what you gain and what you learn, and then you apply it yourself professionally and personally.

In addition, there is the rich network of people of different backgrounds and variety of education and experiences that make up the AF community. The diversity or the nature of diversity that I could see in UNITAR – that was really eye-opening for me. I not only learned the skills, and benefited from the teachings, the lectures, and the presentations, I came to cherish the relationship and rapport that I built with so many people, starting from Humaira Kamal, to Dr. Michael Fors, to Berin McKenzie, to Mihoko Kumamoto herself, and to all other Resource Persons not only from Afghanistan, but from Canada, Britain, and the United States. I can list all the names because I have created that kind of bond with like-minded people. This helped me to return to Afghanistan after the Fellowship as a Fellow and transfer the learnings and knowledge to my colleagues and to my family, to my friends' and social circles, and spread the word. Then, when I had the opportunity to become a Coach, I learned a lot – not only trying to help the Fellows, but also to learn from them. It's all the learning, and the Fellowship design is a kind of catalyst for you to learn and apply, and, at the same time, to gain a lot of social capital around the globe. Wonderful; for me it's been very transformative, and I still try to apply and implement what I learned and what I gained from UNITAR in my daily routine, work, and my office with my team members.

Can you give us an example of how you apply some of the learning in your daily work now? What was your project in the AF, and did you get to implement the project afterwards?

My project was to develop a communication strategy for the Ministry of Public Works (MoPW). I developed that project and implemented it partially at MoPW. But soon after, I moved from the MoPW to the Office of the President, the Presidential Palace at the end of 2014, where we founded the National Procurement Authority, a new organization to reform public contracting and public procurement. So that was another platform for me to apply some of the skills that I had learned and also my project. In terms of skills, we had to create our team from zero. We started recruiting people, and then applying all the team development theories and models we learned from UNITAR like the Tuckman Model and the DISC Model – how we motivated the team to work with us. Since it was a newly established, newly founded organization, strategy communication was desperately needed. I applied my project to that need. Also, due to all those efforts that we made, our organization was marked as the bright spot in the Afghan Government by Transparency International. There is an official report on that. We became a group of people, who were UNITAR Fellows and Coaches at NPA, as we recruited some of the AF alumni to build our team. We tried to conduct some of the presentations of UNITAR internally for our new recruits. We requested some Fellows and Coaches to prepare an orientation for the team and start the team building process.

When I came to the Ministry of Finance three months ago, I had been at NPA for a long time, more than four years. Last month, I had a team building session for my Ministry of Finance Team. So, I explained to them what we learned from the Tuckman Model about team development, how to motivate teams, and boost their spirits. These were the practical aspects that I tried to apply and implement, during the last seven years till now, from 2014 to date. It's been a long time, but I still remember and cherish all those memories from UNITAR, and it feels like it was just last week or last month.

It is really wonderful to hear how the legacy of the Fellowship left its impact on you. You brought the training back to Afghanistan and to your teams. On that note of good memories, would you like to share with us any other memories from the Fellowship?

> If you ask me to share only one or two memories, it's too few, you know because I have so many great memories from the Fellowship, not only in Kabul but also Abu Dhabi, but particularly in Japan, Hiroshima. If I mention a couple of them…well, the food. I tried sushi for the first time (laughs) in my life, the Japanese food. I have many memories from the Peace Memorial Park and the Peace Memorial Museum, the road walk we took from our hotel there, we went to the Universal Studios and Miyajima Island. But the most interesting memory for me, which I remember and won't forget, is my meeting with the Hiroshima Governor. I met him and it was impressive, the meeting we had. After that - my interview with NHK, the national TV of Japan. I still have the recording of me, the video which went on air, and I think it was March 2016 if I'm not mistaken ….

Given the AF goal of developing leaders for transformational change, how have you been able to apply the lessons from AF in your projects after the program? Please share examples if possible.

> In one simple sentence, I can say that I have applied every bit of what I learned during the program on my daily life at the family level — to my children, with the social circle of friends, and on the professional level with my team-mates, peers, subordinates, and even superiors.

Have you had the chance to engage with any AF alumni community activities or alumni-driven initiatives since graduating from the program?

Yes, I stayed engaged in the program and its alumni network through becoming Coach, Resource Person for the Afghan program, and Mentor for the South Sudan program. I also helped the program coordinator in his interactions outside of the Fellowship sphere on the program of Afghan Women Leadership program in Japan.

What do you think of the current economic, social, or political environment in Afghanistan? How has it affected your life? How has the Covid-19 pandemic impacted the country and yourself?

These are tough questions indeed. The ground reality is that by the time I am writing this response to these very questions, the situation in Afghanistan is extremely worrisome due to increased levels of violence and atrocities. I am concerned as every human being should be in this type of situation. In the bigger picture, I also see it as a moment of opportunity within a crisis, to play as much as a small role to protect the republic, to protect the basic rights of my children, my wife and my fellow country men and women. Despite all the concerns, increased threats for me personally and my family, and being in war since I was born to being in war at the very existing moment, not only the war on terror and the darkness of Taliban violence but also Covid, I try to motivate and create vibes for myself every morning to generate passion within me, within my team at the Ministry of Finance, and within my circle of friends, to survive these extremely difficult times with resilience, tenacity, and hope.

What is your vision for Afghanistan? How do you think you can contribute to that?

My vision for my beloved Afghanistan is flourished with the substance of peace, unity, diversity, liberty, prosperity, and sovereignty under a flying tricolor flag. My daughter can go to school, my friend has a job, the poor have their basic needs met in a peaceful condition, a jubilant music concert of local pure Afghan music can be held on the streets of Kabul and other parts of the country with no worry about bombings, explosions, or incidents that take human lives. That's the Afghanistan known for its past 800-year history of richness with love of humanity, culture, arts, philosophy, and civilization — as put beautifully by the poet Rumi, "If the house of the world is dark; Love will find a way to make windows!"

Carrying the Torch Forward:
Capacity-building, Hope and Karaoke
Nigel Gan[46]

Reflecting on the Afghan Fellowship brings back so many memories, and I am honored to have been the project manager for the last several cycles of the Fellowship. The Fellowship is such a meaningful program, challenging the role of international organizations by highlighting how developmental support should, if it wants to be effective, build capacity in a way that is sustainable in the long term and that empowers community members to address community needs. The multi-layered and reinforced learning approach — including through the several levels of faculty and different learning engagements provided to Fellows — has informed many other programs, both inside and beyond UNITAR. The impacts too go far beyond the Fellows themselves: I could see the ripple effect it had on all those who engaged with the program, whether as staff, Resource Persons, or even Hiroshima citizens who met the Fellows. Finally, and most importantly, it was clear the Fellows' projects made a positive impact on those living in Afghanistan.

The Fellowship changed my life too. While this may seem a bit cliché, looking back I understand the program's catalytic effect. The Fellowship informed and refocused the kind of work I want to do, and I continue to benefit from the experiences, lessons, and friendships gained along the way.

---

[46] Former UNITAR Hiroshima Office staff, in charge of the Afghan Fellowship

The pivotal moment for me was the final day of the 2015 Fellowship Cycle. In the Ballroom of the Oriental Hotel in Hiroshima, over 70 Afghans had just spent an intense week developing their project proposals, under the expert and guiding eyes of the stalwarts of the Fellowship: Dr Michael Fors, Professor David Eaton, and Shona Welsh, as well as the dedicated international mentors, Afghan Resource Persons (ARPs) and coaches. They were exhausted. Yet, as the final presentations and feedback came to a close, the energy in the room rose to a crescendo. Under the bright lights, Fellow after Fellow shared their story and their resolve to make a difference in their community, in their office, and in their country. This energy and enthusiasm, in the face of the stark challenges they faced, moved me. I was humbled to be part of it. I felt that here, I could make a difference and contribute to something bigger than myself. Making a difference — no matter how small, even just one person — would be worthwhile. It was this feeling that convinced me to turn down a job offer from the Australian Government and join UNITAR full-time. I was soon the Fellowship project manager, and the rest, as they say, is history.

Looking back, I think the saying "standing on the shoulders of giants" is very relevant here. The structure of the program, the dedication of the Coaches, ARPs, Mentors, Resource Persons and UNITAR staff, the staunchness and commitment of Mr. Sokout made it such a unique and dynamic programme.

I am thankful to all the Fellows, Coaches, ARPs, RPs, Mentors, UNITAR staff. These connections, friendships and memories have had a lasting effect, changing who I am and helping me grow. I also want to take this opportunity to particularly thank Sokout, whose experience and steadfastness helped me grow as a project manager. As you would have read, Sokout's pivotal role helped focus and ground the Fellowship, as well as other programs we ran in Afghanistan. I am grateful to be able to call him my friend.

Here are just some of the memories I often recall, reminding me of both the good times spent together and the Fellows' perseverance in the face of daily challenges.

- Fellows sitting in the Hiroshima Peace Park at all hours of the day and night. They were just enjoying the tranquility and the ability to be out at 1 a.m. by themselves.
- Three Fellows joining a video conference while driving somewhere in India.
- Hearing about the successes of projects that had been implemented, and hearing about new projects these Fellows had developed.
- Numerous late nights in hotel lobbies working to isolate real needs, develop effective change plans, and working on pitches.
- The planning and avalanche of emails and phone calls working to organize the 2019 workshops, when additional funding became available at the last minute, allowing us to hold the workshop in Singapore.
- Singing karaoke with the Coaches, ARPs, and RPs.

And examples which constantly highlighted the reality of Afghanistan:

- Numerous phone calls dropping out as armored personnel carriers or helicopters thundered past.
- Hearing the Fellow's experiences about daily life in Afghanistan. Although each story is unique, I was struck by the inhumanity of the security threats and constant pressure they all face.
- Speaking to Sokout, mere moments after he had been hit by glass from a nearby explosion, yet he was as calm as ever.

These experiences have helped define me and will stay with me.

Lessons learned from the AF also informed the development of other UNITAR program in Iraq, South Sudan, Syria and more. It was fulfilling to see how the program evolved and to watch the South-South cooperation expand, with Afghans becoming coaches or resource persons for participants from those countries. The Fellowship also played an integral role in the development of the UNITAR Women's Leadership Program for Afghanistan, which ran in 2018 and 2019, with many AF Fellows being key resource persons supporting this program. These experiences and lessons have helped define me and will stay with me – and they continue to live as even now, in my current role at UNAIDS, I am developing new leadership and women's empowerment program.

I have seen Afghans' resilience and passion, and I remain hopeful that they can surmount the challenges they face. To build an inclusive society. To be free. To be safe

Vignettes from Fellows - courtesy UNITAR
archives (2003 to 2019)
Friba Quraishi[47]

In her role as a mentor and leader, Friba Quraishi counted as a personal achievement guiding a team of Fellows, as they developed their group project — facilitating a group of people with disparate opinions wasn't always easy! However, Friba believed her work was well worth it, as the Fellows gained real confidence in what they learned and their abilities through the UNITAR Fellowship Program for Afghanistan's blend of activities and group work. For some Fellows, the program involved their first trip outside Afghanistan, and their experiences and study in Hiroshima left a lasting impression.

Friba was born in Kabul in 1985 and graduated with a BA from the Department of English at Kabul University. She worked as an adviser for the University Support Workforce Development Program.

After participating in AF as a Fellow in 2012, Friba returned as a Coach and Afghan Resource Person in 2013 and 2014 respectively. In 2015 she served as a Mentor for the first cycle of the UNITAR South Sudan Fellowship Program, and she participated as a panel member assigned to critique the gender focus of projects during the cycle's final workshop.

---

[47] Adviser, Afghanistan University Support Workforce Development Program (USWDP); UNITAR AF 2012 - 2016 Fellow, Coach, ARP, and Mentor

When she was a Fellow, Friba worked on a project on gender mainstreaming for the Ministry of Rural Rehabilitation. The project created a gender working group and network, comprising of representatives from various Ministry projects, which worked to improve gender mainstreaming at the project and beneficiary levels.

Friba said she wanted to participate in the Fellowship because it "focused on developing Fellows' capacities and sharpening their skills; and it provided a forum to exchange views and experiences amongst Fellows, in order to learn about each other's challenges and successes." After participating in the program as a Fellow and in various mentor positions, Friba noticed that participants' perception and outlook positively changed, and a change in their behavior followed. After workshops, Fellows would try to put into practice what they learned. For example, after learning about teamwork, Fellows working together in a group divided tasks among group members and worked toward the group's main goal. Similarly, the DiSC test, which gave Fellows a chance to reflect on their work styles and personality, as well as those of their team members, was one of the most useful activities of the program.

Friba developed skills both personally and professionally through her mentor and leadership roles with UNITAR, skills such as time management, networking and coordinating. She commented that she learned something new at every cycle and got the opportunity to work with diverse teams. Throughout her association with UNITAR and the Fellowship, inspired by the people of Hiroshima, Friba constantly aspired to adapt lessons she learned in Japan to Afghanistan.

Abdullah Fahim[48]

"Teams need to accept diversity. If we can't accept diversity in a team, how can we accept it in our country? We can't succeed if we don't do so."

Dr. Abdullah Fahim, Medical Director of the French Medical Institute for Children, UNITAR AF Program Fellow

AF Fellows of the 2016 Cycle, representing various sectors, worked in teams to develop project proposals to address organizational and/or community needs. Dr. Fahim's group project was to create a sustainable, village-level agricultural supply shop, that could provide farmers with hybrid seeds, fertilizer, and tools. More than just providing supplies, the shop would also educate farmers on how to best use the products; the project was gender conscious and outlined plans for how women could participate as well. If farmers grew a large crop, they could then sell the surplus, growing the local economy — a typical example of a small project transforming the way business was conducted in one community.

As required in a training on leadership, communication, and teamwork, Dr. Fahim was particularly attentive to the dynamics in his group. Although he had the most work experience of all the team members, he focused on striking a balance between leadership and support, and allowing the other members the freedom to

---

[48] Medical Director, French Medical Institute for Children; UNITAR AF 2016 Fellow

even critique his ideas. Contrary to cultural dynamics, the team achieved a free atmosphere, and although conflict still existed, it could be overcome. This was his most meaningful experience from the Fellowship.

While visiting Hiroshima for Workshop III during the 2016 Cycle, Dr. Fahim was struck by a similar cooperative attitude from the people of Hiroshima, an attitude which had clearly helped them reconstruct their city. Dr. Fahim said that one of the most positive aspects of the program overall was the opportunity to experience Hiroshima firsthand.

The program's learning-by-doing methodology also positively impacted Dr. Fahim. He noted that participatory practical exercises were key to internalizing and utilizing what the Fellows learned. He said the training made his work style more results-oriented and that he "moved with more clarity and strength through distinguishing needs rather than wants, which improved results and increased customers and staff satisfaction." Thanks to the UNITAR Fellowship, he "better understood his environment."

In his own work as medical director of the French Medical Institute for Children, Dr. Fahim has been able to utilize what he learned about evidence-based planning and activities in UNITAR's training. Thanks to these skills, he successfully conducted patient satisfaction surveys, analyzed the data, and planned to effectively address the concerns that were raised therein.

Mina Naikmal[49]

"It is essential to encourage women, as well as train them in leadership and effective decision-making," Mina Naikmal, Program Specialist for the Afghanistan Ministry of Finance, 2016-2019.

Mina participated as one of 29 Fellows in the UNITAR Fellowship Program for Afghanistan 2016 Cycle, which focused on capacity development for Afghan professionals in leadership, teamwork, and project development and implementation. A passionate and motivated professional, she wanted to participate in the Fellowship to learn how to work effectively in a diverse team, while also developing her own capacity as a team member.

"The program helped me define, develop, and lead a team consisting of people with different ideas and behaviors," Mina said. Learning techniques of effective leadership and team building helped Mina empower other women to take initiative as leaders.

During the Fellowship, Mina's group worked on a project related to an online contract monitoring system for the Afghanistan Ministry of the Interior and Ministry of Defense. As was quite common, the system already existed, but ministry officials were unfamiliar with how to use it. The project proposed on-the-job training, as well as

---

[49] Human Resources Specialist, Internal Audit Directorate, Ministry of Finance; UNITAR AF 2016 – 2018 Fellow, Coach

instructional manuals and videos, to improve officials' capacity to work with the system.

Along with teamwork, leadership, and communication skills, Mina said she learned how to concretely plan out the activities and steps necessary to implement this – or any – project. She learned how to identify organizational needs and develop projects to address them as well. In her experience, comprehensive project development can play a critical role in social change thorough collaboration with various organizations, including initiatives for women's empowerment.

During the Fellowship's third workshop, held in Hiroshima, Mina was inspired by the local people's commitment to reconstruction following the atomic bombing, particularly stories of women's efforts.

Mina believes the training's well-designed combination of theory and practice helped her achieve her goals. She continued her association with the Fellowship as a Coach for the 2018 Cycle, during which she successfully guided her team of Fellows as they worked to develop a project proposal about beekeeping in Afghanistan's

Bamyan Province. In addition to her continued role with UNITAR, she successfully implemented in her workplace a project designed to utilize her Fellowship training — the project summary, below, was featured in a newspaper in 2018:

Mina Naikmal (26), who works for Afghanistan's Ministry of Finance and is one of this year's Coaches, successfully implemented a project she developed through the Fellowship. The project gave women internships with the Ministry, which later onboarded a number of them as staff. The result was an increase in the number of women working in the Ministry's Intern Audit Directorate, from 10 to 23 percent. Ms. Naikmal said the skills she learned from UNITAR helped her through every step of her project.

"Visiting Hiroshima gave me hope to rebuild my country, to fight for peace no matter what the circumstances are," said Ms. Naikmal, who first came to Hiroshima as a Fellowship participant last year. "I am excited and happy to visit this beautiful and peaceful city again, and I wish to adopt Hiroshima's culture to bring change in my country."

Adapted from Annelise Giseburt, *The Chugoku Shimbun* (Originally published on July 3, 2018)

https://www.hiroshimapeacemedia.jp/?p=83763

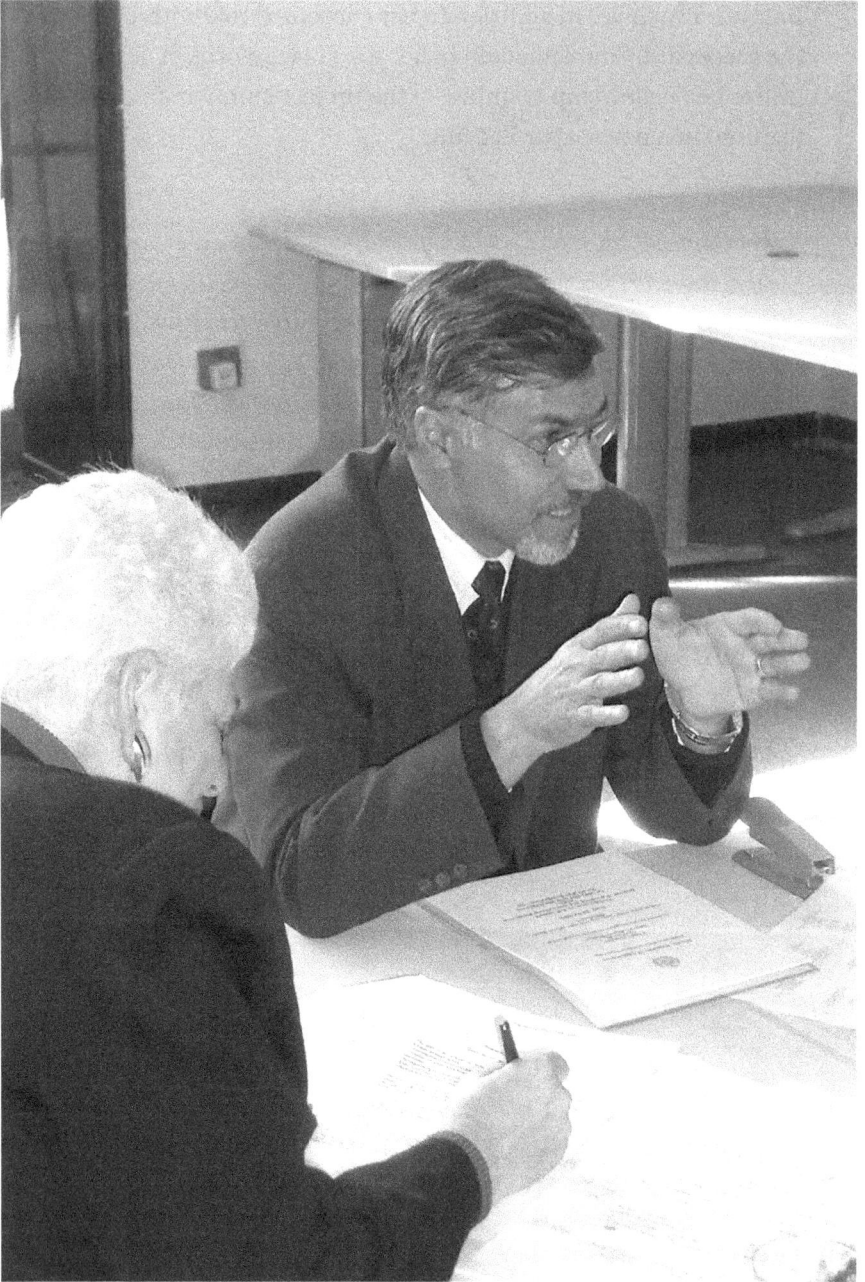

Abdul Rashid Janbaz[50] (RIP)
Success Story

I am one of the UNITAR alumni who joined the Fellowship in 2003/2004, in fact one of the first Fellows of the UNITAR Fellowship Program. It was very encouraging for me to be able to complete the one-year long program. I was selected then as a Coach to facilitate most of the training issues with another new group in 2005. I also was selected as volunteer advisor for the UNITAR program from 2006 to 2009. One of my big achievements inspired by AF was my educational improvement after I graduated from the Fellowship. One of the UNITAR resources from Singapore, who was a Ph.D. holder, encouraged and advised me how to get my higher academic degree easily. He explained the way he used to receive his academic degree, which was very interesting to me. I agreed with his ideas and just copied what he did; initially, I got my master's degree from the University of Wales in England in Business Administration in 2011. My degree was approved by the executive board in the Ministry of Higher Education, and then as I was very motivated to continue my education, I applied to get my Ph.D. as well. Finally, I got my Ph.D. in Management (Economic Management) in early 2014 from India. In fact, the only reason behind my success is the advice of my Singaporean mentor and the opportunities offered by UNITAR. This is my best success story, and what I am proud of most in my life. My family and I can never forget it, and I proudly tell this story to everyone I know, as this is a great example of my career improvement, with many thanks to UNITAR, you are the inspiration which changed my life...

---

[50] UNITAR 2003-04 Fellow, 2005 Coach, 2006-09 AF Advisor; Founding Member of AF Alumni Association - ACTRA

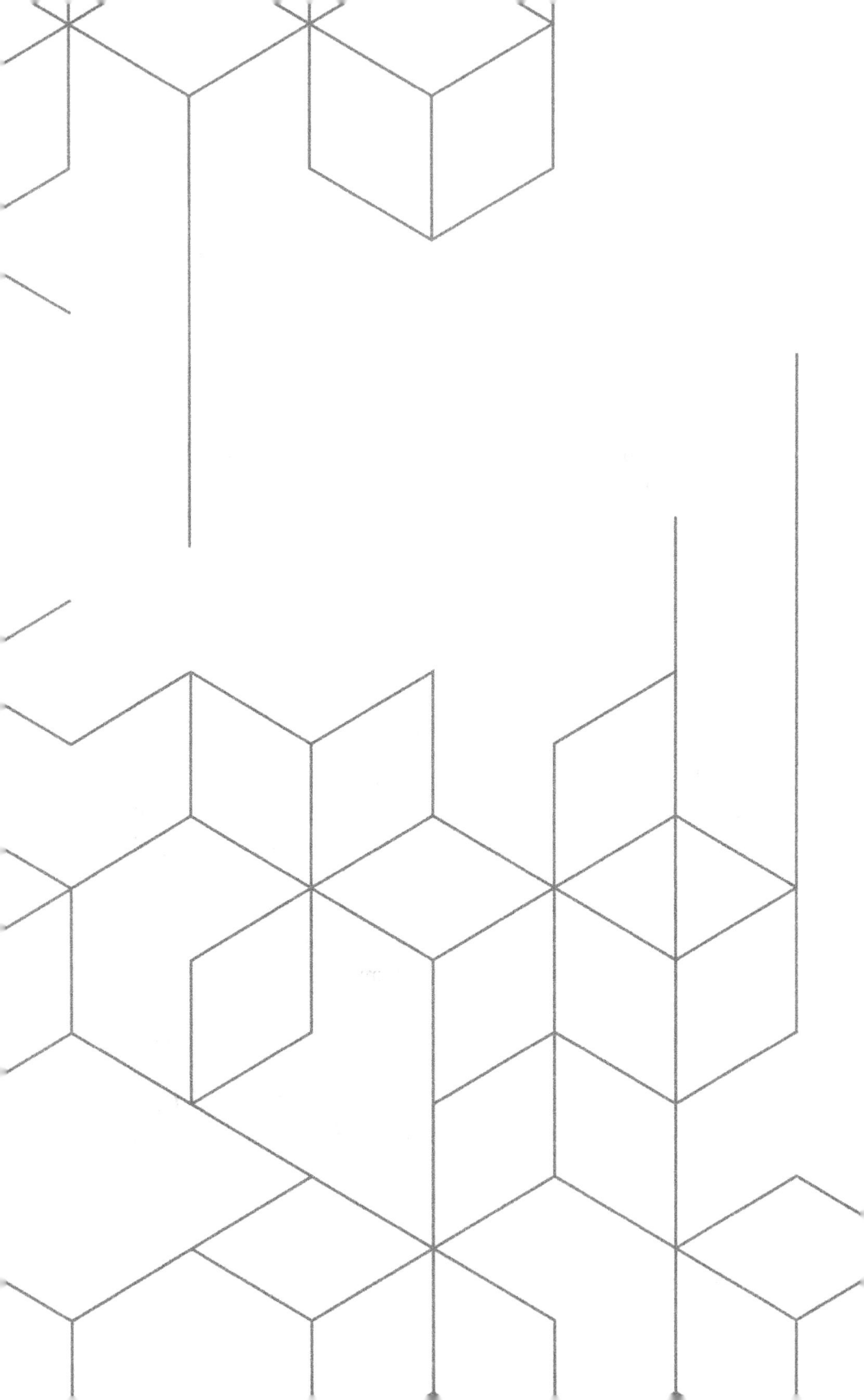

PART V

THE AFGHAN FELLOWSHIP – A QUALITATIVE ANALYSIS

The Afghan Fellowship — A Qualitative Analysis
Yuji Uesugi[51]

Introduction

A single project, no matter how well designed, executed and sustained, cannot create peace all by itself. Hence, it is wrong to criticize the UNITAR Hiroshima Fellowship for Afghanistan (hereafter, the Afghan Fellowship) for not having able to prevent the Taliban take-over of August 2021. It is also beyond my capacity to scrutinize the entirety of a program that lasted over 15 years, and offer an overall evaluation of it. Rather, I seek to share in this chapter my views and insights gained from my own involvement in the Afghan Fellowship as a Mentor and a Resource Person/lecturer in the light of peacebuilding (under)development in Afghanistan in the past two decades.[52]

To the rhetorical question put to us by Humaira Khan-Kamal, one of the interlocutors of the Afghan Fellowship and editors

---

[51]Yuji Uesugi is Professor at the School of International Liberal Studies, Waseda University, Japan. He served as AF Mentor and Faculty Member from 2007 onwards.

[52] Maybe my most useful contribution to the Afghan Fellowship revolves around the fact that I had the opportunity to supervise the doctoral research of Shamsul Hadi Shams in Hiroshima University, who later worked for the Afghan Fellowship. In 2012, Shams submitted his successful doctoral thesis entitled, *The Impacts of Post-Taliban Reconstruction Strategy on the Viability of Intra-Afghan Conflict Settlement*. Being an intelligent Afghan national, whose late father was an influential teacher in an Islamic school called *madrasa* where many Taliban were educated, he has made a significant contribution to the Afghan Fellowship as an intercultural translator and bridge-builder. I also had the opportunity to serve as a deputy supervisor for one of the three UNITAR Musketeers, Sharapiya Kakimova, who wrote a doctoral thesis on *Public Administration Reform (PAR) in Afghanistan's Reconstruction*.

of this volume, namely "Was it all a waste?", my answer must be "Definitely not". Talented human resources with a right mindset are needed everywhere, in state-building, peacebuilding, business, public administration, and schools, to name but a few. Having been involved in higher education at Hiroshima University (at the time of my engagement with the Afghan Fellowship) and currently at Waseda University in Japan, I am a strong believer of the importance of continuous learning, as well as the need to wait a while for such investments to bear fruit. In other words, the results of education and training should be judged by their long-term rather than their immediate impact.

While the continuous funding of the Afghan Fellowship by external donors (including Hiroshima Prefecture and City) for over 15 years is indicative of its impressive track record and success, it does not mean however that the program did not face any challenges. My involvement in the Afghan Fellowship was at its nascent phase, and I have witnessed several technical challenges as Musa Kamawi, an Afghan Fellow and an Afghan Resource Person, outlines in his contribution to this volume. For example, in the beginning, the internet connection was often not available, reliable, or fast enough to have stress-free communication between war-torn Afghanistan and Hiroshima. Some Afghan Fellows did not have adequate command of English. Poor internet connection and the lack of proficiency in the working language made it very difficult for us to even communicate. Due to these problems, in the worst case, after an hour of struggling to be connected, we were able to just greet each other. When I was serving as a Mentor, I was tasked to supervise one of the groups, and as I had to make a business trip to the United States, I held regular consultation meetings with the Afghan Fellows from there. Because the Wi-Fi in a hotel was very weak, and the best reception I got was in a bathroom, I had to operate my session from the bathroom, sitting on a toilet seat at 1 AM due to the time difference! In today's era of high-speed internet and online communication, a new normal especially after COVID-19, I can share this as a funny story, but the episode shows how challenging it was to conduct online training in the earlier stages of the program.

In the following, what I will offer first is a brief sketch of the literature on evaluation in the field of peacebuilding. This allows us to appreciate the analytical and/or evaluative framework with which the Afghan Fellowship will be examined. Then, referring to frameworks of peacebuilding evaluation, such as "Quality Peace" (Joshi and Wallensteen 2018; Wallensteen 2015), "Measuring Peace" (Caplan 2019), "Reclaiming Everyday Peace" (Firchow 2018), and "New Directions in Peacebuilding Evaluation" (d'Estrée 2020), I shall endeavor to provide a set of critiques of the Afghan Fellowship. Over 400 Afghan Fellows went through this program, and many of them assumed important administrative positions in the ministries of the (late) central government, while others joined non-governmental organizations or were employed by foreign organizations and entities in Kabul. Since it is impossible to follow the career path of all the Afghan Fellows, I shall examine the two focuses of the program: the mindset of servant leaders and local ownership. The purpose is to measure the impact of the Afghan Fellowship upon the peacebuilding process in Afghanistan, by illustrating the plausible contributions it has made on Afghan society in the last 15 years. Because I did not have a chance to interviews Afghan Fellows nor did I have an opportunity to visit Afghanistan to confirm the impact the program had on Afghan society, the following should not be read as the findings of rigorous academic research. Instead, I shall take the advantage of hindsight and draw on my expertise as a peacebuilding expert, who has visited and studied Afghanistan.

Literature on Peacebuilding Impact Assessment
Exploring linear causal links between inputs and outputs through mechanical quantitative analysis is not an appropriate methodology

for assessing dynamic and multifaceted peacebuilding efforts. This is because many things, including unexpected developments, affect the trajectory of a certain project/program/intervention, and unlike natural scientific experiments that can control these variables in a laboratory, it is extremely difficult to find a clear causal relationship between a specific intervention and the situational change brought to the scene (Hunt 2016). It is often difficult to clarify even the correlation between the two. This is because peacebuilding processes involve complex and interactive dynamics in which various factors are intertwined, but existing assessment frameworks tend to apply a short timeframe and to claim direct causal relationships and sustainability of the planned effects and outcomes. Even though a particular intervention is short-lived, and its initial beneficiaries are limited in number, it can still have a positive impact on medium- to long-term peacebuilding so long as it has led to desirable changes in local contexts, or in the attitudes and behavior of local stakeholders. But in most of the conventional evaluations of peacebuilding intervention, these after-effects are either underestimated or overlooked.

Existing Evaluation Frameworks
In the field of peacebuilding, because many projects are donor driven and donor governments need to present the positive outcomes of their assistance to their taxpayers or supporters, project evaluation is bound to be shortsighted. For example, the Organization for Economic Cooperation and Development, Development Assistance Committee (OECD/DAC) offers one of the most used frameworks for assessing development cooperation, in which six evaluation criteria—relevance (is the intervention doing the right things?), coherence (how well does the intervention fit?), effectiveness (is the intervention achieving its objectives?), efficiency (how well are resources being used?), impact (what difference does the intervention make?), and sustainability (will the benefits last?)—are identified (OECD 2021).

While it includes two potentially medium- to long-term criteria, i.e., impact and sustainability, most evaluation efforts have been carried out when the intervention is still being implemented or has very recently ended, which makes it very difficult to meaningfully apply these criteria in the assessment. The OECD/DAC admits that "Evaluation will often take place during the lifespan of the intervention or may occur at a point where sustainability is not yet evident" (OECD 2021). Similarly, impact by nature should also last "long enough" because the transformative effects of the intervention can be vanished, nullified, or even become irrelevant due to changes occurring in its surroundings, like the fall of the beneficiary Afghan government, that was established in the aftermath of the US invasion of Afghanistan.

Among the six criteria, relevance is the most important one as it asks if the intervention's objectives and design respond to the needs of beneficiaries and continue to do so if circumstances change. The intervention becomes counter-effective to peace if it aims for "wrong" purposes and is implemented for "wrong" beneficiaries. However, the answer to the question of right or wrong becomes uncertain in the long-term peacebuilding perspective, and if we ask follow-up questions such as "peace for whom?" or "what kind of peace to aim for?" For example, many talented former Afghan Fellows still work in the Taliban-led government as even authoritarian and illiberal regimes need the capacity to govern and, equally important, perhaps the Afghan Fellows need to survive and support their families. Does this mean that the Afghan Fellowship has contributed to, though unintended, a "wrong" objective? Should contributing to the "illiberal" governance of the Taliban regime be seen as an unintended outcome of the program?

Thus, the question of relevance needs to be seen in the light of changing circumstances, which makes evaluation a never-ending, continuously readjusting endeavor, requiring a 360-degree assessment of the surroundings as peacebuilding is often undertaken in a fragile situation susceptible to external influence and factors that could be changing rapidly. While the OECD/DAC criteria include the criterion of coherence, advocating for placing the intervention in the whole or big picture of development (judging from the point of view of seeking compatibility with other interventions), proper evaluation of the intervention should be conducted not only from the perspective of compatibility with other interventions, but also from the societal development caused by constant and unforeseeable interactions of various social factors, actors, and other variables.

Likewise, the criterion of effectiveness is dependent of the criterion of relevance as it questions if the intervention is achieving its objectives, which is determined by the objective-setting exercise of the project formulation and design. An effective apparatus can be used to realize both benign and evil objectives. For example, the Holocaust might have not been possible if Nazi Germany did not have an effective apparatus capable of handling complicated logistics, administration, finance, procurement, and management.

Alternative Frameworks for Evaluation
These evaluation criteria employed to measure short-term direct effects of an intervention may be suitable for donors who require an instant proof of the value of their investment, but they are not always suitable for assessing the medium- to long-term impacts of human resource development like the Afghan Fellowship. Then, what are better alternatives to these existing approaches? A major trend in impact assessment in the field of peacebuilding is to measure the plausible "contribution" rather than the direct causal "attribution" of an intervention (d'Estrée 2020, 11-12; Hughes 2016; Hunt 2016; Firchow 2018; Caplan 2019).

What is contribution analysis in the context of measuring the impact of human resource development in peacebuilding? A case study is a common method of contribution analysis used to explore and establish causal relationships and correlations between intervention and outcomes. Contribution analysis is characterized as providing plausible evidence of the changes that a particular intervention may have had (Hughes 2016). By accumulating plausible evidence, a "contribution story" is established (d'Estrée 2020). It is the role of a contribution story to explain the result chain of why and how a certain initiative contributed to or produced a particular outcome. The result chain includes linkages not only to intended changes, but also to unintended or unexpected changes. Contribution analysis assesses not only changes that are desirable, but also those that are not desirable (it remains to be examined for what, and for whom, though). In building a contribution story that explains why and how a certain change has taken place, it is necessary to listen not only to local stakeholders but also to the public at large. This requires ethnographic approaches to evaluation, which rely on knowledge of local culture, history, and conflict dynamics (Millar 2014; Caplan 2019, 107-8). In addition, it is also important to consider the reasons why the impacts are sustained over a long period of time, as well as the factors and paths that have secondary or indirect impacts on the ground, such as knock-on effects, ripple effects, and trickle-down effects.

"Outcome mapping" technique can be used to verify impacts on a relationship, and it is useful for examining the correlation between the changes in people's perceptions of their leaders in the government, for example, and the actual improvement of the attitudes and behavior of the leaders (Hunt 2016). Sayed Maqbool, an Afghan Fellow from the 2009 cycle, highlighted in this volume that the key to success was to ensure that other Afghans in the country shared and believed in what he calls the "Fellowship mindset." The Afghan Fellowship focused on working with potential leaders in Afghan society to enhance their "servant leadership" mindset, expecting that their behavioral change would contribute to societal transformation. In the post-Taliban Afghanistan, however, perhaps after the initial honeymoon phase, ordinary people never developed confidence in their government and in the Afghan Security Forces, which were established, trained, and equipped by their allies and friends from the West. The Afghan Fellowship had offered training to over 400 Afghan civil servants in 15 years, and one can claim that such an effort clearly has left a positive impact on the attitudes and behavior of these Fellows, and these positive changes at the individual level have led to various institutional reforms of the Afghan government, such as the Ministry of Finance, the National Procurement Authority, and the Ministry of Commerce and Industries, as Sabahuddin Sokout argues in his chapter of this volume. So far, however, such reform initiatives have not caused fundamental transformation in the system of governance in Afghanistan, which allowed the Taliban to topple Ashraf Ghani's government so easily, as soon as the United States abandoned it. Continuous monitoring of people's perception of their relationship with the government over time will allow us to identify collective cognitive changes among them, which could lead to structural transformation in the society. I must admit, however, that this would be time-consuming and costly, and I cannot apply such a comprehensive and long-term approach in this chapter.

Instead, what I can propose is that this volume, particularly stories shared by Afghan stakeholders such as the Afghan Fellows and Coaches, should be re-read as a collection of contribution stories. To navigate such an endeavor for readers in the international community, what I shall employ in the following is a trend in peacebuilding called the "local turn". In the literature of peacebuilding, it is suggested that the goals of peacebuilding must be closely associated with the local people and aligned with the local context, considering the nature of the terrain where peace is being built (Leonardsson and Rudd 2015). Because different local stakeholders may have diametrically opposed interests, it is also essential that the concept of "locals" be unpacked, and its dynamic and fluid nature be captured. Upon establishing the contribution story of the Afghan Fellowship, therefore, "complexity thinking" (Brusset, de Coning, and Hughes 2016) is introduced, and ethnographic approaches (Caplan 2019) are employed to explore the footprints and to map out the outcomes of the program. Through this ethnography-based understanding of social and political change (Brusset 2016), local voices are incorporated into measurement and evaluation (Firchow 2018).

As I pointed out, I did not have a chance to visit Afghanistan after the Afghan Fellowship was terminated in 2018, to conduct the ethnographic analysis. In lieu of it, the testimonies presented in this volume by some Afghan Fellows and other associated interlocutors and participants of the program are used as sources for ethnographic reference. After almost two decades of ceaseless effort, the local capacity of the Afghan government, including its security forces, has been upgraded to a certain degree and the assistance offered by the international community should have improved to better accommodate local needs. Nevertheless, the Afghan government was stigmatized as corrupt according to the survey results presented by Alisa Tukkimaki in this volume. I believe that the Afghan Fellowship should be revisited from a local peacebuilding perspective with an aim to contribute to a series of discussion on "measuring peace consolidation" (Caplan 2019, 4, 104-22).

Critique of the Afghan Fellowship
The Context in which the Program was Pursued

When the Taliban collapsed in December 2001 with the Northern Alliance marching into Kabul with support from the United States, it was already obvious in theory that peace and stability for Afghanistan required the participation of majority Pashtuns in the discussion over how to rule the country. At the peak of the excitement and serious aftereffects (trauma) of the 9.11 attacks, it was difficult in practice for the US leadership to transform its winning

mentality to a conciliatory one, but I thought back then that a negotiated solution with the Taliban must be explored if we really wanted
to bring peace and stability in Afghanistan. In a meeting where several US State department officials were present, I advocated for a
negotiated settlement between the Afghan government (dominated
by the members of the Northern Alliance) and the Taliban, but my
proposal was flatly rejected by one of the participants from the US
government, saying it is impossible to negotiate with "terrorists."

In Japanese, the Afghan government was labelled as a "castle
built on loose sand (house of cards)," and a considerable amount
of money was poured into such a fragile or illusionary castle (for
example, the Japanese government provided about US$7 billion
to Afghanistan in two decades). In ancient Chinese philosophy, it
was believed that it was the god or heaven that decided who should
rule the world. The god would remove a ruler if he or she diverted
from the rule of right. According to this logic, sooner or later,
the Afghan government established with support from outsiders
would be removed by the order from heaven as it strayed from the
rule of right. A series of peacebuilding support provided by the
international community was seen as mere "life extension measures," and as soon as they were terminated, the fate of the Afghan
government would come to an end.

Then, why did the international community support the Afghan
government if it was doomed? The United States intervened in
Afghanistan to disrupt terrorist networks in the region and especially in Pakistan, and to degrade any ability they had to plan and
launch international terrorist attacks. This primary objective of
the US involvement in Afghanistan was maintained throughout,
from George W. Bush to Barack Obama, and then Donald Trump.
In this sense, the US involvement of Afghanistan was a "success"
as it prevented the second 9.11 attacks on the US homeland by Al
Qaeda from happening for about 20 years. So, it was the cost that

the international community had to pay to achieve the primary objective of the United States. The "life extension measures" provided to the Afghan government by the international community was counted as one of these expenditures.

As pointed out by Michael Fors in his chapter in this volume, when Obama won the US presidential election in 2008, we were in the middle of a workshop held in Hiroshima. I still remember vividly that the people in the venue surrounded a large TV in the hall covering the election results. Many of us, including the Afghan Fellows, jumped for joy when we learned that Obama had won. As Michael Fors recalled in his chapter, the Afghan Fellows literally danced with Fors (not Dances with Wolves). This episode illumined two important points: one about the Afghan Fellowship and the other about the US engagement in Afghanistan. Most of the participants of the Afghan Fellowship, including Fellows, Coaches, Mentors, Resource Persons, staff of the UNITAR, were like-minded people, cerebrating the victory of Obama and sharing optimism for the future of Afghanistan. They identified themselves as liberal peace-loving citizens and expressed dissatisfaction with the US policy pursued under George W. Bush. None of them expected the hasty US withdrawal from Afghanistan. They expected some changes in the US policy but not in the direction of weakening the US support for peacebuilding in Afghanistan. This episode revealed an inconvenient truth that the newly elected US government controlled the fate of the Afghan government, not the Afghan leaders. In August 2021, we all witnessed that the Afghan government collapsed when the US President Joe Biden decided to withdraw the remaining US troops from Afghanistan.

Human Resource Development of Afghan Technocrats
Obviously, the goals of the Afghan Fellowship did not resonate with the primary objectives of the US involvement in Afghanistan. Then, why was UNITAR allowed to undertake and continue this

project for 15 years? Because it focused on human resource development of Afghan technocrats, particularly those who worked for the finance and procurement sectors. According to Michael Fors, many alumni of the Afghan Fellowship were found in leadership positions in the Agha Khan Foundation, the National Procurement Agency, and the President's Office. After the fall of the previous government, I am not sure how many of them still work with the current government. Human resources are worth investment in most circumstances as any government needs talented people to administer it. In particular, the Afghan Fellowship focused on offering leadership mindset and administrative skills useful in project management and procurement.

The first Islamic Emirates of Afghanistan, also known as the Taliban regime, was good at controlling people with strict rules which were associated with fear of harsh punishment. However, during the five years of rule by its first administration, economic growth was not seen, and women and ethnic minorities suffered from discrimination. For the current Taliban regime, to learn the lessons of its previous "failed" experience and to enjoy the support of ordinary people, it needs to employ as many capable civil servants as possible to run the country smoothly and effectively, without depending too much on the fear of ordinary people. It is a good sign that many of the former Afghan Fellows were allowed to keep their positions in the government even though their ministerial leaders have been replaced. The investment of the Afghan Fellowship could bear fruit under the new Taliban regime, whether it was intended or not.

Ironically, the conditions are favorable now for the Afghan Fellows to demonstrate their potential as servant leaders and effective public servants. Insecurity caused by the Taliban offensive was the most serious bottleneck for the Afghan Fellows to work effectively in the government. Now that the Taliban rule, and have claimed general amnesty for those who worked for the previous government, civil servants do not have to worry about their safety, and they can concentrate on working for their country. Since the Taliban face economic devastation and international isolation incurred by the sanctions by the West, dedicated service and devotion of the former Afghan Fellows are needed more than ever. In the previous government, the situation was non-permissive, and the safety of government officials was not guaranteed as they became vulnerable targets of the Taliban offensive. But now they do not have to be afraid for their physical safety. Hence, the Afghan Fellowship Program was not a waste as many Afghan Fellows may still have a chance to take the advantage of their past learning. Hopefully, their dedication will be rewarded properly since in the previous Taliban regime, government officials were not provided with sufficient salary which forced them into corruption so as to survive and support their families — thus losing the incentive to serve the people.

At the same time, with hindsight, one can make a critique of the program design of the Afghan Fellowship, as it focused on recruiting liberal individuals in the society. From the point of view of local peacebuilding, jirgas (traditional assemblies of leaders in Afghanistan) had the potential to bridge the central government and rural communities in Afghanistan. Religious leaders, elders, and warlords have been very powerful and influential among the ordinary people in the rural areas. They are known in the literature of peacebuilding as powerbrokers or gatekeepers, whose presence is critical for bridging different communities and orchestrating various peacebuilding endeavors in their sphere of influence. Unfortunately, from the standpoint of promoting liberal peace, these powerbrokers are often labelled as spoilers or illiberal agencies, who can jeopardize liberal peacebuilding.

Such a bias prevented these actors from being selected as Afghan Fellows (perhaps, they were not even considered as legitimate candidates for the Afghan Fellowship). It would have been useful if prominent players (or promising members) in jirgas were recruited as Afghan Fellows. Perhaps, it would not have been practical to train elders or ideologues, who were either too old or too eccentric to learn from others. However, promising young religious leaders, and sons or daughters of tribal elders and warlords could have served as a bridge between the "Fellowship mindset" and traditional customs and norms. They could have translated foreign knowledge and skills into ones that fit well in the local context. Although it was beyond the scope of the Afghan Fellowship to envisage such a critical function of bridge-building, with hindsight, working with these "illiberal" elements in Afghan society would have contributed to the infiltration of the "Fellowship mindset" or the spirit of servant leadership deep into the hinterland.

In other words, many of the Afghan Fellows were clean, innocent, enlightened, liberal, and bright individuals, who belonged to a different universe from the corrupt and greedy but powerful gatekeepers in the Afghan government and communities. Perhaps other human resource development programs oversaw the engagement with these illiberal elements or already influential leaders, and the Afghan Fellowship should be evaluated in the light of complementarity and coherence as what the Afghan Fellowship was trying to achieve was a drop in the ocean. At the same time, at least occasionally, the "liberal" Fellows, who belong to the promising next generations, could have been paired with "illiberal" but prominent powerbrokers in their on-the-job training assignments of the Afghan Fellowship.

Local Ownership: Key Interlocutors of the Human-centered Approach
One important element in program design worth noting is what Alisa Tukkimaki describes in her paper (Annex A of this volume) as follows: "Structurally and logistically, the Afghan Fellowship is a top-down program whereas its core values, resources, and

sustainability lie in its bottom-up approaches." While the Afghan Fellowship was a UNITAR initiative, and key stakeholders included US citizens such as Professor David Eaton of University of Texas and Michael Fors of Microsoft, the program was led initially by three female UNITAR Musketeers whose backgrounds were close to the region where Afghanistan is located: Nassrine Azimi (Director of the UNITAR Hiroshima Office, originally from Iran), Humaira-Khan Kamal (Afghan Fellowship Team Leader, originally from Pakistan), and Sharapiya Kakimova (UNITAR Afghan Fellowship staff, originally from Kazakhstan). This gave the Afghan Fellowship a multicultural flavor and non-Western outlook, which contributed positively to the purpose of encouraging local ownership. Visions projected and leadership demonstrated by the three Musketeers were very instrumental in maintaining the top-down structure of the program; at the same time, their mindset and approaches were very useful for promoting local ownership. As the Afghan Fellows were not recruited from the bottom of society in Afghanistan, it may be misleading to identify the Afghan Fellowship as having bottom-up approaches. At the same time, because the program was designed to promote local ownership, it possessed genuine bottom-up characteristics. For example, after completing the cycle of training, outstanding and committed Afghan Fellows were given the chance to serve as Mentors and Resource Persons for the next cycles of training.

Another symbolic embodiment of local ownership can be found in the presence and dedication of Sabahuddin Sokout, who started as a Fellow in 2005, became a Coach in 2006, and an Afghan Resource Person in 2007, and since 2007 has served as a Faculty/Mentor and UNITAR Afghan Fellowship Representative in Afghanistan. The manner through which Sokout performed his role in the Fellowship at the Afghan end, contributed to and impacted the memory, behavior and the "Fellowship mindset" of the Afghan Fellows, as their testimonies included in this volume illustrate, as well as on the larger

Fellowship community. Sokout's engagement, together with tireless efforts by many Afghan Coaches such as Sayed Mobin Shah, M. Ayaz Azizi, and Samad Yadgari, was both symbolic and substantive, to make the Afghan Fellowship truly locally owned. I wish I had had the chance to read the rich personal histories and profiles of the Afghan Fellows and Coaches included in this volume when I served as a mentor located in Hiroshima.

Final Remarks

Over a decade ago, in a volume entitled, Toward Bringing Stability in Afghanistan: A Review of the Peacebuilding Strategy (Uesugi 2009a), I proposed some policy recommendations to the international community involved in peacebuilding in Afghanistan. I advocated for promoting three changes in the peacebuilding strategy: (1) a regional approach; (2) human security; and (3) popular support (Uesugi 2009b). As statements presented in the survey conducted by Alisa Tukkimaki in this volume indicated that Afghan government officials saw the presence of Pakistan and Iran had a negative impact on the security situation in Afghanistan, a regional approach (not only focusing on Afghanistan but perceiving dynamics in Afghanistan in relation to the regional circumstances) is still relevant. Due to the security challenges, some of the sessions of the Afghan Fellowship were conducted in neighboring countries. More involvement of Pakistan and Iran could have been envisioned in the Afghan Fellowship, including inter-regional leadership training and discussion for the future of the region with leaders of these neighboring countries.

Promoting human security for the Afghan people, not for US strategic interests, is still an important peacebuilding policy for Afghanistan in the context of the post-Taliban takeover. It will be in this challenging period that the servant leaders are needed more than ever. In addition to the 400 alumni, who can act as effective public servants in their government institutions, as I argued above, we could have also trained "hybrid" bridge-builders, who could travel across cleavages and translate between traditional elements in the rural society and the central government as these bridges are essential for generating and sustaining popular support in Afghan society. The Taliban regime has maintained successfully the overall security, so that ordinary people now do not have to worry about their physical safety. Under such circumstances, Afghan society could move into the next phase in which a myriad of challenges could be tackled substantively. The new government must provide social and public services to their constituents (particularly in the areas of education and health), protect the rights of minorities, generate robust economic growth, and address the challenges of corruption and criminality, all of which were the goals of international coop-eration for the past two decades. This time these efforts should not be led by expatriates, but now it is high time that the international community encourage and support "true" national/local ownership. It is hoped that in this endeavor, the Afghan Fellows would play important roles in various sectors of society. Whether the Afghan Fellowship has produced a sufficient number of serious and capable servant leaders able to work with the Taliban regime (chosen by the god/heaven at least temporarily) for the ordinary people (not for the donors) can be seen only in the years to come. This would prove to be living evidence of my answer to Humaira Khan-Kamal's ques-tion, "Was it all a waste?"

Reference

- Brusset, Emery. 2016. "Seeking Simplicity: A Practical Appli-cation of Complexity to Evaluation." In Complexity Thinking for Peacebuilding Practice and Evaluation, eds. Emery Brus-set, Cedric de Coning, and Bryn Hughes. London: Palgrave Macmillan. Kindle.

- Brusset, Emery, Cedric de Coning, and Bryn Hughes. 2016. "Introduction." In Complexity Thinking for Peacebuilding

Practice and Evaluation, eds. Emery Brusset, Cedric de Coning, and Bryn Hughes. London: Palgrave Macmillan. Kindle.

• Caplan, Richard. 2019. Measuring Peace: Principles, Practices, and Politics. New York: Oxford University Press. Kindle.

• d'Estrée, Tamra Pearson. 2020. "A Refresher on Evaluation."
In New Directions in Peacebuilding Evaluation, ed. Tamra
Pearson d'Estrée, 3-18. Lanham and London: Rowman & Lit-
tlefield International. Kindle.

• Firchow, Pamina. 2018. Reclaiming Everyday Peace: Local
Voices in Measurement and Evaluation After War. Cambridge, New York, Port Melbourne, and Singapore: Cambridge University Press. Kindle.

• Hughes, Bryn. 2016. "Thawing Ceteris Paribus: The Move to
a Complex Systems Lens." In Complexity Thinking for Peacebuilding Practice and Evaluation, eds. Emery Brusset, Cedric
de Coning, and Bryn Hughes. London: Palgrave Macmillan.
Kindle.

• Hunt, Charles T. 2016. "Avoiding Perplexity: Complexi-
ty-Oriented Monitoring and Evaluation for UN Peace Operations." In Complexity Thinking for Peacebuilding Practice
and Evaluation, eds. Emery Brusset, Cedric de Coning, and
Bryn Hughes. London: Palgrave Macmillan. Kindle.

• Joshi, Madhav, and Peter Wallensteen, eds. 2018. Understanding Quality Peace: Peace- building after Civil War.
Oxon and New York: Routledge.

• Leonardsson, Hanna, and Gustav Rudd. 2015. "The 'Local
Turn' in Peacebuilding: A Literature Review of Effective and
Emancipatory Local Peacebuilding." Third World Quarterly
36 (5): 825-39. DOI: 10.1080/01436597.2015.1029905.

• Millar, Gearoid. 2014. An Ethnographic Approach to Peacebuilding: Understanding Local Experiences in Transitional
States. Abingdon and New York: Routledge. Kindle.

- OECD. 2021. Applying Evaluation Criteria Thoughtfully. https://doi.org/10.1787/543e84ed-en

- Uesugi, Yuji, ed. 2009a. Toward Bringing Stability in Afghanistan: A Review of the Peacebuilding Strategy, IPSHU English Research Report Series No. 24, Institute for Peace Science, Hiroshima University.

- Uesugi, Yuji. 2009b. "Breaking the Vicious Cycle of insecurity: Counter-insurgency in Afghanistan." In Toward Bringing Stability in Afghanistan: A Review of the Peacebuilding Strategy, ed. Yuji Uesugi. IPSHU English Research Report Series No. 24, Institute for Peace Science, Hiroshima University.

- Wallensteen, Peter. 2015. Quality Peace: Peacebuilding, Victory, and World Order. New York: Oxford University Press.

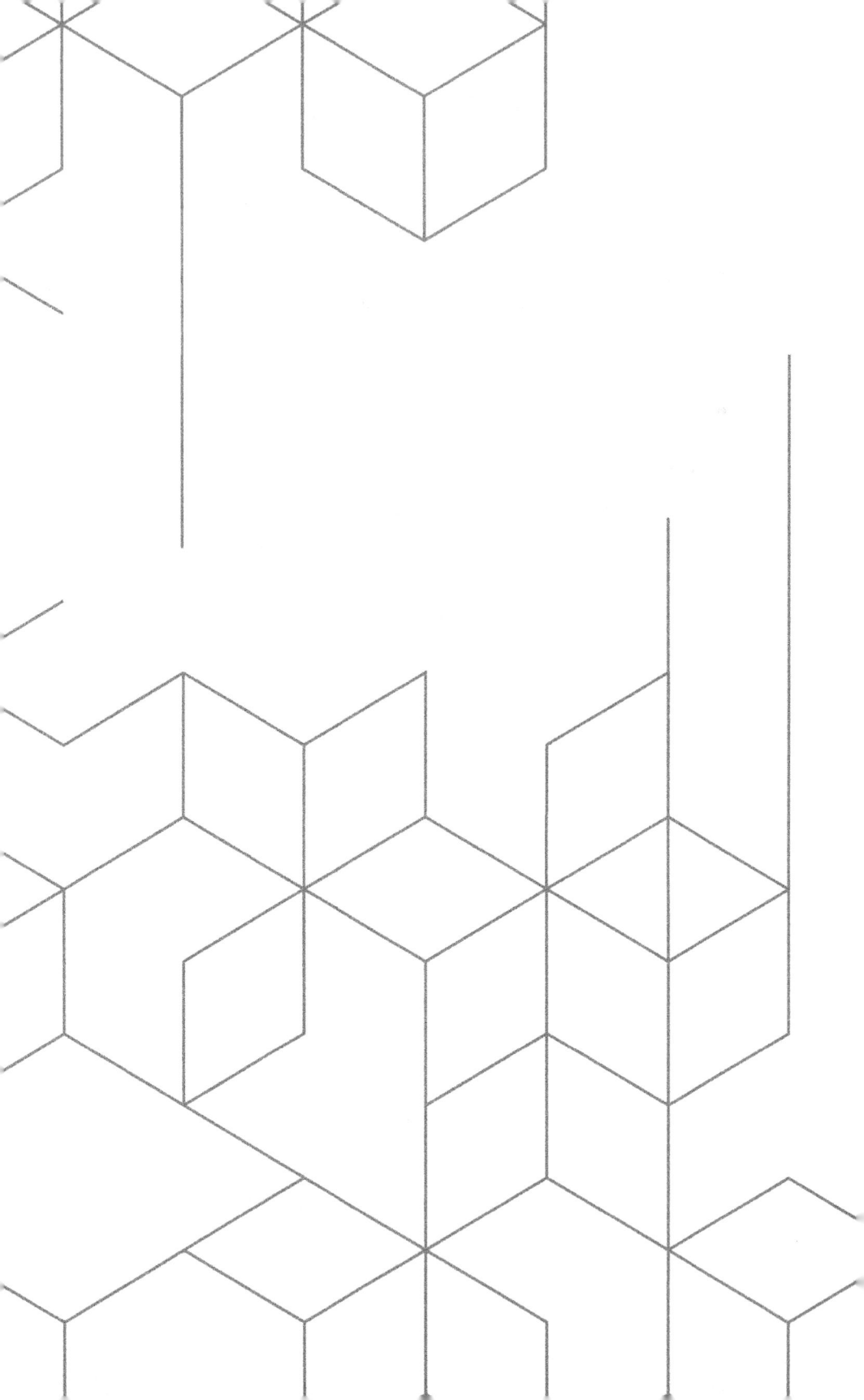

PART VI
IN CONCLUSION

A Poem in Pashto
Jamal Nasir[53]

کندهار می د بابا په قباله دی

که پنجشیر دی که واخان دی وطن زما دی

هره لوپښت می د نیکه او بابا گور دی

په هر گام باندي لحد او کفن زما دی

هر غاټول یی زما له وینو رنگ اخیستی

دا په وینو روزل سوی چمن زما دی

له نیکه راپاتی سوی په میراث دی

دا د مشکو رباتونو خــــتن زما دی

سرداري یی زما په پچه ده ختلی

له آمو تر مست هلمنده مامن زما دی

که تاجک دی که اوزبک دی یو افغان دی

ددي خاوري هزاره ترکمن زما دی

چی فکرونه د نفاق پالی په سر کی

امتیاز یی د وهلو کشتن زما دی

بنه یی زما دي ، بد یی زما دي هر څه زما دي

ددي خاوري ارغوان او زغن زما دی

دلته هره تیره کاڼی بدخشان دی

دا لالونه، غرونه غرونه دمن زما دی

Kandahar is my forefather's possession, Punjshir and Wakhan is my homeland

Every inch of this land is my ancestor's ownership, and on every step even the bones of the dead in the graves are mine

The red roses are watered by the blood of sacrifice of its patriotic sons

The ownership of this country has passed to me from our grandfathers and its beautiful roadways and thoroughfares are blessed with aroma of heavens.

The Kingship of this land is given to me and from Amu River in the north to Himland valley to its south are all mine.

Tajiks and Uzbeks are all Afghans, Hazaras and Turkmens are all ONE and sons of this homeland

Anyone who divides us into groups and ethnicity; I will be the one to demolish and destroy such individuals

All ups and downs, all good and bad shades of this homeland are mine. The negative minds and positive both belongs to us

---

[53] AF 2008 Fellow, Coach

د ازل تقسیم باغوان یم پیدا کړی

دا بهار دا لاله زار او ګلشن زما دی

دا مورچل مورچل پکتیا او دا ښبربریتي

چي فلک به کوږ ورګوري دښمن زما دی

که میرویس دی که اکبر که مسجدي دی

هره توره، هر میدان او تورزن زما دی

فتحه زما ده، فخر زما دی، جشن زما دی

شهید زما دی د ویرژلو شیون زما دی

چي په زړه کبڅه درتبر نسي اسمانه

چي پرون می د نیکونو و ننـ زما دی

عبدالباري جهاني

Here every stone, and mountain are Badkhshan, full of Emeralds and Rubiesand precious stones are mine

God gifted me this land full of fresh water, orchards and gardens and its flowers, trees and fruits are mine

The high peak mountains of Paktia are mine and anyone has bad attention towards my homeland is my enemy

Mirawais, Wazir Akbar and Masjidi and all the great freedom fighters are mine whom have bravely conquered every battle.

All the proud of conquests are mine, all the achievements of battles and martyrs are mine

Do not doubt, as yesterday this land was property of my forefathers that's why today its ownership belongs to me.....**by A. Jahani**

A Poem in Dari and Commentary
Raed Quraishi[54]

نام : سید فیض‌الرحمن
تخلص: راند
نام خانوادگی: قریشی

بنده یکی از اشتراک کنندگان برنامه خوب و گران ارز UNITAR در سال ۲۰۱۵ از سهم وزارت تحصیلات عالی بودم. این برنامه که در کابل ، ابوظبی و شهر هیروشیمای جاپان برگذار گردیده بود ، در کل یک برنامه آموزشی در عرصه علوم مدیریتی ، رهبری ، پلانگذاری و بخش های متعدد و مختلف دیگر بود. برای من این برنامه خیلی آموزشی بود و مهم تر این که چیز های تازه و نو را در بخش پروپوزال نویسی ، مدیریت و رهبری آموختم که قبلا ندیده و نخوانده بودم. فضای درسی چنان دوستانه ومحترمانه بود که هیچ انسانی احساس دل تنگی و بیگانگی نمی کرد و گویا که همه اعضای یک خانواده اند. برخورد مردم هیروشیما و همپذیری و کوشش آنان برای عمران کشور و ملت شان شگفتی آور بود. آن جا جز به کارکرد نو زحمتکشیدن به چیز دیگری نمی اندیشیدند. مهم ترین اینکه ، بانوی کهن سالی که از سانحهٔ بمباران هیروشیما در جنگ دوم جهانی زنده مانده بود ، چیز های جالب و شنیدنی از چشم دید خود برای ما قصه کرد که سراپا اندرز و درس بود. به هر حال از کابل تا ابوظبی و تا هیروشیما ، این سفر آموزنده ، دوست داشتنی و تجربه آور بود و حالات و کیفیات ما و آن مردم مصداق این بیت شیخ اجل حکیم سعدی شیرازی بود:

بنی‌آدم اعضای یک دیگر اند
که در آفرینش ز یک جوهر اند
چو عضوی به درد آورد روزگار
دگر عضوها را نماند قرار
سعدی

من از برگذارکنندگان این برنامه زیبا و آموزنده اظهار سپاس و امتنان می‌نمایم ، علی‌الخصوص شخصیت با دانش و مهربان جناب صباح‌الدین سکوت که سکوتش سرشار از فریاد های وطن دوستی است. من در آخر این بیت ابوالمعانی بیدل را به تمام برگذار کنندگان و اشتراک کنندگان این برنامه پیش کش می کنم:

به محفل شمع تابان در گلستان رنگ و بو باشی
الهی هر کجا باشی بهار آبرو باشی
بیدل

باعرض ارادت و محبت
س . ف (راند قریشی)
کابل
۲۹ جوز۱/خرداد/۱۳۹۹

---

[54] AF 2015 Fellow

یک پارچه شعر از خودم

جهان گرفته دلش از جهالت از جنگ و ...
ازین شرارت و انسان کشی و نیرنگ و ...
ازین مذاهب و ناباوران دین و بشر
ازین کتاب و ازین برگه ها و فرهنگ و ...
ازین منابر و وعاظ و شیخ و روحانی
ازین کنشت و ازین فتنه های افرنگ و ...
دلش گرفته ازین نابرابری ها و ...
ازین ترازوی دیرینه سال و پاهنگ و ...
جهان جهان فریب است و پول سالاری
جهان جهان دروغ است و فتنه آهنگ و ...
جهان حکایت یک کودک فلسطینی
جهان نگاره‌ی پیری و اخم و اژنگ و ...
جهان جهان بدی بود ما ندانستیم
جهان سوّم و آوارگان از جنگ و ...
ر.ق. ...

The world is tired of ignorance and war...

Of these chaos and killings

The world is disillusioned with these numerous religions and the unbelievers of divinity and humanity...

And suffering of these books and pages...

The world is tired of these priests and propagators...

And of these theses minarets, sheikhs, prayers and priests...

The world is tired of these inequalities ...

And from these old scales and beams...

The world is a world of deceit and capitalism...

The world is a world of lies and cunning...

The world is the story of a Palestinian child

The world is the portrait of our anger and senescence...

The world is not a reasonable place for us

The Third World and the refugees from the war...

S.F.Ra'ed Quraishi

Hiroshima Reflections
Jennifer Hatfield[55]

In 2004 I emerged from the Kabul Airport into the direct sight of a Canadian tank. The soldier was aiming a very large gun in my direction, and I felt a dislocation and a traumatic jolt that I will never forget. The devastation I saw as we drove to the guesthouse was harrowing. I was a visitor, but all around me were people who had lived through this utter catastrophe. The loss of schools, hospitals, homes, cultural centers, and historical buildings. Everywhere I looked I saw loss. Many bombs had destroyed the city over decades of war.

The reason for my trip to Afghanistan was to meet with members of the Ministry of Health and the newly formed Ministry of Women's Affairs. This work was part of an international research project on domestic violence. The University of Calgary in Canada had been invited to learn from our Afghan colleagues and local women about the issues they faced, and the efforts being made to address this leading health issue. We were seeking a way forward together to create new policy that would guide the ministries in reducing violence in the family. I was so deeply moved by the resilience and commitment of my new Afghan colleagues and friends. Returning to Canada, I wondered how I could stay connected to this remarkable community.

---

[55] Jennifer Hatfield was Associate Dean Global Health and International Partnerships from 2009-2014 and Associate Dean Strategic Partnerships and Community Engagement in the Cumming School of Medicine 2014-2019. Dr. Hatfield served as an AF Mentor and Resource Person for multiple cycles.

Not long after my time in Afghanistan I was approached to be a Mentor for the UNITAR Fellowship Program for Afghanistan. I was very fortunate to be involved for several years, once again working with remarkable leaders in the emerging civil service. It was this engagement that brought me to Hiroshima three times as part of the annual leadership training of the Afghan Fellows. Each visit was a life altering event. In this brief section, I have the honor of sharing just a few of the reflections of the Fellows who participated in the Hiroshima experience.

Following the devastation of the atomic bomb, Hiroshima declared itself a City of Peace. The prefectural government decided to commit itself to supporting leadership development in countries impacted by war and conflict. This support was financial, cultural, and educational. Hiroshima determined that its legacy would be investment in reconstruction and peace building. The UNITAR Afghan Fellows were invited annually to visit the city, to learn about this approach to post conflict reconstruction and to meet with A-Bomb survivors. Each element of the visit was structured to share, in the most personal way, the possibility of re birth and renewal in the wake of utter destruction.

I was asked by Humaira Kamal to reflect on the experiences of working with the Fellows during our Hiroshima visits. I have been able to review many of the written reflective notes that Fellows wrote following our visit to the Peace Park and our time with the survivors. I have sought to capture some of the key themes and to share a sample of the moving messages that flowed from the Fellows during our time together. This is just a snapshot of the many wonderful notes written during our visits. Not all of the quotations are attributed to specific individuals as some were handed in without names. However, where possible I have quoted as accurately as possible and provided the name of the authors.

It is important to set the context for these reflections as we remember that approximately 80,000 people died immediately when the bomb fell on August 6th, 1945. The total fatalities rose to 146,000 people in the months that followed. The utter destruction of the city and the legacy of radiation poisoning created a toxic legacy and suffering that has lasted for 75 years. The last 75 years have also seen a refocusing of energy into urban development. The stark contrasts of devastation and re birth were shared though the sculptures of the Peace Park, the realistic reenactments of events at the Memorial Museum, and by the individuals we met who shared their harrowing stories of survival.

In a November 23rd, 2011, an article in the Asahi Shinbun newspaper entitled, So Tell Me about Hiroshima, a Japanese journalist recounts the story of Mr. Shinuaku. This soft-spoken gentleman was one of the survivors we met in Hiroshima. He was 19 years old the day the bomb was dropped and had worked all night at a car manufacturing plant. Exhausted from his labor, he had gone home to bed in his modest house. Soon after he lay down, there was an enormous blast and his vision was blocked by a cloud of dust. "In a flash he was thrown into a cloud of darkness. He thought he had died and gone to another world." Over the following days he walked endlessly to find friends and relatives. He saw women and children who had lost their clothes and even skin in the force of the blast. He remembers trucks carrying away the dead. He witnessed great suffering and loss of life. The damage to his city was overwhelming but he had survived. In the decades to follow he went on to be a successful businessman working on the reconstruction of the city. In 2008 he left his business life behind and decided to share the story of his experience with as many people as possible. He felt the story must be told and more people should know about the war and the nuclear weapons. He gives 150 lectures a year to groups from all over the world and to children at schools throughout Japan.

Our trip to the Peace Park and Museum and our meeting with a survivor were central components of a busy schedule of cultural and educational activities in Hiroshima. It is impossible to describe the impact of these experiences on all of us, but a reflective writing exercise gave an opportunity to express some of the strong emotions that we felt after bearing witness to the survivors' stories and the Peace Park Museum's depiction of the history of the destruction. These reflections were shared during our round table discussions and kept at the UNITAR office in the hope that one day they might be part of the Afghanistan Fellowships' historical record.

One of the most poignant messages came in the form of a letter Shirzad addressed to his mother. It captures the heartfelt emotion and the pain we felt, as we learned about the human cost of war.

"Dear Mom
I kiss your hands and greet you from Hiroshima.

You know Hiroshima is the city that was heartlessly bombed by an atomic bomb and still has many documented stories in the chests of its survivors and ancestors.

It was a surprise what we learned [as we] watched facts about the Hiroshima atomic disaster. However, what I saw and what I heard was what I have seen with my own eyes in Kabul, but there is a difference. We are dying dozen by dozen and they died thousand by thousand. We are dying by shooting but they were burned alive. We are waiting to die but they encountered the "Little Boy" (the bomb) that burned out their sweet children and their respected moms and dads. Here, everything is speaking and shedding tears... while telling the story of the land, the trees the river, the ruins, the memorial and over the peace park, is singing the song of peace.

Katsufumi Shintaku, the 86-year-old survivor of the war, told us the same story of the war and his story took me 10 years back to Kabul. I remembered my assassinated father who was red colored by his blood. Shintaku has hundreds of stories in his chest."

The deep emotion expressed in this letter was echoed by Abdul Ari Balakarzai, another Fellow who expressed the shock we all felt at the scale of the devastation. His reflection is full of tenderness and an awareness of the innocent lives lost. He also introduces the two key themes of reconstruction and long-term security that were noted by many of the Fellows. He wrote,

"A bomb dropped at 8h15 am on Aug 6, 1945. Killing 90,000. The next day Nagasaki killing more than 60,000.

It was not the fault of those innocent children who were playing in the streets and were killed.

I call upon all armed countries to sign a non-proliferation treaty... to have a secure world for the sake of their children.

It gives me great hope that this city has been rebuilt again, after it was massively destroyed and faced starvation.

All humans are brethren, and we should give more space in our hearts for co-existence, for discussions of hope and social cohesion."

It was a wonderful realization for the Fellows that they found kindred spirits in their Japanese hosts. The solidarity of shared experiences of war created an energy and a catalyst for imagining a hopeful future for Afghanistan.

Dr Mohammad Saber Perdes, a Fellow from November 2008, wrote a letter that so powerfully captures the impact of the survivor's story.

"I want to write to you about the most important experience of my life which made me hopeful for the future.
In fact, I believe in [a] strong decision and its power but
I never felt it on my skin before. Today I was privileged
to meet one of the survivors of the first atomic explosion
back in 1945- in the Peace Museum of Hiroshima City.
His name is Mr. Shintaku and he is 83 years old.

While I was listening to his sayings, I visualized the
scenes he was talking about. I was about to cry because
all his experiences were very sad and full of grief. He witnessed the death of thousands of people yelling for help
and asking for water. He has been a very courageous
man and he has been the luckiest person of Hiroshima
City, for he not only survived the explosion but also didn't
develop any keloids and has lived a healthy life up to now.

I would like to say that the most important lesson I
learned from my trip to Hiroshima and visiting the Peace
Museum was that we can also rebuild our war-torn country only if we have a strong decision and put our country
first. Long live Afghanistan."

One of the most painful and powerful moments for me was when
I saw how the trauma of the day at the Peace Park evoked painful
memories and experiences in my Afghan colleagues. The traumatic
stress experienced by so many Afghans is a daily reality and witnessing the stories and images of trauma in Hiroshima triggered
suffering as well as emotions of hope. The Fellows were profoundly
courageous to bear witness to the experience of war in Japan while
themselves in the grips of so much conflict and violence at home.
Jamal Nasir's impressions of visiting the Peace Park speak to this
shared trauma in a personal and immediate way as he recounts a
recent loss of a dear friend. His reflections brought the individual

impact home and I reflected on the thousands of friends lost in war and the legacy of these losses on children in Japan and Afghanistan.

"It was indeed a very sad moment and touching as well... you just stop as a living person and think about those who had lost their life and their dear ones. The A-Bomb, Hiroshima's destruction on that morning.

Afghanistan is one of the countries that has had the same experience. Every Afghan can write a book on his life... full of sorrow and touching moments... I can't describe in words, but I lost my dearest friend two weeks ago and it is very hard for me to go to his home and meet his kids... his son always asks me what happened to his dad...why is he not coming home? My heart aches and I do cry wherever I am by myself... I cannot cry in front of them... I am pretending but his wife and kids lost interest in life... I would say peace is the most beautiful thing in the world... Love and let others live.

Afghans and Afghanistan very much know the value of peace, but we are victims of war and conflict...still we are always a peace-loving people, and we will bring peace to Afghanistan region and finally to the whole world."

Hangama Hamid shared this same sentiment when she drew a comparison between the Japanese and Afghan experiences. In her reflection, we see the reoccurring themes of protecting and teaching the next generation.

"The Afghan people have had similar experiences as the Japanese people... it is better to try to rebuild our country, passing our memories of war to our next generations and encouraging them to have more consideration for peace building... not [to] spend time and energy and funds on war."

Ahmed Fawad Akbari also shared his concerns for the lessons that need to be shared with youth.

> "The Japanese used the consequences of war to tell their future generations and those who have nuclear weapons to promote peace."

Many Fellows focused their reflections on the importance of sharing a global message. Their comments reflect a cry of the heart to those in power to address the terrible consequences of war. Looking beyond Japan and Afghanistan there were calls to action like the one written by Gul Afghan Saleh in 2008.

> "Dear Honorable Mr. Obama, New President of the United States,
>
> First of all, I would like to congratulate you on your success. Second, I would like to express my feelings from visiting the Hiroshima Peace Memorial Park and meeting a survivor of the Atomic Bomb that burned Hiroshima City in 1945. The reason I am doing so is to appeal to you for launching a campaign to destroy all atomic bombs from the globe. You are the most important person who can play the key role in such an effort. You take the lead and ask/force other countries to follow you. The Hiroshima tragedy should never happen again. Human beings need peace. Please do this for the sake of God, for the sake of innocent children, for the sake of the mothers, for the sake of humanity, for the sake of your country and the for the sake of God's creatures. This should be your first responsibility. Also please put all your efforts to bring peace and stability in our warn-torn Afghanistan and other parts of the world where people suffer from the war and conflict. If you try, I am sure God will help you to success. I pray for peace and prosperity in the world."

As I look back and reflect on the sentiments shared by the Afghan Fellows, I am again made aware of the tremendous importance of the UNITAR program. The leadership training was structured to provide key skills to these remarkable emerging leaders. Team building, project management, leadership skills, and human resource development were taught through intense curriculum and many hours of in person and online classes. However, it was the experiential learning in Hiroshima that strengthened resolve and focused the Fellows on resilience, rebuilding, and hope. It was in Hiroshima that Fellows deepened their sense of shared solidarity. So many of the Fellows spoke of the need to seek peace and were impressed with how Japan took on the responsibility of fostering peace globally.

Nasir Ebrahimkhail noted in his reflections,

> "Japan and the Japanese can play a huge role in mobilizing other countries for a nuclear free world. The Japanese's have the message of forgive but do not forget."

Another personal reflection from one of the Group VI Fellows in 2009 captures several lessons learned:

> "I appreciate the patience of the people of Japan... they never thought of taking revenge after the atomic bomb was thrown at them. This gives me a clear message to be patient in every difficult moment of life.
>
> Everybody has the right of <u>peace and security</u> for herself or himself. It has come to my knowledge that war is not the solution of a conflict. If people have conflicts they should sit around and find out a peaceful solution to it. After the atomic bomb dropped <u>reconstruction</u> started immediately, which is also a good lesson learned."

Zainulabuddin Hamid a Fellow from 2008 also calls for peace in his heartfelt reflection.

"In 1945 we had big human damage and we lost more than 100,000 people...they were in their homes, some were on the road, in school, some children were away from their family. Therefore, I have a message to the people of the world PLEASE PLEASE think about peace- instead of war, instead of atomic competition... until people can live in peace."

In one of the most poignant pieces of writing that emerged from the groups was provided by Mahbooba Abawi in November 2008. It captures so many of the themes and feelings we all experienced. This poem provides us with enduring images of the sacred and moving experiences of the Hiroshima visits:

To you, the people who suffered from the Atomic Bomb

To you, the bravest creatures of the world

To you, the champions who reached the peak of success

To you, the establishers of your developed city

I am proud of you and your struggles

I admire your patience and your hard work

I don't want to remind you individually

The very painful event again

I don't want to say that thousands of people died

They are alive in all the people's hearts forever

I remembered and I saw the atomic bomb remaining

How all human beings were killed on blood and fire?

All people together died at once

I don't want to remind you about the hopelessness

I want to congratulate you, congratulate you

By rising from the ashes, the people of Hiroshima gave hope and inspiration to the world. To be beside my Afghan colleagues as they processed the stark realities of war, and the challenges of reconstruction was an honor and privilege. Seeing the courage, they display in the face of trauma was humbling. Through the Hiroshima experience many fellows came to a deeper understanding of the leadership they wished to embody and the peace they seek to secure. Their sincere reflections both haunt and inspire me, and I am glad we have captured them for future generations.

Afterthoughts Post-August 2021
December 7, 2021
Jennifer Hatfield

Four months have gone by since the fall of Kabul. I ask myself: What did the Hiroshima experience and the Fellowship program teach us about how to handle this utter catastrophe? What did we learn that can help us now?

We learned that innocent people did survive the worse situation that can ever be imagined or experienced. We learned we can never avert our gaze from the darkest moments of human history.

I listened to my Afghan colleagues then, and I listen to them now. They have taught me that from the ashes of loss and trauma, hope and a future can emerge if we stand in solidarity.

Epilogue
Japan to Afghanistan —A Silk Road Friendship
Masanori Nagaoka[56]

It seems that I have had some kind of connection to Hiroshima and to Afghanistan all my life.

Like most Japanese school students making a field trip to Hiroshima, I visited that city for the first time with my elementary school in 1980. My initial memories of the city, including the Hiroshima Peace Memorial Park, were of well-maintained landscapes surrounded by a tranquil atmosphere where no one could have ever imagined a nuclear explosion...

My next visit to Hiroshima was in 2014, when I started serving as one of the facilitators of UNITAR's World Heritage Sites Series in Hiroshima for three consecutive years. The UNITAR Series provided a unique opportunity for policymakers and national officials from developing countries, including Afghans, about how best to manage and conserve World Heritage sites. Meanwhile, I was fortunate to have worked for several years with the late Prof. Ikuo Hirayama, a renowned artist and former UNESCO Goodwill Ambassador, who was born in Hiroshima and was very active in the safeguarding of the world's cultural heritage, including that of Afghanistan.

---

[56] Dr. Nagaoka is Head of Culture Unit, UNESCO Office in Cambodia. He previously served at the UNESCO Office in Afghanistan.

Some years later, when I worked at the UNESCO Office in Afghanistan, Nassrine introduced me to some of the Afghan Fellowship participants, and I was reconnected to Hiroshima again through these young professionals: they were polite, receptive, vigorous, and full of energy as if they had determined to initiate reconstructing their country in speed.

Then a few months ago, Nassrine spoke to me about this book and asked me to contribute a paper about what safeguarding Afghanistan's cultural heritage could mean — what was done these past years, and what remains to be done yet in the future — and I wholeheartedly accepted the invitation to write this chapter.

Background

During my assignments in Afghanistan for nine years in total, I encountered many challenges in both security and programs, but there was always hope, and the deep motivation of Afghan colleagues with whom I worked.

UNESCO worked in close cooperation with the Afghan authorities, to safeguard and promote cultural heritage, cultural diversity, and human rights in the country. Its activities in Afghanistan re-affirmed UNESCO's mission as stated in the Preamble to the UNESCO Constitution, which aims to promote peace through humankind's intellectual and moral solidarity. To this end, UNESCO continued to assist Afghan authorities in delivering projects to safeguard Afghanistan's tangible and intangible cultural heritage and to promote public awareness among Afghan people about the value of preserving their heritage for future generations. Cultural heritage resources were mobilized, for example, by utilizing historical monuments that galvanized community support around their historical and contemporary symbolic values; myth, ritual, and religion that coalesce communities around movable, immovable, tangible, and intangible heritage ideals. It was argued that if efforts to preserve cultural heritage were to be sustainable into the future, they must be considered within a broader appreciation of the development context that integrated conceptions of intangible and tangible cultural heritage within a unified development model. UNESCO also sought to promote cross-cultural awareness and dialogue concerning Afghanistan's heritage as a valuable component of the world's natural and cultural heritage that enriched us all through an understanding of its contribution to history, art, and science.

Afghanistan or Ancient Ariana, as many ancient Greek and Roman authors referred to the region in antiquity, can be acknowledged as the multi-cultural cradle of Central Asia, linking East and West via historically significant trade conduits, that also conveyed ideas, concepts, and languages as a cultural by-product of fledgling international commerce. From this historical intercultural dialogue, Afghanistan and a number of countries on the Silk Route had benefited and significantly contributed to helping construct identity, self-esteem, pride, memories, and dignity in each county. As a result, contemporary Afghanistan became a multi-ethnic, multi-lingual society with a complex history stretching back many millennia. The numerous civilizations attested to in the archaeological record, both indigenous and foreign, constitute an extremely important account of the history and archaeology of Asia.

Afghanistan is, unfortunately, also a nation fragmented by a history of protracted conflict, exacerbated by geographic isolation for many communities with limited or unequal access to infrastructure and resources, both regionally and demographically. Having faced considerable adversity concerning the preservation of history and national identity that occurred from the late 1970s to 2001, significant steps needed to be undertaken to address the country's multiple challenges: the rehabilitation process in Afghanistan addressed these issues when the nation was to unify under a common objective, fostering a veracious society free from conflict, and where ethnic diversity was recognized for its social, cultural, and economic benefits rather than seen as a hindrance to particular developmental objectives. Part of the solution to this problem lies in the promotion of a positive public discussion to promote inter-cultural understanding and to raise awareness of the potential that such discourse had to contribute to the broader goals of rapprochement, peacebuilding, and economic development in Afghanistan.

Culture during the Civil War from the 1970s

During the civil war, the capacity of the Ministry of Information and Culture (MoIC), responsible for cultural heritage management in Afghanistan, was steadily eroded as skilled personnel continued to flee the country. Nonetheless, amidst the destruction, there were glimmers of hope and acts of self-sacrifice to secure some of the most significant items from the collections. The story of the Bactrian Gold is one such example, where the National Museum staff clandestinely moved the collection into the vaults of the Presidential Palace during the 1980s to protect it from potential threats, until its re-emergence in 2003. Another was the ad-hoc inventory and the removal of the remainder of the Museum collections in 1996 to a "safe house" at the Kabul Hotel while the Museum building was under rocket fire, and the Duralaman area was in dispute by Mujahedeen factions, merely weeks before the arrival of the Taliban in Kabul. There is no doubt that these acts saved many of the important materials from disappearing completely or being irrevocably damaged.

Efforts to Preserve Afghanistan's Cultural Heritage

After the end of the civil unrest until 2021, concerted efforts by the international community and the Afghan authorities had attempted to address the many challenges confronting cultural heritage preservation in Afghanistan, both contemporary and historical, with varying degrees of success.

On a practical level, there had been significant steps forward regarding cultural heritage preservation in Afghanistan as a result of the return of the international community since 2001, and concerted efforts to address key issues and priorities by the newly established government, national and international proponents. The Afghan Government, which had ratified the World Heritage Convention in 1979, has also ratified the 1970 UNESCO Convention on the Means of Prohibiting and Preventing the Illicit Import, Export, and Transfer of Ownership of Cultural Property, the 1995 UNIDROIT Convention on Stolen or Illegally Exported Cultural Objects, the 2003 Convention for the Safeguarding of the Intangible Cultural Heritage, and the 2005 Convention on the Protection and Promotion of the Diversity of Cultural Expressions. Revised national legislation for the protection and promotion of culture in Afghanistan in 2004 introduced to implement them has positively impacted the illicit traffic of antiquities and cultural heritage preservation in general.

However, the implementation of the law was yet in its early stages as agencies such as UNESCO tried to improve the capacities of the relevant Afghan authorities and also encouraged a culture of safeguarding movable heritage, which was largely non-existent among the general population. Unfortunately, the illicit traffic of antiquities and the organized looting of archaeological sites remain the greatest threats to Afghanistan's cultural heritage and may well continue for the foreseeable future within the present context of poverty, lawlessness, and conflict, that has gripped much of the country. Notwithstanding, the new laws had certainly had a direct and positive effect on raising awareness of the problem at the government level as an important first step.

Gains were also made at the policy level, although this too needed further strengthening and development on a range of issues including protecting movable heritage, safeguarding and promoting tangible and intangible heritage, and the protection and long-term management of historic urban heritage throughout the country. These issues have been identified in several international forums as of primary concern to the preservation of Afghanistan's cultural heritage along with a range of other important issues. To this end, the International Coordination Committee for the Safeguarding of Afghanistan's Cultural Heritage (ICC) was formed in 2002 to coordinate all international efforts for the safeguarding of cultural heritage in Afghanistan. UNESCO was requested to assist with coordination efforts by the Afghan Government and published recommendations concerning the types of measures to be taken.

H.E. Dr. Raheen, the former Minister for Information and Culture, also established a Heritage Management Advisory Board in 2013 to assist the government in specific areas of expertise in heritage management and conservation, and to enhance coordination in the sector. This Board has already had a measurable impact on improving coordination and capacity in the culture sector to act quickly to challenges facing heritage in provinces across the country and to provide practical solutions to existing problems. Activities and initiatives such as this, that can contribute to enhanced coordination, strengthening the capacities of government institutions and their ability to better preserve and manage cultural heritage into the future, are worthy of maintaining and bolstering into the future.

Another positive for Afghanistan has been the two sites, the Minaret and Archaeological Remains of Jam and the Cultural Landscape and Archaeological Remains of the Bamiyan Valley, inscribed on the World Heritage List in 2002 and 2003 respectively, which is a source of cultural pride for many Afghans. The Government had received financial and technical assistance from the international community with a view to their effective long-term management and preservation, e.g., Japan, Italy, Korea, Switzerland, Greece,

Germany, the World Bank, and so forth. In turn, these efforts were having a positive effect on building the capacity of Afghan heritage-related institutions, such as the Institute of Archaeology and the Historical Monuments Department, as well as encouraging a more coordinated effort from different Ministries of the Afghan Government through the creation of Technical Working Groups and Committees to facilitate better management of the sites.

The site of Mes Aynak in Logar Province, earmarked for extensive copper extraction, is presently the subject of rescue and preventive archaeology carried out by the Ministry of Mines and Petroleum and the Ministry of Information and Culture. This site had been subject to illegal excavation for many years, occupied by various military factions in the 1990s due to its remote location. The mining lease granted to a Chinese firm had brought international attention to the site, and as a result, an important picture emerged of the Buddhist community in the early centuries of the current era, that accrued wealth based on copper extraction and trade, resulting in an urban complex with numerous religious monuments, sculptures, and artifacts which are now being partially recovered.

Efforts of international organizations, most notably the Society for the Preservation of Afghan Cultural Heritage, the Aga Khan Trust for Culture, the Délégation archéologique française en Afghanistan, the Afghan Consulting Cultural Heritage Organization as well as others such as Turquoise Mountain, and a host of national non-governmental organizations, such as the Afghan Center at Kabul University, have also made considerable contributions to the activities of the MoIC concerning both tangible and intangible heritage related programs, and in rebuilding civil society. Many of the aforementioned organizations conducted numerous conservation programs on historical monuments in the provinces of Bamiyan, Ghor, Balkh, Kabul, Herat, Ghazni, and Tashqurghan, thereby further contributing to practical and visible gains for the Afghan community. UNESCO is proud to have been contributing to this work through the preservation of the Minaret of Jam, the rehabilitation of the Mausoleum of Abdul Razzaq in Ghazni, the consolidation of the Buddha niches, and the restoration of the ancient Islamic citadel of Shahr-e-Gholgholah at the Bamiyan World Heritage Site, the Musalla Complex in Herat including the stabilization of the 5th Minaret, and the restoration of the Gawhar Shad Mausoleum.

Another landmark was the substantial restoration of the National Museum of Afghanistan. The building, dating from the early 20th century, has now been fully repaired and expanded, pending plans for a new building, and can once again house the Nation's moveable cultural heritage adequately. Elements of the museum's collections, that had been kept safely with organizations around the world for years, have been returned during the past 12 years, such as the objects brought back to Kabul by the Bibliotheca Afghanica and a further hoard of confiscated objects inventoried and returned by the British Museum.

Furthermore, many of the National Museum's collections had been inventoried and conserved by UNESCO and others by 2021, with an initiative being undertaken to digitize the records in multiple languages, overseen by the Oriental Institute of the University of Chicago in collaboration with the National Museum of Afghanistan. The Museum was steadily becoming one of Kabul's more popular venues for heritage education once again with occasional new exhibitions, such as the ongoing display showcasing finds from Ancient Bactria, along with a policy to encourage schools to visit regularly.

Afghanistan also had an exhibition of the Bactrian Gold and the Ai Khanoum collections traveling the world, marking the heritage sector as one of Afghanistan's few income earners at an international level. In addition, the exhibition helped to project a positive image of Afghanistan in the face of the more typical media coverage, that merely highlighted the conflict within the country. Although security will remain a particular challenge to be overcome for the institution before a full exhibition of the best of its collections can be safely reinstalled, the National Museum of Afghanistan set policies for the safeguarding of movable heritage, that elaborated the necessary future steps towards fulfilling its institutional mandate to effectively inform and educate Afghan society. A cultural space was established in Bamiyan province by UNESCO, the Ministry of Information and Culture, and the provincial government just in August 2021. It is hoped to provide a further opportunity to preserve and exhibit Afghan cultural heritage and will be strongly connected with the local community by providing an educational space on heritage as well as training opportunities on professions associated with culture and heritage conservation.

Despite what could be characterized as a general lack of visibility concerning heritage issues in Afghanistan, the last few years have witnessed a noticeable increase in interest among both the Afghan and international communities including the media. Culture in its broadest sense, including cultural and creative industries such as locally produced film and contemporary art, is beginning to gain increased recognition both at home and on the international stage. There was also an increase in national tourism in various provinces, in addition to a small number of returning international tourists, predominantly to Bamiyan province and the Wakhan Corridor in Badakshan province, forming a logical starting point for economic development through conservation endeavors, alongside aspirations for community heritage education and awareness. The international donor community too had become increasingly aware of the potential contribution of culture to development in Afghanistan, and numerous new and ongoing projects that employ culture as a central pillar of development had been receiving support, especially since 2014.

Future Progress and Challenges

Though there is uncertainty in many contexts in Afghanistan after August 2021, what is certain is that international assistance is still required and will be needed for perhaps another generation or longer. For Afghanistan, international assistance cannot solve all the problems nor preserve all heritage, but eventually, these need to be protected and promoted by the Afghans for their people. Assistance will have to continue to be targeted where it can make the highest impact, which is a combination of emergency intervention at sites in particular danger, such as both of Afghanistan's World Heritage sites in Bamiyan and Ghor provinces, as well as policy development and strengthening local capacities in specific parts of the heritage sector.

Efforts to preserve cultural heritage in Afghanistan must also be seen in the context of it being placed low on the agenda of general security and development policies and priorities in a country with one of the lowest standards of living in the world. Therefore, a challenge for organizations working in the profession within Afghanistan is to raise awareness of the greater role that culture can play in peace and development, and to explain their projects and objectives about broader goals that address a wider range of pertinent issues, such as poverty alleviation, health, education, national identity, and the state-building processes. Another step is to encourage the wider international community to be more innovative in their approaches to incorporate the peacebuilding and human-rights approach in cultural initiatives into both policy and broad-based developmental projects. This strategy will help draw more funds into the sector, broaden its relevance based on basic human needs in the country, and more importantly, mobilize culture in working towards a peaceful, sustainable country.

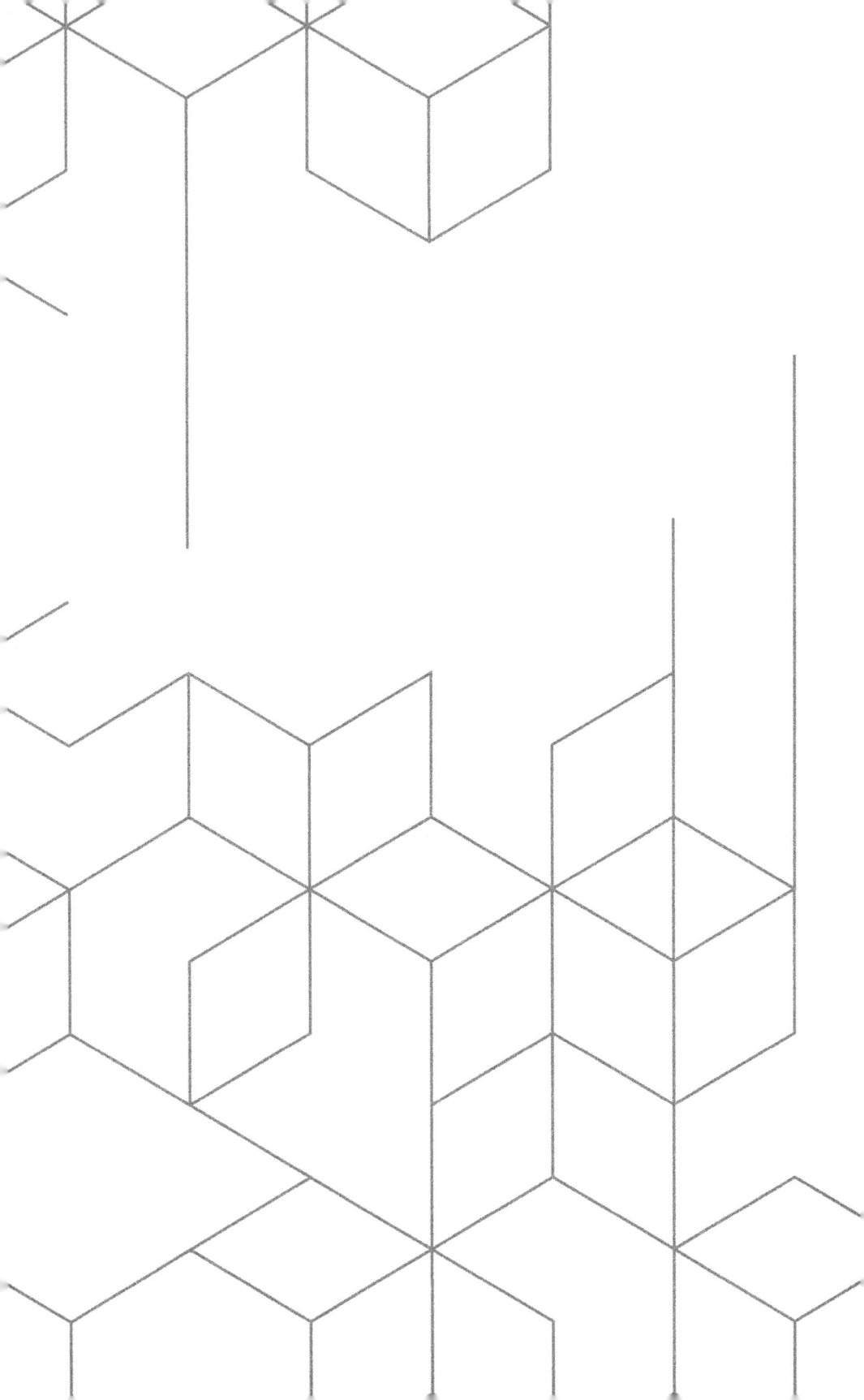

APPENDICES

سوله

صلح

ساني

平和

A survey in three parts
Alisa Tukkimaki[57]

Editors' Note:

Ten years later we find this survey to still be deeply mean-ingful, as it gives the reader a window into the unfiltered, uncensored voices of Afghans trying to build their coun-try on the frontlines in 2011. Sadly, still today those views and analyses remain true and relevant in many ways. The survey has been minimally edited for clarity.

Part I:
Top Down or Bottom-up?
Research Notes and Reflections on my 2011 UNITAR Fellowship

I began my University of Calgary Fellowship with UNITAR ques-tioning whether or not the Afghan Fellowship program, a UNITAR program, was a top-down or bottom-up post-conflict development program. After experiencing the eight-month cycle I had my answer. The program was both.

---

[57] Alissa Tukkimaki was 2011 University of Calgary Fellow to UNITAR and worked on the Fellow-ship for the 2011-12 Cycles

Structurally and logistically the Afghan Fellowship was a top-down program whereas its core values, resources and sustainability lay in its bottom-up approaches. Before this fellowship I thought the two development methods worked in isolation, but now it was clear that in the case of post-conflict reconstruction both methods work best in tandem. This is how I have came to see this relationship work within the Afghan program:

The UNITAR Hiroshima Office provideds the structure and logistics within which the program's framework was built. Here UNITAR had the capacity and support to maintain the program, through which funding was secured, partnerships made and maintained and staff mobilized to ensure the quality and standard of the program. This was the top-down piece, as the structure offered by UNITAR. In this particular situation, the capacities of the Afghan Fellows had to be built first before they could take ownership over their own country's development. Here top-down was vital as it provided the succinct framework and concrete tools needed to build local capacity, which a post-conflict Afghanistan was unable to provide for itself.

Yet the program was more bottom-up than one would first realize. Where UNITAR appeared to have all the decision-making power over the Fellowship, it was in fact the Afghan Fellows who control the direction and sustainability of the program. Resourceful, the UNITAR team had greatly stretched their relatively small funding sources through bottom-up community development approaches. By tapping into local Afghan resources to cut costs, the UNITAR team also tapped into local expertise, partnerships, and solutions. Through eight years of working and listening to local Afghans, the program itself was nearly completely dictated by the expressed needs of the local program participants. It is this relationship that earned the Fellowship such a high standing within Afghan communities and also contributed greatly to the success and sustainability of the program. Each year as Fellows graduated from the program a handful were asked to return the following year as mentors or coaches. In addition, graduates were asked to nominate their co-workers and employees for the program. This was truly local ownership as you had Afghans mentoring Afghans, supporting each other and recognizing the value and merit of the program for others. Overall, it is this distinct balance of development approaches that led to the success of the program.

Lastly, my own reflections of the Fellowship boil down to people. From afar the program appeared top-down heavy but from a closer, more intimate look, it was the small handful of passionate and dedicated UNITAR staff and the brave Afghans themselves that made the program bottom-up. This for me was further reflected in the evaluation questionnaires I summarized as nearly all Fellows commented on the importance of generating social capital during the workshop and having a chance to relate and network with like-minded people. Here, everyone recognized the need to connect with one another and to generate community in order to understand each other and work cohesively to reach a common goal. That was community development; breaking bread, sharing stories and investing in human capital. In the end, for myself, bottom-up community development is about listening to the voices of the local people and working with, not "for them", to create change. The Afghan Fellowship program did that.

Part II: Survey Project Overview
The State of Afghanistan in 2011: A Questionnaire for Afghans

This survey explores Afghanistan's governance, security and future through the eyes of Afghans living in Afghanistan in 2011. The goal is that through unfiltered communication a genuine conversation regarding the true wants and needs of Afghans can take place.

This project was sparked by the recognition in 2011 for a need for Afghans to have their voices heard through an unfiltered medium.

Questions were created based on the context in which I came to know the Fellowship participants: within governmental and NGO community development projects in Afghanistan.

All participant responses are their personal views and do not reflect the views or opinions of the organizations or government bodies they work for. Responses were not edited in any way and all responses remain anonymous.

Part III contains the questions asked of the 2011 Afghan Fellows and some of the responses received.

Part III: Survey Questions and Responses

Governance/State: Legislative

L1. How do you see the government's structure changing once NATO troops leave?

- After the leaving of NATO troops there will be no government in place.
  Female, Doctor from the Ministry of Public Health
- About 65% of the government ministries and independent agencies ordinary budget is covered by the national revenues and the remaining shortage is covered by the foreign aid. The Developmental Budget is fully funded through the foreign aid. It is hoped that, in a few years, the Government will be able to cover the ordinary budget fully from the national revenues. Increase in national revenues directly depends on improvement of security and stability in the country and private sector development. In a scenario where foreign aid to be reduced, the government will have to take action to reduce the size of the Government Ministries and Agencies. Actions may include merging similar function ministries with each other, mandatory early retirement, and reduction of contracted (not civil servant employees.)

It should be clarified that the cost of the Afghanistan National Army and Police is much higher than the civil service. In case if the international community continues to support the civil service in terms of budget, I do not think there will be drastic change in the civil service system.
Male, development project worker

- It's difficult to predict, however I personally think it would lead to extreme centralization.
Male, student

- In the long term, NATO will surely leave, so there might be some structure for the government to continue governing. According to most people's ideas, the US forces after a long plan and program entered in Afghanistan and they won't leave Afghanistan in a short time easily. It was a program for them to reside in central Asia and Afghanistan was a suitable place for them to stay, plunder, or despoil. There are many places in Afghanistan having precious mines or chemicals, and on that place the US and other forces are having compound. What do we get from this issue? They are not here to protect Afghan people as many Afghan people are dying every day, but they are engrossed in despoil of the Afghanistan mines. According to a survey, the western, especially the U.S., are spending about 60 percent of the world's energy and food; however, their recourses are untouched. Where are they getting their energy and food from? It is an unanswered question.
Collective response from males and females, their group wishes to remain anonymous

- I think some local leaders will forcefully make it decentralized, at least in their areas of control.
Male, Senior Program Manager, energy & water

L2. How do you think the Afghan government will continue to protect women and girls in terms of education?

- As mentioned above, in current situation it will be a bit difficult to protect the women and girls' rights in terms of education, but in the long run, once the course of thoughts and behavior of the citizens are changed, the level of the education, as a whole, will be increased. It will definitely be protected. The current momentum is that going, if continued for a longer period, will assure these rights for our women and girls.
  Male, wishes to remain anonymous

- Never!!!
  Female, Doctor from the Ministry of Public Health

- The government promises not compromising with women rights, but we are not sure to what extent they are able to. They may be able to do so in the cities, but definitely not in the provinces and rural areas. This needs long-term commandment, support, and community mobilization from social and religious point of view. All these without the interventions of the UN or the international community support are not possible.
  Female, professional for an international organization in Kabul

- The achievements of the Ministry of Education have been promising. The Ministry of Education has built thousands of schools in cities, districts, and villages. The enrolments of children have increased considerably. And recently it was announced that, in the coming years, education will be provided to all who can attend school. Education is free and with equal access to both girls and boys....
  Male, development project worker

- It solely depends on how the government would be able to bring security. Once security is in place the education for girls will be protected. Otherwise, the insurgents have many times destroyed the schools for girls and threatened them for going to school.
  Male, student

- The Afghan government would hardly be able to protect its leadership for a couple of months, but nothing is expected of them in terms of protecting women and girls' education.
  Male, Senior Program Manager, Energy and Water

Governance/State: Executive
E1. How is the government structured now, it is centralized or decentralized?

- It is a centralized government, and the Afghan constitution and government laws are equally applicable at central and provincial levels.
  Male, wishes to remain anonymous

- Overall, the government is centralized now. However, some of the places due to existence of Taliban are not secure as well as corruption in the country threatens the government centralization. Because of fear for the Taliban, people are compelled not to obey the government and put the existence of the government in question.
  Collective response from males and females, their group wishes to remain anonymous

E2. After NATO troops leave, where do you think government money will be allocated, in national portfolios like defense and security or into social programs like education and health?

- The government money will be sent to international bank accounts of the high authorities of the government and some foreign advisors. There will start fighting a civil war. No time for spending money.
  Female, Doctor from the Ministry of Public Health

- Unfortunately, in the very beginning the international community had the wrong judgment of the situation and thought that they can solve Afghan problems within months, and therefore they gave top priority to military operations and lost the balance between the military part and development. As it is crystal clear that the Al-Qaeda and Taliban who were supposed to be washed out overnight, emerged as powerful opponents and for the last 10 years are on their feet and fighting back. Therefore, the opposition which is resisting even in the presence of international community, needs more attention, and, in order to cope with the situation, government will channel majority of funds to defense and national security rather than social programs and development. Even the so-called transition is not fully linked with development aspect and has more concentration on the military part.

Male, Deputy Director for District Delivery Program (DDP) of Independent Directorate of Local Governance (IDLG)

- Due to the existence of Pakistan to the East and Iran to the West, the Afghan government is compelled to allocate most of its money for defense and security issues. It is something generally known, and people know about it and have no objections, they admire government to work on security and defense issues.

Collective response from males and females, their group wishes to remain anonymous

E3. What do you think will happen to Afghanistan's natural resources like oil?

- Considering the natural resources of the world, those have been used from decades and will be depleted somehow in the near future, and the untouched under the soil resources and especially oil, will definitely attract the international community for huge investments, and countries in power to come back to Afghanistan under the cover of the security forces, civilian aid, and strengthen the Afghan government groups and extract this industry. Currently, there are also huge interests from the international community to extract this industry, but the lengthy and bureaucratic administrative systems and processes of the government discourage investors from coming to Afghanistan.

Male, wishes to remain anonymous

- If a strong government is in place and security improves, the natural resources will be used effectively, but otherwise no. In any case, Afghanistan needs a lot of assistance from the international community to assist and invest in this sector. But even after involvement of the international community, greater monitoring and accountability mechanisms are needed to ensure the transparency of the process and that the revenue comes as public property and is spent appropriately and in a balanced way by the government.

Female, professional for an international organization in Kabul

Civil Society

C1. What role do you think local municipalities will play in Afghanistan's future?

- If I rightly understand the word municipalities, they are just bound for development activities like construction of roads, sewage system, etc. and they do not have any political role. But we have local governance bodies in Afghanistan at grassroot levels. They have played important roles in the past, are playing at present (even if not 100%) and for sure will continue to play the roles in future. However, there is need for certain transparency that there should be people in those bodies who should be elected and not selected.

Male, Head of Kabul Revenue Department for the Ministry of Finance

- Well, they can play a good role in bringing order to the city, ensuring cleanliness of cities, implementing cities' master plans, bringing people closer to the government, ensuring proper housing schemes, enforcing relevant laws in the country, ensuring safeguards issues particularly on the environment and creating green zones, reducing pollution, etc. In the past, municipalities were elected positions in Afghanistan, but not now. The government has promised to make it again elected which will be a desired option. Of course, there is a severe need for the capacity building and strengthening of the municipalities in order to enable them to play their role effectively.

Female, professional for an international organization in Kabul

- Local municipalities have not played any role in the past and they are not expected to play any major role in the future, mainly because the mayors are selected instead of being elected.

Male, Senior Program Manager, Energy and Water

C2. To what extent is the government engaging civil society to participate in political and social governance?

- Outwardly, it looks that people or civil society are participating in political and social governance but actually that's not in real terms, we faced LOYA GIRGA in near past about a month ago there were true representatives of the people, but the percentage was very much low.

Male, Head of Kabul Revenue Department for the Ministry of Finance

- Civil society has a major role in the political and social governance. Civil society was a part of the Bonn and other important conferences held in connection to Afghanistan. While on the local level, civil society is working side by side with different government institutions. At village and district level they are busy with CDCs (Community Development Councils) and

DDA (District Development Authority). Even in some areas projects are implemented through the civil society e.g., education, agriculture, health, etc.

Male, Deputy Director for District Delivery Program (DDP) of Independent Directorate of Local Governance (IDLG)

C4. What type of reconciliation work do you know of that has taken place between different tribes in Afghanistan?

- Gladly, we have a very strong peace mechanisms within tribes in Afghanistan in form of Local Girgas which throughout history have resulted very positively. I would like to share with you experience of my father who was member of Parliament in 1969 and said that in our Province, Paktia, there were only two criminal cases in central court of the province and the rest were totally solved through local tribes through these local Girgas headed by the elders and whose order was followed 100%.

  Male, Head of Kabul Revenue Department for the Ministry of Finance

- Afghan tribes and ethnicities do not have any major problems with each other. They have been living side by side for thousands of years, but after the collapse of the pro-Soviet regime racial and ethnic matters came into surface. The military fractions and parties have misused people's loyalty and have put them into fight with each other. On the other hand, the neighboring countries started to provoke their loyal tribes in Afghanistan against others. A wider-based government that consists of real members of people will play a significant role in stability, peace, and equality between Afghan tribes.

  Male, development project worker

- I think we don't require a lot of reconciliation among the different tribes in Afghanistan. Reconciliation should be done in between Pakistan and Afghanistan. Pakistan should be

pressurized to work with Afghanistan in bringing peace. Taliban are representing Pakistan in Afghanistan.
Male, student

C5. What role do you think Community Councils play in the future of Afghanistan?

- Well, if the Community Councils are really built by and for the local people, they can play a vital role in improving the lives of the people. Currently, they are built by order of political parties, armed groups, and government with focus on their interests not the people. In simple words, the current community councils are just like a stage shows, which entertain you for a while but do not exist in reality.
  Male, wishes to remain anonymous

- Their role will not be visible in such a complex situation of Afghan society. The future of Afghanistan is related to a strong central government with good economic support. In this situation, the Community Council itself is not strong and healthy.
  Female, Doctor from the Ministry of Public Health

Security
S1. How do you think security is going to be administered in Afghanistan once NATO troops leave?

- The causes of the Afghan conflict are not only internal, but rather a multi-dimensional conflict. I think powers in the West and the East, and the neighboring countries' proxy wars meet and compete in Afghanistan. Afghanistan is important for India and Pakistan, and it is obvious that none of them wants Afghanistan to get closer to its rival. Both countries have nuclear power and in the past years they fought several times with each other. On the other hand, China has become an emerging superpower in terms of technology, economy, and its ambitious modern arm agenda. The central Asian countries have resources of oil and gas, and they are important for the future of world. The old Russia seems to gain gradually its lost status for being a powerful country both in terms of having natural resources and military technology. On top of all, the 3000 km long border issue between Afghanistan and Pakistan is still not resolved. Afghanistan must strengthen its border with Pakistan, Iran, China, Turkmenistan, Uzbekistan, and Tajikistan. The long border with Iran and Pakistan can at any time be used by these countries to destabilize the security in Afghanistan, which is a practice in the past 30 years. The Afghan border police is not able to control the border by any mean. Moreover, they do not have air support and technology to watch the border areas. I think NATO and the US government have not been serious to help the Afghan Army to be self-sufficient and have the required arms and technology to resist against Taliban. The years from 2011 to 2014 will be important for Afghanistan to see how much the US Government and NATO will be assisting Afghan armed forces (Air force, border force, police force, and ground forces.)

Male, development project worker

- The country is not ready yet for such a transition. Besides other factors like honest reconciliation process, building trust between communities and the government, social and economic development, and improving the governance at sub-national level, we need strong, well-trained, and well-equipped army and police. The high level of corruption and lawlessness further increase the gap between people and government, which can further deteriorate the security situation.

Male, Deputy Director for District Delivery Program (DDP) of Independent Directorate of Local Governance (IDLG)

S2. What do you see as on-going or reoccurring security threats to Afghan people?

- Direct interventions of ISI, CIA, Iran, Taliban, and local armed parties. I have to mention that nowadays we hear that USA is doing negotiation with Taliban and Taliban will come again to Afghanistan. These kind of news makes all people of my country very upset, and women think that again they will lose opportunity of working outside home and again we have to wear BURQA. We don't want Taliban again and please tell your audience at the end of your presentation not to let other powers to play with the people of Afghanistan and to stop this game.
  Female, Doctor from the Ministry of Public Health

- Pakistan and Iran are two countries that never want a peaceful and prosperous Afghanistan beside them...... The US Government and international alliance have provided only light weapons to the Afghan National Army and Police forces and, unfortunately, there are no Air Force, artillery, tank, or other logistical support provided to the Afghan forces in the past ten years. On the other hand, the drug mafia is very active in Afghanistan that produces 95% of the world opium. The alliance of international drug mafia, corrupt Government officials, warlords and neighbor country officials contribute to sustaining war and conflict in Afghanistan, because they can make billions of dollars from such illegal businesses.
  Male, development project worker

- Afghanistan is dependent on its neighbor countries. Most of our imports are from Pakistan, Iran, Uzbekistan, and Turkmenistan. We need to manage the expectation of all key stakeholders in the region. This can play a major role in limiting the ongoing security threats (insurgency, etc.) to the country.
  Male, Deputy Director for District Delivery Program (DDP) of Independent Directorate of Local Governance (IDLG)

S3. Do you think the Afghan police force is ready to take over security? Please explain.

- Not at all due to following reasons:
    a. They are not well trained.
    b. They lack strong leadership.
    c. They need money for their expenses. So they will leave the army to find a safer job and more money. Most of them will join the opposite side.
    d. During the 30 years of war, the psychology of young generation has changed.
    Female, Doctor from the Ministry of Public Health

S4. What do you think will be the role of the Afghan military in terms of security efforts?

- The international community could have made optimal and better use of the billions of dollars spent in Afghanistan. Instead of spending on expensive and unfamiliar military technology and equipment for Afghanistan, cheaper and familiar military equipment that proved to be effective could have been bought from the Russia or the previous Russian states. The Afghan air forces have made almost no progress so far, because they have been told that when a neighbor country attacks Afghanistan the international air forces will take action against it. Peace talks with the opposition with an Afghan framework and agenda which did not happen in the past ten years have to be resumed. I think the Afghan National Army (ANA) should not be involved in large fighting, especially in the civilian areas, because the ANA will lose its image between the people as an impartial force. Instead, it will be very good to strengthen the borders with Iran and Pakistan that people cannot travel without border cross documents. It will also help in combating the drug trafficking.

Male, development project worker

- All security measures will collapse.
  Male, Senior Program Manager, Energy and Water

S5. How do you feel about the NATO troops leaving and why?

- I don't believe they plan to leave. I think they will stay and
  have to stay longer. Because they have to reach their goals.
  Female, Doctor from the Ministry of Public Health

- Apparently, they will leave without any big achievement in
  hand due to fact that we still face threats from neighboring
  countries and their interventions. We still don't have fully
  equipped Army after 10 years. We still can't produce a single PhD internally in our own institutions after 10 years.
  So I think they should leave but their civil presence should
  remain but backed by sincere commitment and not just
  window dressing.
  Male, Head of Kabul Revenue, Department for the Ministry
  of Finance

- It's their failure. They are leaving at a time where Afghanistan is still suffering from bad security. And there hasn't been
  any progress or improvement in the area of security. Perhaps,
  they accept their failure and want Afghanistan to turn into a
  center for terrorists again.
  Male, student

- As stated above, there is a lack of adequate transfer of capacity and expertise to local police and national army and equipping them as required to cope with current insecurity threats
  both internally and ability to protect Afghanistan borders.
  Afghanistan has no quick response mechanism and resources
  in term of Air force to respond in situations needed, neither
  does the army have heavy machinery, weapons, etc. Furthermore, not adequate transfer of capacity and expertise

in provincial budgeting, planning and service delivery taken place from international to local.

Male, Deputy Director for District Delivery Program (DDP) of Independent Directorate of Local Governance (IDLG)

S6. What do you expect will happen with the Taliban once NATO troops leave?

- They will once again get the chance to weaken the government, even take over and implement their rules and once again become a severe threat for the rest of the World.
  Female, professional for an international organization in Kabul

- Taliban are Afghans and I think some elements in the current Afghan administration have not started true talks with them in the past 10 years. The government was not able to segregate good people from the bad people among its armed opposition. I also think that the government of Afghanistan does not have one enemy that can be called Taliban, but there are many small military fractions independent from Taliban. In some areas bad governors made people take side of the opposition. Ironically, none of the big criminals and those who have looted the government property, land mafia, drug mafia has been sentenced in the past ten years. Why cannot they be sentenced and put into court? The answer is because they have backing of the government and superpowers. E.g., The Kabul Bank scandal whereby hundreds of millions of dollars of the Bank have been misused, but the government has not charged any one in public because senior government officials are involved in this case.
  Male, development project worker

- They would be resurrected with support from the neighboring countries.
  Collective response from males and females, their group wishes to remain anonymous

S7. How is Afghanistan's relationship with its neighboring countries like Iran, Pakistan, and China?

- Currently, the relation of Afghan government with its neighboring countries is based on diplomacy and fake picture the world can see. Until the interests of these three countries are not considered in the structure of the government, these relations will never be real and based on honesty
Male, wishes to remain anonymous

- As said that in politics, there is no enemy and no friend but interests. Currently, I think the relationship with all the three countries are that it should not have been e.g., with Pakistan we have ongoing blame game, with Iran also not good due to expected strategic agreements with US and rest of the allies and with China that's good but not to extent to which it should have been due to many factors, mainly due to US presence but still we have some big projects with China namely the AINAK copper project, world's biggest copper mine.
Male, Head of Kabul Revenue Department for the Ministry of Finance

- Afghanistan is dependent on its neighbors and, therefore, need to think of all stakeholders in the region. Thousands of refugees still living in Pakistan and Iran while on the other hand, we are depended on the exports from Pakistan, Iran, China, Uzbekistan, and Turkmenistan. The country needs to have a long term healthy and friendly relationship with our neighbors.
Male, Deputy Director for District Delivery Program (DDP) of Independent Directorate of Local Governance (IDLG)

S8. Do you think the security situation in Afghanistan is improving or getting worse?

- It is getting worse day by day in spite of existence of NATO troops.
Female, Doctor from the Ministry of Public Health

- In the early years after the fall of Taliban one could visit every part of the country without any threat, even I went to Kandahar, Helmand, and some other provinces by road. But now I can't which means that security has gotten worse — peace is what I will call a sort of pseudo peace. For the future, I have some hope but if the allies do some basic and strategic tasks like fully equipping Afghan Army and police and sincerely using their influence to make all countries, whether neighboring or regional or international to take sincere part in Afghanistan's reconstruction (reconstruction does not only mean making roads).
Male, Head of Kabul Revenue Department for the Ministry of Finance

NGOs

N1. In what ways do you think Afghan NGOs are encouraging civil society to be politically engaged?

- I could not see any major activity in this regard but normally I am 95% against NGO's. They don't do to extent they spend and are the only cause of inability of government to improve its capacity. NGO's hire people with comparatively good qualifications often with much more salary. Too few people are left with some good qualification for the government offices and that results in a gap and inability of the government. I don't have exact statistics but most of the government employees have only till 12th grade education, so what one can expect to do in the best interest of the government except corruption.
Male, Head of Kabul Revenue Department for the Ministry of Finance

- There is a need for a close cooperation and coordination between the NGOs and government. The government still needs support from civil society in term of their access to different areas and the expertise in some specialized fields.
Male, student

N2. Where do local NGOs in Afghanistan get funding and is this sustainable?

- They don't have any internal sources for funding, they receive their funding from the international organizations and PRT's (Provincial Reconstruction Teams of International Forces), and they do not have any sustainability in the future. If the international community and forces leave Afghanistan, they will collapse on the same day.
  Male, wishes to remain anonymous

- Actually, the only and best supporter of the Afghan NGOs is the Japan Embassy (GAGP Unit). Few other supports existed as well, but they have no credibility nowadays as their aims are different and against Afghan religions and cultures.
  Collective response from males and females, their group wishes to remain anonymous

N3. Do you think international NGOs should continue to play a role in Afghanistan's development? Please explain.

- Not at all, not even as a 1%, because their mandates are built on self-interest and financial earnings.
  Male, wishes to remain anonymous

- No. They must stop. Most of the money which was expected to be used for the reconstruction of Afghanistan is now in the pocket of NGO presidents and other NGO workers. It is better for the Afghan people that the money should be used by the government itself.
  Female, Doctor from the Ministry of Public Health

- One of the negative aspects of INGOs and NGOs was working independently with no consultation and coordination with line Ministries and Agencies. The NGOs have to play a positive role in harmonizing with the line Ministries strategies and developmental plans and projects. Successful

projects leave positive impact and image in communities and win the hearts and minds of people. In long run, the NGOs have to have strategies and leave the job to the Government institutions. There should be always a transfer of knowledge and capacity building plans in each of the project to avoid aid-dependency.
Male, development project worker

Last thoughts
L1. What are your hopes for Afghanistan's future?

- Well, if we analyze the performance and achievements of the international community and forces in the last 10 years and before that, it is really not what the people of their own countries expected and what we expected. Because they have always seen us through the eyes of Pakistan and other neighboring countries, and have never tried to look into our eyes and hearts to know what exactly we want. This really weakens the hope and trust of Afghans in the international community and really gives us no hope for a brighter future of this land. But if we, Afghans, stand and decide to build our country, it is possible to have a real government by the people and for the people. Not the government of international community and neighboring countries.
  Male, wishes to remain anonymous

- I have no hope for a better future. I think everything is getting worse.
  Female, Doctor from the Ministry of Public Health

- Despite all the problems and present situation of Afghanistan, I am hopeful for the future. I think a good movement has been started. Our young generation realize the importance of peace and the hardships of war. They are doing their best to get better education and fill the gap of professionals in the country. I hope Afghanistan, with the support of these young

professionals and the international community and learning from its past, soon will be among the developing countries and move towards development and enjoy peace and prosperity it deserves just like any other country in the world
Female, professional for an international organization in Kabul

- A free, strong, and independent state that has a strong economy by using its underground wealth and human capital. My hope is that Afghanistan lives with its neighbors side by side with full diplomatic protocols, not like now that they are directly interfering in Afghanistan and making negative use of the Afghan refugees in their countries. Afghanistan can be a hub for business between the central Asian countries and the world. Unless Afghanistan becomes a strong nation, Pakistan and Iran will not accept it as an independent state. Although Afghanistan is far behind Pakistan and Iran in terms of economy, literacy rate and military strength, a committed and honest leadership can bring the country back to normal.
Male, development project worker

- We believe that each conflict and problem have its end and solution. The end of Afghan conflict is in peace and reconciliation process. This needs a strong political well and commitment at all levels, and implementation of holistic and balanced interventions rooted in Afghan knowledge and priorities.
Male, Deputy Director for District Delivery Program (DDP) of Independent Directorate of Local Governance (IDLG)

- Peace, security, safety, and freedom without strangers' interference.
Collective response from males and females, their group wishes to remain anonymous

- I have already lost my hope.
Male, Senior Program Manager, Energy and Water

L2. What do you see being Afghanistan's biggest struggle?

- This question has two perspectives, first is the struggle of the people, and second is the struggle of the government, that both together create Afghanistan. Struggle of people is to have civil rights; governments ruled by law and norms and have a government that is selected by people. Struggle of the government is to assure its stability for a longer period and have international supports for their wishes and objectives, even if that is against the national interests and wishes of people.
  Male, wishes to remain anonymous

- Our geographic location in the middle of Asia among Pakistan, Iran, China, and Central Asian countries is our biggest challenge that causes the powerful countries to interfere in our affaires for reaching their strategic goals. Our biggest struggle is to get rid of these interferences.
  Female, Doctor from the Ministry of Public Health

- To some extent ignorance, mostly illiteracy, and some black sheep.
  Male, Head of Kabul Revenue Department for the Ministry of Finance

- Its economy and insincere neighboring countries. Of course, security is on the top of the list.
  Female, professional for an international organization in Kabul

- Corruption in the government, for which the government has never been honest and have further contributed to defaming the country. Government officials became millionaires by bribing, misuse of authority, and collection gifts. The higher the position, the higher the level of corruption. Security challenges, Illiteracy, Drug cultivation, addiction to it and trafficking and not being able to appoint honest people to key government positions
  Male, development project worker

- Security and poverty.
  Male, student

- A struggle for peace and reconciliation and an end to the current conflict, strong and well-equipped army and police, economic and social development.
  Male, Deputy Director for District Delivery Program (DDP) of Independent Directorate of Local Governance (IDLG)

L3. What do you think the international community can do to support Afghanistan?

- This question is not just a right question for me but each and every individual. If the international community really supports the Afghan Land, they do what they did in Kosovo and other similar societies to build a government by the people and for the people, arrest and punish those criminals currently in the government, and give real support to Afghan government to fight against the interference and intelligence services of the neighboring countries. To strengthen the armed forces of Afghanistan will help Afghanistan to stand on its feet and be in the line of the developed countries.
  Male, wishes to remain anonymous

- Yes, they can if they only help Afghanistan because it is Afghanistan, not because it is beside Pakistan, Iran, and the Middle Asia.
  Female, Doctor from the Ministry of Public Health

- Take into consideration Afghanistan's interests without taking into consideration their hidden agendas.
  Male, Head of Kabul Revenue Department for the Ministry of Finance

- Change the existing government key elements that have criminal background, who committed mass killing of innocent people and are clearly blamed for looting public property and are involved with drug mafia. It is a pity that criminals became key political faces in Afghanistan. The international community has not only kept quiet, but dealt with them by buying their loyalty and giving them immunity and safety. Fighting corruption should be on top of all agendas, reward and punishment should take place. Afghanistan is not suffering from lack of resources for its post conflict reconstruction, but from corruption and misuse of resources. The international community has to fulfill its commitment to channel its funds through the government system. (This was pledged in Kabul conference July 2010). According to the decisions of the conference 50% of the total aid in two years will be provided through the government system. Currently only 20% of the foreign aid is provided through the government and for the remaining 80% the government is not aware of how it is spent and where.

Male, development project worker

- Anti-corruption programs to be practiced and settled in Afghanistan.

  Collective response from males and females, their group wishes to remain anonymous

L4. Where do you see Afghanistan in five years?

- I don't see much multifaceted development in Afghanistan in five years to come because it has taken 30 years to destroy and will take much longer to rise to even where Afghanistan was in the 1980s.

  Male, Head of Kabul Revenue Department for the Ministry of Finance

- In a better position, financially and politically, but security would still be a challenge.

  Female, professional for an international organization in Kabul

- Considering the existing pace of development and the government, I have to carefully comment about the future of Afghanistan in the coming five years. Afghanistan needs the support of the international community to sustain the existing programs for post conflict reconstruction and development. To make sure the government has a continuous support from the international community, it should establish accountability system for the use of resources. As a project manager, I always recall "value for money" and "rate of return" aspects for the funds are spent and will be spent for developmental projects in Afghanistan. There is weak area that the donors and international community should address immediately, and that is to find out about the quality of outputs produced and the impact of large projects in Afghanistan. Moreover, if the international community is committed to strengthen the Afghan government in the development and reconstruction agenda, they need to assess all their past projects for their success and failure. A lessons-learned list to be prepared, in order to not repeat the same mistakes again. Moreover, as promised in the Kabul Conference (July 2010) the donor community has to channel their funds through the Government system, in order to avoid parallel structures (projects). [This pledge is still not fulfilled.] The government accountability system has to be strengthened and it has to be made accountable, responsible and answerable, if international funds were not used effectively and efficiently. If the government accountability function is not improved and the key officials are not made answerable for use of resources, and if a strict "reward and punishment" system is not in place, I do not think the future five years will be better than the past 10.
  Male, development project worker

- We believe in mutual respect and love peace both for ourselves and others. We want to be among the peaceful, strong, and developed nations of the world. I am sure the world will see us there in the coming five years Inshallah.
  Male, Deputy Director for District Delivery Program (DDP) of Independent Directorate of Local Governance (IDLG)

- I see Afghanistan being in the state that it was a decade ago.
  Male, Senior Program Manager, Energy and Water

APPENDIX B

Sample Syllabus for Credits at University of Texas at Austin

	LYNDON B. JOHNSON SCHOOL OF PUBLIC AFFAIRS
	THE UNIVERSITY OF TEXAS AT AUSTIN
	P. O. Box Y • Austin, Texas 78713-8925 • (512) 471-4962 • FAX (512) 471-1835

	***UNITAR Hiroshima Fellowship for Afghanistan* 2010 Cycle**
	2010 UNITAR Hiroshima Fellowship for Afghanistan

Syllabus for Course on Leadership and Management

COURSE TITLE: **Leadership and Management**

COURSE SUBTITLE: Executive Development and Professional Capacity Building in the Afghanistan Civil Service

SUPERVISING FACULTY MEMBER: David Eaton, Ph.D.

E-MAIL: eaton@mail.utexas.edu

CLASS MEETINGS: Four workshops, each 4 days in length, Six video-conference seminars (4.5 hours each), 6 to 7 web-enabled, one-hour audio conferences with faculty, 6 to 7 project work sessions with Coaches, study-trips to government and private institutions, and one 3-day After-Action Review/Lessons Learned Seminar at the conclusion of the course.

CONTACT HOURS: A minimum of 191 class contact hours

COURSE DURATION: May through November 2010

ADMINISTRATIVE ASSISTANT: Jayashree Vijalapuram, SRH 3.348, jayashreev@mail.utexas.edu, 512-471-8959

RESOURCES and PARTNER INSTITUTIONS: UNITAR Hiroshima Office, Afghanistan Independent Reform and Civil Service Commission, University of Calgary, Microsoft Corporation, Singapore International Foundation, Hiroshima Prefectural Government and Hiroshima University.

Description of UNITAR

The Fellowship for Afghanistan is a program of the United Nations Institute for Training and Research in cooperation with the University of Texas at Austin (UTA) and its other partners. UNITAR was established as an autonomous unit within the United Nations in 1965. Training and capacity building for government officials, scholars and representatives of civil society from developing countries in the general areas of peace and security and economic and social development are its main mandate. The Hiroshima Office (HO), which started operations in July 2003, is the newest extension of the UNITAR family. While its goals and methodologies are consistent with UNITAR's, its activities are designed to focus on the specific needs of the Asia and Pacific regions. Each year HO organizes training workshops and symposia around six thematic areas. The Fellowship for Afghanistan is the longest and most intensive of these programs.

Description of the Participants

The Fellowship is intended for the direct use and benefit of a selected group of senior and high potential Afghan public sector officials, university representatives and NGO leaders, as well as other relevant individuals playing an influential role in Afghanistan's reconstruction. They are selected based on specific criteria established by UNITAR and partners, such as background, motivation, seniority and role in their department.

Description of the Course

This is an executive development course, which extends over a eight-month period. Teaching will primarily take place during a series of four, four to five-day workshops and the six video-conference seminars. Workshops/seminars will focus mainly on a single subject so that the particular set of skills can be fully developed and absorbed by the Fellows. Topics will, in part, be determined by the requests and needs of the Fellows, but will in general include organization development and change, project planning and implementation, proposal writing, leadership, team-building, coaching and facilitation, human resource development and management and post-conflict reconstruction. Workshops/Seminars will be lead by experts on the particular subject being taught and will include faculty from the University of Texas, the University of Calgary, Microsoft Corporation, Hiroshima University, Lamb and Lamb Associates, and the Singapore International Foundation.

Throughout the duration of the Fellowship, participants will be divided, based on their professional foci, into groups of five or six. Each group will be assigned a Mentor and a Coach, with whom Fellows will stay in regular communication, to help guide them though the Fellowship and to the successful completion of their projects. Mentors are experts, practitioners, or academics in various disciplines, and based in different countries. They communicate with their group via email, UNITAR scheduled video conferences, and audio-web sessions. A majority of Mentors will travel to Dubai or Hiroshima to meet their Fellows in person and lead workshop sessions. Coaches are the mentoring arm based in Afghanistan, selected each year from the increasingly committed and capable pool of highly professional graduates of the previous Fellowship Cycle, and provided further training to act as facilitators for the Fellowship activities at the group level. Each Mentor/ Coach team commits to oversee at least one group of Fellows for the duration of the Fellowship.

An additional module of the course will focus on increasing the reliance on/ expanding the roles of Afghan colleagues and the Alumni network, by having successful Afghan Coaches from 2010 apprentice as junior faculty members at workshops, seminars, and through the cycle.

Once the main resource persons have been identified for a workshop, they will be connected to the Afghan junior faculty, and requested to work with them to develop the material and deliver the training. This would ensure that we have a set of Afghan resource persons better prepared to teach the same curriculum.

This will be further supported by an increase in the number of Coaches to be trained, and prepping the coaches more with a detailed coaching-for-coaches module, so that their role can be further expanded.

Team Projects

Throughout the Fellowship, each group of Fellows will work on and develop a substantive organization development or change project which may or may not include training as a tool to transfer select skills and knowledge to members of their ministry or related organizations. This will involve each Fellow conducting an organizational needs-assessment within his or her organization before the first workshop. The team will decide together the final list of issues to be addressed in their project, and the methodology or tools to address them with. Each Fellow will then be assigned one section of the project to pursue and in the case of training, the section for which to develop a curriculum. Members of each team will coordinate with each other, to ensure no overlaps in content and also help each other if needed in getting material for the content. Mentors and Coaches will advise on how the project will come together and flow as part of one plan.

The team projects will include three major assignments.

1) *Assignment I* - Each Fellow will undertake a needs assessment in her/his workplace to determine capacities required (and not just restricted to training requirements), to do the job in his/her organization/department. This is an individual assignment, and should address both the needs and capacities of the organization/department and the Fellow's own role and skills. The assignment will be submitted as a written report.

2) *Assignment II* - Assignment II is a team assignment, to develop a first draft concept paper for the team project (1 to 2 pages) (1 submission per team). The team of Fellows (4 or 5) is required to select a project, based on the findings of the Organizational Needs Assessments conducted by the Fellows as the first assignment. This project should address common organizational needs, or the needs of the common sector/specialization (for example health sector, or

the function of admin and finance), identified through Assignment I, and should be an organizational development or change project, which could be a training programme, or an organizational restructuring programme, etc..

3) *Assignment III - .* The assignment will report, through a formal presentation involving all group members, on the development of a *detailed plan* for the team's organizational development or change project[58]. This report should also be submitted in written form prior to Workshop III. The report/presentation should include:

1. expected project outcomes
2. specific objectives
3. justification (why this is important)
4. environmental analysis
5. key stakeholders and their expectations
6. a comprehensive action plan for developing and implementing the project
7. a description of how the project will be monitored and evaluated

Each team member should have a distinct role in the presentation, and should also discuss lessons learned from the different stages of developing this project, including the needs assessment. If a proposal for funding from donors is a part of this project, a draft of the proposal should be submitted to Mentors for feedback. The final proposal draft with Mentor feedback incorporated, should be attached to the report. In case the project is on training, a draft of the curriculum should also be submitted.

---

[58] Although actual implementation of the team projects is beyond the scope/time frame of the Fellowship and is not a requirement for completing the Fellowship, the Fellows are encouraged to make the best use of their work in the Fellowship assignments for capacity building in their organizations.

Project work sessions will be set up twice a month, where groups will be required to meet to discuss progress and problems with their individual roles among the group, with Coaches, and through email or web-conferencing with Mentors, and also do project-related research.

Each group will give a formal presentation describing and evaluating their work to an expert panel at the third workshop in Hiroshima.

Grading Policy

Participants will be graded on their attendance and participation in workshops, video conferences and audio-web conferences. They will be expected to complete the 3 major assignments as well as several workshop-specific assignments. Each participant will apply the lessons learned in workshops to complete a Fellowship-long team organizational development project.

Assignments will be weighted as follows:

- Attendance at workshops, video conferences and audio-web conferences and submission of regular update reports: 40%
- Team project and individual and project assignments: 50%
- Final presentation: 10%

Readings

Readings will come from the texts and on-line resources listed below as supplemented by other readings to be added as the course proceeds.

1. Guidelines for conducting organization or needs assessment – Howard & Sue Lamb, Lamb & Lamb Associates
2. – Howard & Sue Lamb, Lamb & Lamb Associates
3. Examples of Environmental Factors in Afghanistan – Howard & Sue Lamb, Lamb & Lamb Associates

4. Development of human resources, Part 1 -- Beyond Training, A perspective on improving organizations and people by <u>Robert H. Rouda</u> & <u>Mitchell E. Kusy, Jr.</u>, <u>Technical Association of the Pulp and Paper Industry</u>

5. How to conduct a Needs Assessment, by Michael Fors, Microsoft USA

6. Motivation: The Not-So-Secret Ingredient of High Performance, Excerpted from Performance Management: Measure and Improve the Effectiveness of your Employees, Harvard Business School Press 2006

7. *Sample Project Selection Criteria*, Dr. Tawab Saljuqi, Ministry of Public Health, Afghanistan

8. *Facilitating Brainstorming"*, *excerpted from Facilitation Skills for Team Leaders* by Donald Hackett and Charles L. Martin

9. *Assignment III Addendum – Guidelines for submitting curriculum*, (Duffie Vanbalkom and Lorne Jaques, University of Calgary);

10. *Brief guide to Business Writing* (Kenneth G. Brown, and David J. Barton, University of Iowa); c) *Guidelines for writing reports* (compiled by Lia van Ginneken);

11. *Project Management Issues and Considerations: Project report writing* (Slides by R. Max Wideman);

12. *Some tips for creating effective Power Point Slides* (Howard and Sue Lamb, Lamb & Lamb Associates).

13. Six Step Problem Solving Process", excerpted from Facilitation Skills for Team Leaders by Donald Hackett and Charles L. Martin

14. Team Life Cycle, excerpted from Facilitation Skills for Team Leaders by Donald Hackett and Charles L. Martin

15. Handling difficult team members, excerpted from Facilitation Skills for Team Leaders by Donald Hackett and Charles L. Martin

16. Project Plan Template by Michael Fors, Microsoft Corporation

17. Learning to Teach: Preparing a training of trainers workshop, *by Jane Vella, Save the Children and OEF International Washington;*

18. Participatory learning and action: Trainer's checklists;

19. Instructional Design Criteria Checklist, *by Michael Fors, Microsoft Inc.;*

20. Other learning activities, *by Howard and Sue Lamb, Lamb & Lamb Associates;*

21. Techniques for Encouraging Participation, *by Howard and Sue Lamb, Lamb & Lamb Associates;*

22. Leading Effective Discussions in Class, *by Howard and Sue Lamb, Lamb & Lamb Associates.*

23. Guidelines and Suggestions for Group Facilitators, by Howard and Sue Lamb, Lamb & Lamb Associates

24. Some tips: Presenting information to groups, by Howard and Sue Lamb, Lamb & Lamb Associates

25. Presentation on Leadership and Its Role in Organizational Development, by Lorne Jaques, University of Calgary

26. Presentation on Stakeholder Analysis, by Lorne Jaques, University of Calgary

27. Clear Leadership: How Outstanding Leaders Make Themselves Understood, Cut Through Organizational Mush, and Help Everyone Get Real at Work, *by Bushe, G.R. (2001)*

28. The Road to Empowerment: Seven Questions Every Leaders Should Consider, *by Quinn, R.E. (1997)*

29. Glossary of terms for the DISC test, by Afghan Coaches 2007

30. Presentation on DISC Workstyles, by Michael Fors, Microsoft Corporation

31. Presentation on Facilitation Skills, by Michael Fors, Michael Corporation

32. Excerpt from the 2007 UNITAR Hiroshima Fellowship final evaluation report – notes on roles of Mentors and Coaches, by UNITAR AF team

33. Presentation on Team Development, by Michael Fors, Microsoft Corporation

34. Presentation on Project Success, by Michael Fors, Microsoft Corporation

35. Project Plan Worksheet, by Michael Fors, Microsoft Corporation

36. Examples of completed worksheet, by Zabiullah Azizi and Gul Afghan Saleh, Coaches, 2008 UNITAR Fellowship for Afghanistan

37. Presentation on Elements of a Project Proposal, by Leo Zonn, University of Texas at Austin and Sabahuddin Sokout, BCURA Afghanistan & UNITAR Afghan Resource Person

38. Additional Reference -- Case Study 1 – Proposal for Sarobi Suspension Bridge, *by Sabahuddin Sokout, Baz Construction Unit for Rehabilitation of Afghanistan*

39. Additional Reference -- Case Study 2 – Proposal on Delivery Health Services, *by M. Yasin Nezami*

40. Additional Reference -- Case Study 3 –Reshkhor Milking Cows Project, *by Mohammad Omar*

41. Additional Reference -- Case Study 4 – Drinking Water Capacity Building in Under-served Areas of Blantyre, Malawi, by University of Texas at Austin

42. Brief guide to Business Writing by Kenneth J Brown, Ph.D. and David J. Barton B.A., University of Iowa

43. E-mail: Structure and Use

44. Guidelines for writing reports, compiled by Lia van Ginneken, NetworkLearning.org

45. Team Development' by Michael Fors, Microsoft USA

46. Thinking about Organizations as Open Systems *by Howard and Sue Lamb, Lamb & Lamb Associates*;

47. Worksheet 1 - My Organization *by Howard and Sue Lamb, Lamb & Lamb Associates*;

48. Worksheet 2 -- Environmental Analysis for My Organization *by Howard and Sue Lamb, Lamb & Lamb Associates*;

49. Worksheet 3 -- Stakeholder Messages *by Howard and Sue Lamb, Lamb & Lamb Associates*;

50. SIPOC Model for Assessing Work Processes *by Howard and Sue Lamb, Lamb & Lamb Associates*;

51. Worksheet 4 -- SIPOC *by Howard and Sue Lamb, Lamb & Lamb Associates*;

52. G.R.P.R. Model *by Howard and Sue Lamb, Lamb & Lamb Associates*;

53. Worksheet 5 - GRPR Model *by Howard and Sue Lamb, Lamb & Lamb Associates*;

54. The Differences between Factual Data, Opinions, Conclusions and Recommendations *by Howard and Sue Lamb, Lamb & Lamb Associates*;

55. Defining Cultural Norms *by Howard and Sue Lamb, Lamb & Lamb Associates*;

56. Worksheet 6 - Cultural Norms *by Howard and Sue Lamb, Lamb & Lamb Associates*;

57. Roles in the Organization Change Process *by Howard and Sue Lamb, Lamb & Lamb Associates*;

58. Managing the Three Stages in the Organization Change Process *by Howard and Sue Lamb, Lamb & Lamb Associates*;

59. Why Individuals Resist Change *by Howard and Sue Lamb, Lamb & Lamb Associates*;

60. Developing a "Critical Mass" of Support for the Change *by Howard and Sue Lamb, Lamb & Lamb Associates*;

61. Adult Learning Theory by North Central Regional Educational Laboratory

62. Using Adult Learning Theory by Annette DiLello, Director, Product Development, Knowledge Impact and Kelly Vaast, Project manager, Knowledge Impact.

63. Its all in the design: Eight steps to planning an effective training event based on Jeary, T. and Gerold, B. *Training Other People to Train: A Workshop on Training Adult Learners*. West Des Moines, IA: American Media Publishing, 1999; and Showers, B., Joyce, B., and Bennett, B. Synthesis of Research on Staff Development: A Framework for Future Study and a State-of-the-Art Analysis. *Educational Leadership* November 1987: 77-87.

64. Guidelines for Training of Trainers, International Labour Organization (ILO) Technical Intervention Area Summary Notes: TIA-F, September 2002

65. Introduction to the Training of Trainers by W. Duffie Vanbalkom, University of Calgary

66. Coaching/Facilitation Skills – *Michael Fors, Microsoft Inc.*

67. Leading People, an Organizations Greatest Asset, Prof. W. Duffie VanBalkom, University of Calgary

68. Tips for Managers for Conflict Resolution, Yuji Uesugi, Hiroshima University

69. Is there any need to analyze conflict? By Okello Sunday Angoma, University of Birmingham

70. Background on Balance Score cards, by SIF – Chin Hooi Yen, Patsian Low and Ernest Lee

71. Background on Competency Based Approach -- by SIF – Chin Hooi Yen, Patsian Low and Ernest Lee

72. Presentation on Tools of Effective Performance Management - by Singapore International Foundation – Patsian Low and Ernest Lee

73. Presentation on Result-based Management by Phil Cox, Plan:Net and University of Calgary

74. Presentation on Training as a tool for Capacity-Building – by Shona Welsh, University of Calgary

75. Guidelines for Effective Training Facilitation, by Howard and Sue Lamb, Lamb and Lamb Associates

Suggested/optional readings:

a. Community building games and activities. What should we be looking for? By Gavin Peat, University of Calgary;

b. Let's Learn and Play! By Biljana Vukčević, Belgrade;

c. Addressing the Spiritual Dimensions of Adult Learning: What Educators Can Do by Jane Vella, *From the New Directions for Adult and Continuing Education* a publication of Jssey Bas

d. Peace-building in an Inseparable World by Jonathan Moore, Harvard University

e. UN will pick-up pieces in Iraq, if US will let it, Op-ed by Jonathan Moore, Boston Globe 2003

f. Leadership Theory and Practice – Peter G. Northouse, Western Michigan University, Sage Publications

g. Ten Ways to Think About Leadership – *by W. Duffie Van-balkom, University of Calgary*

h. Leadership: Spheres of Interest -- *by W. Duffie Vanbal-kom, University of Calgary*

i. Leading Complex Organizations -- *by W. Duffie Vanbal-kom, University of Calgary*

j. Managing Change -- *by W. Duffie Vanbalkom, University of Calgary*

k. Using the Four Lenses Worksheet -- *by W. Duffie Vanbal-kom, University of Calgary*

l. Mapping Change Process Worksheet *by W. Duffie Vanbal-kom, University of Calgary*

m. Basics of Project Design and Project Management – *Pre-sentation by Jobaid Kabir, University of Texas at Austin*

n. Risk Management and Project Scheduling *Presentation by Jobaid Kabir, University of Texas at Austin*

o. Project Budgeting, Tracking and Control *Presentation by Jobaid Kabir, University of Texas at Austin*

p. Project Reporting and Closing *Presentation by Jobaid Kabir, University of Texas at Austin*

q. Proposal Writing for Fundraising *Presentation by Jobaid Kabir, University of Texas at Austin*

r. Orientation to Microsoft Project and Team Exercise *Pre-sentation by Jobaid Kabir, University of Texas at Austin*

s. Monitoring and Evaluation *Presentation by Jobaid Kabir, University of Texas at Austin*

t. Discovering Your Authentic Leadership – Bill George, Peter Sims et al, Harvard Business Review, February 2007

u. In Praise of the Incomplete Leader – Deborah Ancona, Thomas W. Malone et al, Harvard Business Review, February 2007

v. Great Leaders know that all Changes must start both at the Top and the Bottom: The Whole Human System must Change – Michael Ba Banutu-Gomez, Rowan University, Glassboro, New Jersey, The Business Review, Cambridge, Vol. 6, Num. 1, December 2006

w. Richard Beckhard and Wendy Pritchard, *Changing the Essence: The Art of Creating and Leading Fundamental Change in Organizations*

x. Daryl R. Conner, *Managing at the Speed of Change*

y. Stephen G. Haines, *Systems Thinking & Learning*

z. Richard G. Weaver and John D. Farrell, *Managers as Facilitators: A Practical Guide to Getting Work Done in a Changing Workplace*

aa. Edgar H. Schein, *Organizational Culture and Leadership*

bb. Lee C. Bolman and Terrence E. Deal, *Reframing Organizations*

cc. Suresh Srivastva, David L. Cooperrider and Associates, *Appreciative Management and Leadership*

dd. Steven W. Floyd and Bill Wooldridge, *The Strategic Middle Manager*

ee. Daniel Goldman, *Emotional Intelligence: 10th Anniversary Edition*

ff. *Kouzes and Posner,* The Leadership Challenge

gg. Peter Block, *Stewardship*

hh. Peter Block, *The Empowered Manager*

ii. Ronald Heifetz, *Leadership Without Easy Answers*

jj. Geoffrey Bellman, *Getting Things Done When You are Not in Charge*

Class Schedule

Orientation Workshop
May 2010
Session I: Introduction to the Fellowship
Session II: Introduction to Coaches and Fellowship groups
Session III: Tools for Distance Learning
Session IV: Management of Productive Meetings
Session V: Communication Tools for Organizations I – Written
        Communication
Session VI: Communication Tools for Organizations II – Verbal
        Communication
Session VII: Web Seminar I on Leading HRM and HRD
Session VIII: Web Seminar II – How to Conduct an Organization
        Needs Assessment
Session IXI: Introductory VC for group to meet their mentors,
        followed by planning session with Coaches

Workshop I: Leadership and Organizational Development for
Performance and Result
July 16 - 22, 2010
Session 1: Coaching individuals and groups, and Team Building
        within the Fellowship and beyond - **Joint working**
        session with Fellows, Coaches and Mentors
Session 2: Introductions on Leadership and Organizational
        Development
Session 3: Why it matters?
Session 4: Non-achievement, Types of Development
Session 5: Refreshment exercise
Session 6: Organizations
Session 7: Leadership – Reflection from Afghanistan
Session 8: Reflections and journaling
Session 9: Review and Goals
Session 10: Performance II

Session 11: Leadership II
Session 12: Leadership II cont'd
Session 13: Performance III
Session 14: Reflections and journaling
Session 15 and 16: Team Challenges and Exercises involving
Fellows, Coaches and Mentors

Workshop II: Project Planning and Proposal Writing
July 22 – 24, 2010
Sessions 1 - 4: Project Planning
Session 5: Review of Project Planning
Sessions 6 - 8: Proposal writing and Fundraising
Session 7: Review of proposal writing and Fundraising

Workshop III: Leading Change and Project Implementation in Organizations
November 1 to 7, 2010
Session 1: Team Presentations on Organization Development and Change Projects, and expert panel review
Session 2: Review of Team-building and Team performance through the Cycle
Session 3: Team Exercise and Debrief
Session 4: Journaling
Session 5: How to Implement a Project – Criteria for Success
Session 6: Selling Your Project Idea to Ensure Implementation Buy-In & Ownership
Session 7: An Overview of Organizational Development and Performance
Session 8: Assessing Fit with the Implementing Organization
Exercise: Presenting your Project's Fit within the Organization
Session 9: Measuring the Success of Your Project
Exercise: Presenting your Indicators for Success
Session 10: Supporting the Project & Assessing Success

Session 11: Change and Transition Management

Session 12 Planning for Team Working Time – Creating the Project Implementation Plan

Session 13: Team Planning to achieve outcome: A Project Implementation Plan Presentation to a Panel

Session 14: Group work on Team Exercise and Assignment

Session 15: Team Exercise Presentations to Panel

Session 16: Team Exercise Debrief

Session 17: Lesson Learned from the Fellowship; Next Steps.

Video-conference Seminars

Web Seminar Series on Human Resource Development and Management 2010

Web Seminar I: Leading people, an organization's greatest asset: An introduction to human resources management and development May 2010, UNITAR

Web Seminar II: How to conduct a needs assessment
May 2010, Lamb & Lamb Associates

Web Seminar III: Practical Tools for Effective Performance Management
August 2010, Singapore International Foundation

Web Seminar IV: Result Based Management
August 2010, University of Calgary

Web Seminar V: Planning for Training as a Organizational Development/Change tool.
October 2010, University of Calgary

Web Seminar VI: Tools for Conflict Resolution
October 2010, Hiroshima University

Additional activities:

- Field trips to representative and relevant Japanese/UAE organizations to review production systems, health services, educational institutions, environmental organizations etc.

- Seminar on global leadership by Senior Officials from donor countries

- Roundtable with the Ambassador of Afghanistan to Japan and Japanese experts on the role of peace memorials as tools of rebuilding a nation's soul in post conflict reconstruction.

- Discussion on Japanese assistance to Afghanistan with emphasis on capacity building

- Audio-web conferences with Mentors (once a month), and project work sessions are held twice every month.